EARLY MUSIC HISTORY 13

EDITORIAL BOARD

EARLY MUSIC HISTORY 13

STUDIES IN MEDIEVAL
AND
EARLY MODERN MUSIC

Edited by

IAIN FENLON
Fellow of King's College, Cambridge

CAMBRIDGE
UNIVERSITY PRESS

Published by the Press Syndicate of the University of Cambridge
The Pitt Building, Trumpington Street, Cambridge CB2 1RP
40 West 20th Street, New York, NY 10011–4211, USA
10 Stamford Road, Oakleigh, Melbourne 3166, Australia

© Cambridge University Press 1994

First published 1994

Phototypeset in Baskerville by Wyvern Typesetting Ltd, Bristol
Printed in Great Britain at the University Press, Cambridge

ISSN 0261–1279

ISBN 0 521 47282 2

SUBSCRIPTIONS The subscription price (excluding VAT) of volume 13, which includes postage, is £48.00 (US $89.00 in USA and Canada) for institutions, £31.00 (US $52.00 in USA and Canada) for individuals ordering direct from the Press and certifying that the annual is for their personal use. Airmail (orders to Cambridge only) £9.00 extra. Copies of the annual for subscribers in the USA and Canada are sent by air to New York to arrive with minimum delay. Orders, which must be accompanied by payment, may be sent to a bookseller, subscription agent or direct to the publishers: Cambridge University Press, The Edinburgh Building, Shaftesbury Road, Cambridge CB2 2RU. Payment may be made by any of the following methods: cheque (payable to Cambridge University Press), UK postal order, bank draft, Post Office Giro (account no. 571 6055 GB Bootle – advise CUP of payment), international money order, UNESCO coupons, or any credit card bearing the Interbank symbol. EU subscribers (outside the UK) who are not registered for VAT should add VAT at their country's rate. VAT registered subscribers should provide their VAT registration number. Japanese prices for institutions (including ASP delivery) are available from Kinokuniya Company Ltd, P.O. Box 55, Chitose, Tokyo 156, Japan. Orders from the USA and Canada should be sent to Cambridge University Press, 40 West 20th Street, New York, NY 10011–4211, USA.

BACK VOLUMES Volumes 1–13 are available from the publisher at £45.00 ($85.00 in USA and Canada).

NOTE Each volume of *Early Music History* is now published in the year in which it is subscribed. Volume 13 is therefore published in 1994. Readers should be aware, however, that some earlier volumes have been subscribed in the year *after* the copyright and publication date given on this imprints page. Thus volume 8, the volume received by 1989 subscribers, is dated 1988 on the imprints page.

COPYING This journal is registered with the Copyright Clearance Center, 222 Rosewood Drive, Danvers, MA 01923. Organizations in the USA who are also registered with C.C.C. may therefore copy material (beyond the limits permitted by sections 107 and 108 of US copyright law) subject to payment to C.C.C. of the per copy fee of $6.00. This consent does not extend to multiple copying for promotional or commercial purposes. Code 0261 1279/94 $6.00+0.10.

ISI Tear Sheet Service, 3501 Market Street, Philadelphia, Pennsylvania 19104, USA, is authorized to supply single copies of separate articles for private use only.

For all other use, permission should be sought from Cambridge or the American Branch of Cambridge University Press.

CONTENTS

NOTES FOR CONTRIBUTORS

PRESENTATION

Contributors should write in English, or be willing to have their articles translated. All typescripts must be double spaced *throughout*, including footnotes, bibliographies, annotated lists of manuscripts, appendixes, tables and displayed quotations. Margins should be at least 2.5 cm (1″). The 'top' (ribbon) copy of the typescript must be supplied. Scripts submitted for consideration will not normally be returned unless specifically requested.

Artwork for graphs, diagrams and music examples should be, wherever possible, submitted in a form suitable for direct reproduction, bearing in mind the maximum dimensions of the printed version: 17.5×11 cm ($7″ \times 4.5″$). Photographs should be in the form of glossy black and white prints, measuring about 20.3×15.2 cm ($8″ \times 6″$).

All illustrations should be on separate sheets from the text of the article and should be clearly identified with the contributor's name and the figure/example number. Their approximate position in the text should be indicated by a marginal note in the typescript. Captions should be separately typed, double spaced.

Tables should also be supplied on separate sheets, with the title typed above the body of the table.

SPELLING

English spelling, idiom and terminology should be used, e.g. bar (not measure), note (not tone), quaver (not eighth note). Where there is an option, '-ise' endings should be preferred to '-ize'.

PUNCTUATION

English punctuation practice should be followed: (1) single quotation marks, except for 'a "quote" within a quote'; (2) punctuation outside quotation marks, unless a complete sentence is quoted; (3) no comma before 'and' in a series; (4) footnote indicators follow punctuation; (5) square brackets [ ] only for interpolation in quoted matter; (6) no stop after contractions that include the last letter of a word, e.g. Dr, St, edn (but vol. and vols.).

BIBLIOGRAPHICAL REFERENCES

Authors' and editors' forenames should not be given, only initials; where possible, editors should be given for Festschriften, conference proceedings, symposia, etc. In titles, all important words in English should be capitalised; all other languages should follow prose-style capitalisation, except for journal and series titles which should follow English capitalisation. Titles of series should be included, in roman, where relevant. Journal and series volume numbers should be given in arabic, volumes of a set in roman ('vol.' will not be used). Places and dates of publication should be included but not publishers' names. Dissertation titles should be given in roman and enclosed in quotation marks. Page numbers should be preceded by 'p.' or 'pp.' in all contexts. The first citation of a bibliographical reference should include full details; subsequent citations may use the author's surname, short title and relevant page numbers only. *Ibid.* may be used, but not *op. cit.* or *loc. cit.*

ABBREVIATIONS

Abbreviations for manuscript citations, libraries, periodicals, series, etc. should not be used without explanation; after the first full citation an abbreviation may be used throughout text and notes. Standard abbreviations may be used without explanation. In the text, 'Example', 'Figure' and 'bars' should be used (not 'Ex.', 'Fig.', 'bb.'). In references to manuscripts, 'fols.' should be used (not 'ff.') and 'v' (verso) and 'r' (recto) should be typed superscript. The word for 'saint' should be spelled out or abbreviated according to language, e.g. San Andrea, S. Maria, SS. Pietro e Paolo, St Paul, St Agnes, St Denis, Ste Clothilde.

NOTE NAMES

Flats, sharps and naturals should be indicated by the conventional signs, not words. Note names should be roman and capitalised where general, e.g. C major, but should be italic and follow the Helmholtz code where specific ($C_{,,}$ C, $C\,c\,c'$ c'' c'''; c' = middle C). A simpler system may be used in discussions of repertories (e.g. chant) where different conventions are followed.

QUOTATIONS

A quotation of no more than 60 words of prose or one line of verse should be continuous within the text and enclosed in single quotation marks. Longer quotations should be displayed and quotation marks should not be used. For quotations from foreign languages, an English translation must be given in addition to the foreign-language original.

NUMBERS

Numbers below 100 should be spelled out, except page, bar, folio numbers etc., sums of money and specific quantities, e.g. 20 ducats, 45 mm. Pairs of numbers should be elided as follows: 190–1, 198–9, 198–201, 212–13. Dates should be given in the following forms: 10 January 1983, the 1980s, sixteenth century (16th century in tables and lists), sixteenth-century polyphony.

CAPITALISATION

Incipits in all language (motets, songs, etc.), and titles except in English, should be capitalised as in running prose; titles in English should have all important words capitalised, e.g. *The Pavin of Delight*. Most offices should have a lower-case initial except in official titles, e.g. 'the Lord Chancellor entered the cathedral', 'the Bishop of Salford entered the cathedral' (but 'the bishop entered the cathedral'). Names of institutions should have full (not prose-style) capitalisation, e.g. Liceo Musicale.

ITALICS

Titles and incipits of musical works in italic, but not genre titles or sections of the Mass/English Service, e.g. Kyrie, Magnificat. Italics for foreign words should be kept to a minimum; in general they should be used only for unusual words or if a word might be mistaken for English if not italicised. Titles of manuscripts should be roman in quotes, e.g. 'Rules How to Compose'. Names of institutions should be roman.

AUTHORS' CORRECTIONS

It is assumed that typescripts received for publication are in their final form. There may be an opportunity to make minor emendations at the copy-editing stage, but corrections in proof *must* be restricted to printer's and publisher's errors. Any departure from this practice will be at the discretion of the editor and the publisher, and authors may be subject to charge.

EDITOR'S NOTE

Shortly before his death in 1993, Howard Mayer Brown finished the first draft of an extended article, including supporting bibliographies and other apparatus, on the subject of music in France in the second half of the sixteenth century. In choosing to return to material which had interested him since the beginning of his career (it was precisely thirty years since *Music in the French Secular Theater, 1400–1500* had appeared), Howard's purpose was to attract attention to an unevenly studied and at times confusing area, that comparatively dark terrain that lies between the death of Henry II and the achievements of the 'grand siècle'. This was not to deny the interest or importance of the work of D. P. Walker, Frances Yates and others on the Académie, the *ballet de cour* and the phenomenon of *musique mesurée à l'antique*, though it was perhaps to suggest (with characteristic Brownian mischief) that the amount of attention paid to these developments was out of all proportion to their contemporary significance and influence. Certainly the repertory that circulated in the Académie – much of it a kind of *musica reservata* that was published, and then only in part, some decades after it had been composed – represents only a fraction of the music written in France during the second half of the sixteenth century. What of the rest?

The contributions to this volume of *Early Music History* all approach this question in different ways and with different emphases. The original idea had been that Howard's paper, 'the monster that I have created' as he called it in a letter written shortly before his death, distributed to the participants in advance, was to provide the starting point for three days of discussion at King's College, Cambridge, at Easter 1993. Tragically robbed of its *éminence grise*, the seminar, attended by musicologists, literary and theatre historians, was convened never-theless, thanks to the generous support of the Managers of the King's College Research Centre and of the Centre d'Études Superieures de la Renaissance (Tours) and its director, Jean-Michel Vaccaro. The articles in this volume are considered versions, recast in the light of the fruitful experience of those extraordinarily energetic and warmly collaborative few days in Cambridge; they are printed here, together with a revised version of Howard Brown's original text, as a tribute to the memory of a great scholar and true friend.

Iain Fenlon

Early Music History (1994) Volume 13

HOWARD MAYER BROWN

UT MUSICA POESIS: MUSIC AND POETRY IN FRANCE IN THE LATE SIXTEENTH CENTURY

In memory of Jean-Pierre Ouvrard,
who contributed so much to our understanding of French music

I: THE POETS' VIEW OF MUSIC

By praising rulers, whose magnificence formed a crucial part of the world order, Pierre de Ronsard and his French colleagues in the second half of the sixteenth century often depicted the world not as it was but as it ought to be. This idea informs Margaret McGowan's book on ideal forms in the age of Ronsard, in which she explores the ways poets and painters extolled the virtues and the theatrical magnificence of perfect princes following the Horatian dictum *ut pictura poesis*: as is painting so is poetry.[1] McGowan demonstrates the virtuosity of the painters and poets of the sixteenth century in shaping their hymns of praise from the subject matter and ideals of ancient Greece and Rome by following Horace's advice to regard paintings as mute poems and poems as speaking pictures. McGowan shows how artists and intellectuals pursued their goals by creating four kinds of ideal form: iconic forms, sacred images derived from classical literary sources offering princes some guarantee of immortality; triumphal forms that evoke the heroic imperial past; ideal forms of beauty to be found in contemplating the beloved; and dancing forms that mirror rituals of celebration. McGowan claims that such ideal forms were intended to enlighten the ruler himself as much as they celebrated his grandeur in the eyes of others.[2]

The ancient idea that a poem is like a speaking picture and a painting like a mute poem was revived in the late fifteenth century when artists attempted to elevate their work from the

---

[1] M. M. McGowan, *Ideal Forms in the Age of Ronsard* (Berkeley and Los Angeles, 1985).
[2] McGowan, *Ideal Forms*, chap. 1: 'The Perfect Prince', pp. 9–50.

1

level of the mechanical to that of the liberal arts, as the studies of Rensselaer Lee, Ernst Gombrich, John R. Spencer, Mario Praz and others have shown.[3] Although the concept *ut pictura poesis* was not greeted everywhere or by everyone with enthusiasm, it was fertile and flexible enough to stimulate painters and poets throughout the sixteenth, seventeenth and eighteenth centuries. Both in the ancient world and in the sixteenth century, theorists of art and poetry claimed that painters and poets sought to imitate nature and through their presentations to instruct readers or viewers by stimulating their emotions. 'The power to move the mind depended ... on the artist's or the poet's ability to select details from nature and assemble them in a striking way, and these imitations were shaped and perfected according to the rhetorical rules that both arts obeyed.'[4]

These formulations, however, seem to leave music out of the picture, even though it appears to have been centrally important to sixteenth-century French poets. Music, it is true, plays an important albeit subsidiary role in McGowan's book. She refers, for example, to its place in Ronsard's conception of the arts. Music clearly helped to glorify the triumphal forms of the powerful élite and to enhance the appreciation of *la belle forme* of the beloved; and it played a central role, of course, in creating the celebratory rituals of the dance. But McGowan leaves unclear what role music played in the scheme of the world envisioned by the sixteenth-century French intellectual.

How did music relate to poetry in sixteenth-century France? What place did it occupy in the minds of the Pléiade, for example, that centrally important group of French poets led by Pierre de Ronsard and Joachim du Bellay, and including Rémy Belleau, Jean-Antoine de Baïf, Etienne Jodelle, Pontus de Tyard and Jean

---

[3] R. W. Lee, *Ut pictura poesis: the Humanistic Theory of Painting* (New York, 1967); E. H. Gombrich, *Symbolic Images: Studies in the Art of the Renaissance* (London, 1972); J. R. Spencer, 'Ut rhetorica pictura: a Study in Quattrocento Theory of Painting', *Journal of the Warburg and Courtauld Institutes*, 20 (1957), pp. 26–44; and M. Praz, *Mnemosyne: the Parallel Between Literature and the Visual Arts* (New York, 1970). For a study of the relationship between rhetoric and music in late sixteenth-century Italian music, see C. V. Palisca, '*Ut oratoria musica*: the Rhetorical Basis of Musical Mannerism', *The Meaning of Mannerism*, ed. F. W. Robinson and S. G. Nichols (Hannover, NH, 1972), pp. 37–65.

[4] Quoted from McGowan, *Ideal Forms*, p. 51.

Dorat, who attempted to enrich and ennoble the French language and thus to create a French literature worthy of a great nation? Those are the first questions to address in trying to understand French music in the second half of the sixteenth century, for they seem to me crucial to our understanding of music in the Renaissance in general, but especially in the word-oriented world of France at that time, obsessed with its relationship to the ancient world, and selfconscious about its position in the grand intellectual traditions of the West. It is scarcely an exaggeration to claim that we cannot intelligently study French music of this period before we have some notion of music's place in the minds of the intellectuals of the time against which to project individual events and compositions.

Even as late as the sixteenth century music was, of course, in the first place a liberal art, a part of the medieval quadrivium. It was the most tangible manifestation of divine order, of the fact that the universe runs according to rational numbers and proportions. Pontus de Tyard claimed that music embraced all disciplines. It contained in itself all the perfection of symmetry and reflected the image of the whole Encyclopedia.[5] Music as rational order was a medieval idea, but one that maintained its strength throughout the sixteenth century. McGowan, for example, points out that the elaborate choreographies of *ballets de cour* were actually seen as manifestations of the ideal order represented by music.[6] Sixteenth-century writers believed that cosmic influences could actually be drawn to affect human affairs, and they thought that by playing on the emotions of an audience through harmonies and movements finely calculated to echo those of the heavenly spheres their listeners and spectators could be moved to act peacefully.

Pontus de Tyard certainly supported this view. His *Solitaire second* of 1555 is in some sense a traditional *musica theorica*, a treatise squarely within a long and distinguished medieval tradition, but with the addition of new neo-Platonic ideas derived

---

[5] P. de Tyard, *Solitaire second*, ed. C. M. Yandell (Geneva, 1980), p. 71. On Tyard and music, see J. McClelland, 'Le mariage de Poésie et de Musique: un projet de Pontus de Tyard', *La chanson à la Renaissance*, ed. J.-M. Vaccaro (Tours, 1981), pp. 80–92.

[6] McGowan, *Ideal Forms*, p. 230.

3

from his reading of Marsilio Ficino and others. Although he largely repeats and rearranges ideas from Boethius and Gaffurius, with examples drawn from more recent writers like Glarean and Zarlino, Tyard devotes most of the space in his musical treatise to explaining the rational basis of music, and its relationship with world order. The culture of sixteenth-century France was seriously deficient in works of musical theory, save for a handful of practical manuals. (See Appendix 1 for a checklist of printed treatises, an excellent starting point for some more systematic study of French musical theory in the sixteenth century.[7]) Pontus de Tyard therefore deserves to be studied carefully by musicians, and not merely dismissed as a literary dilettante who flirted with a technical subject. He is perhaps the pre-eminent French musical philosopher of the sixteenth century, and hence a primary witness to the intimate connection between music and poetry at that time.

The most distinctive and original part of Tyard's *Solitaire second*, and that which differentiates it from medieval expositions of *musica theorica*, is the strong neo-Platonic framework in which he places his discussion of musical theory. He begins by marvelling at the common desire to live a long and fulfilled life. Mental wellbeing, he writes, is determined by temperance, which can be engendered through the study of the liberal and mechanical arts, but especially through the study of music which offers 'le vray pourtrait de la Temperance'.[8] Music, according to Tyard, is

la science qui considere avec sens et raison la differences des sons graves et aiguz, ou bas et haux, donnant le moyen de bien et harmonieusement chanter. . . . A quoy est requis que l'on scache distinctement toutes les especes de Harmonie, et puis que l'on soit industrieusement exercé à entonner et exprimer disertement les voix en toutes mutations, souz une mesure tousjours bien observée. Tellement que son propre sujet est un chant harmonieusement recueillant en soy des paroles bien dites,

---

[7] For an approach to the expressive content of French music through the writings of theorists, see D. P. Walker, 'La valeur expressive des intervalles mélodiques et harmoniques d'après les théoriciens et le problème de la quarte', *La chanson à la Renaissance*, ed. Vaccaro, pp. 93–105. On the practical nature of French treatises, see A. Seay, 'Jean Yssandon and French Renaissance Theory', *Journal of Music Theory*, 15 (1971), pp. 254–72.

[8] Tyard, *Solitaire second*, p. 71.

innocent time, according to him, when poet and musician were united in the same person. The importance of the union of music and poetry, much discussed in the voluminous literature on Ronsard and music, is stressed in both of his most explicit statements on the subject, his preface to the 1560 edition of Le Roy and Ballard's *Mellange de chansons*, and his *Abbregé de l'art poëtique françois* of 1565.[14] In the *Abbregé* Ronsard writes about music in almost precisely the same way as Tyard, though in much less detail and without Tyard's insistence that single-line melodies are better than polyphony. Or rather, Ronsard claims that poetry was born for music, 'car la Poésie sans les instrumens, ou sans la grace d'une seule ou plusieurs voix, n'est nullement aggréable, non plus que les instrumens sans estre animez de la mélodie d'une plaisante voix' (because poetry without instruments or without the grace of one or more voices is not at all agreeable, any more than instruments without being animated by the melody of a pleasant voice).[15] Ronsard may well have been slightly disingenuous – as we shall see, he probably really meant that music was born for poetry – but in any case he appears to claim, just as Tyard did, that words give music meaning; without them music becomes mere sound.

---

[14] Ronsard's preface is reproduced in, among other places, *La fleur des musiciens de P. de Ronsard*, ed. H. Expert (Paris, 1923; repr. New York, 1965), pp. vii–x, and in Ronsard, *Oeuvres complètes*, ed. G. Cohen (Paris, 1938), II, pp. 979–82. Facsimiles of the prefaces for both the 1560 *Mellange* and its reprint in 1572, and an English translation of the 1572 version, appear in *Le Roy & Ballard's 1572 Mellange de Chansons*, ed. C. Jacobs (University Park, PA, and London, 1982), pp. 12–14 and 25–8. Ronsard's *Abbregé de l'art poëtique françois* is published in a modern edition in, among other places, Ronsard, *Oeuvres*, ed. Cohen, II, pp. 997–1011, and in Ronsard, *Oeuvres complètes*, ed. P. Laumonier, rev. and completed by I. Silver and R. Lebègue, 20 vols. (Paris, 1914–75), XIV, pp. 3–35.

For some of the notable studies of Ronsard and music, see J. Tiersot, ed., *Ronsard et la musique de son temps* (Leipzig and New York, 1903); the special issue of *La revue musicale* (May 1924) devoted to 'Ronsard et la musique', with essays by C. van den Borren, A. Coeuroy, L. Laloy, P. de Nolhac, M. Pincherle, H. Prunières, A. Schaeffner and A. Suarès; R. Lebègue, 'Ronsard et la musique', *Musique et poésie au XVIe siècle*, ed. J. Jacquot (Paris, 1954), pp. 105–19; F. Igly, *Pierre de Ronsard et ses musiciens: sélection des meilleurs poèmes de Ronsard* (Paris, 1955); I. Silver, *Ronsard and the Hellenic Renaissance in France*, 3 vols. (Geneva, 1981); the special issue of the *Revue de Musicologie*, 74 (1988), devoted to 'Les musiciens de Ronsard' with essays by I. Bossuyt, J. Brooks, G. Dottin, G. Durosoir, J.-P. Ouvrard and J.-M. Vaccaro; and J. Brooks, 'French Chanson Collections on the Texts of Pierre de Ronsard, 1570–1580' (Ph.D. dissertation, Catholic University of America, 1990).

[15] Ronsard, *Abbregé*, ed. Laumonier, p. 9.

7

In his *Abbregé de l'art poëtique*, Ronsard even offered two important principles for would-be poets to follow in order that their
poems better accommodate music: the strophes of a lyric poem
should be formally identical so that the same music can be
repeated for each; and masculine and feminine rhymes should
alternate, presumably for the sake of variety in creating cadences
at the ends of musical phrases.[16] In his section on lyric verse
with lines shorter than the twelve syllables making up an alexandrine or the ten appropriate for love lyrics, however, he seems
to qualify somewhat his universal statement that all poetry was
intended for music. He describes poems with shorter lines as
'wonderfully appropriate for music, that is, the lyre and other
instruments' ('merveilleusement propres pour la Musique, la lyre
et autres instrumens'), presumably because their differing short
line lengths offer the musician the opportunity for greater variety
in phrase lengths.[17] His statement implies not only that some
kinds of poetry are better for music than others, but also that
short lyric poems are especially appropriate for performance as
solo songs, accompanied, I would suggest, not by the ancient
Greek lyre, which Ronsard grandly substitutes in much of his
poetry for the instruments that were doubtless mostly used in
the late sixteenth century to accompany singers, the lute or the
guitar. He seems to suggest, in short, that music's real importance
was for setting short lyric poems, whereas in fact his admonition
to vary line lengths for the sake of music makes the most sense.

Throughout his life, Ronsard continued to claim – or at least
to maintain the fiction – that music and poetry were, or should
be, united. In praising the prince or his beloved in ideal terms,
the poet describes himself as singing to the accompaniment of
the lute, the lyre or, in some pastoral poems, a wind instrument.
Margaret McGowan has analysed a number of such poems,
beginning with his very early *Hymne de France* of 1549, in which
the poet says he is singing the praises of France to his lute.[18]
Imitating one of Virgil's *Georgics*, Ronsard lauds the arts and

---

[16] *Ibid.*, pp. 8–9.
[17] *Ibid.*, pp. 27–8.
[18] McGowan, *Ideal Forms*, pp. 79–80. The *Hymne de France* is published in a modern
      edition in Ronsard, *Oeuvres*, ed. Laumonier, I, pp. 24–35.

sciences of his native country, including its marvellous music, of which he writes only that it and poetry were rightly praised in the ancient world for their ability to assuage our *ennuis* with their sweetness:

> La Poésie & la Musique seurs,
> Qui noz ennuiz charment de leurs doulceurs
> Y ont aquis leurs louanges antiques.[19]

McGowan cites a number of other poems in which Ronsard praises music, his king, his beloved, or some French aristocrat or intellectual in terms that involve accompanied solo song or another sort of music, for example, the *Ode à Michel de l'Hospital* of 1550; the *Hymne de l'esté* and *Hymne de l'hiver* of the 1550s; the *Hymne de Henri II de ce nom* of 1555; the *Ode à Monseigneur le Dauphin* of 1555; the *Hymne de l'éternité* of 1556; the *Bergerie* of 1563/4; and *La lyre* of 1569.[20] Such examples of music as a metaphor for praise could easily be multiplied.[21]

We gain, however, a much clearer idea of precisely what Ronsard meant by arguing for the union of music and poetry from the musical supplement to his first book of *Amours*, a collection of 183 sonnets, a chanson and an *amourette*, most of them in praise of Cassandre, published in 1552 along with his fifth book of odes.[22] In the preface to the musical supplement, the editor, Ambroise de la Porte, wrote that Ronsard had deigned to take the trouble to measure his sonnets to the lyre ('il a daigné prendre la peine de les mesurer sur la lyre'). In fact the supplement contains nine compositions, all in four parts: settings of six sonnets, the *amourette*, the *Ode à Michel de l'Hospital* from the first book of odes, and the *Hymne triumphal sur le trespas de Marguerite de Valoys, royne de Navarre* (beginning 'Qui renforcera

---

[19] Ronsard, *Oeuvres*, ed. Laumonier, I, p. 32.
[20] McGowan, *Ideal Forms*, pp. 40 (*Ode à Michel de l'Hospital*), 48 (*Hymne de l'esté* and *Hymne de l'hiver*), 47 (*Hymne de Henri II*), 155 (*Ode à Monseigneur le Dauphin*), 156 (*Hymne de l'éternité*), 35 (*Bergerie*) and 114 (*La lyre*).
[21] On Ronsard's many uses of music as metaphor, see B. Jeffery, 'The Idea of Music in Ronsard's Poetry', *Ronsard the Poet*, ed. T. Cave (London, 1973), 209–39.
[22] The 1552 *Amours* are published in a modern edition, among other places, in Ronsard, *Oeuvres*, ed. Cohen, I, pp. 3–110, and in Ronsard, *Oeuvres*, ed. Laumonier, IV (1925). The musical supplement is published in facsimile in Ronsard, *Oeuvres*, ed. Laumonier, IV, pp. 189–250.

ma vois?') from the fifth book of odes.[23] The compositions were written by the older composers Pierre Certon and Clément Janequin, by the young Parisian Claude Goudimel (who later became a Huguenot), and by Ronsard's friend, supporter and commentator on his poems, the poet and jurisconsult Marc-Antoine Muret. Presumably, these pieces were added to the *Amours* to demonstrate precisely the kind of music Ronsard had in mind in arguing for the union of music and poetry, with examples of all the genres represented in the volume. The fact that the compositions were said to be measured on the lyre, whereas they were in truth published as polyphonic four-part pieces, reminds us that sixteenth-century music as it appears on the printed page is not always what it seems. It is but another example of music presumably intended in the first place as solo song but actually issued in a neutral polyphonic version which had to be adapted for performance, most probably in more than one equally acceptable way.[24] Moreover, four of the six sonnets were each intended to be sung to any number of the other sonnets in the collection. Those capable of being sung to the same music are listed at the end of each of the compositions intended as models.

For example, Janequin's *Nature ornant la dame qui devoyt* could also be used to sing any of the fifty-nine other sonnets listed at the end of the supplement to the *Amours*.[25] Janequin's simple music is typical of the collection as a whole. For the most part each voice sings one note per syllable (only a few accented syllables, mainly those that close each line, are set with relatively

[23] Seven of the nine musical examples are published in a modern edition in Expert, *La fleur*. For some doubts about whether the music for the *Hymne triumphal sur le trespas de Marguerite* was intended for all forty stanzas, see M. Egan-Buffet, *Les chansons de Claude Goudimel: analyses modales et stylistiques* (Ottawa, 1992), pp. 442–3.

[24] The best examples of music published as apparently vocal polyphony but performed in a variety of ways are the commemorative editions of Italian *intermedi*, on which see, among other studies, H. M. Brown, *Sixteenth-Century Instrumentation: the Music for the Florentine Intermedii*, Musicological Studies and Documents 30 (Rome, 1973). The early sixteenth-century repertory of frottolas constitutes another large group of compositions published as vocal polyphony but either intended primarily as solo songs, or else most often performed in that way. There are also, of course, the innumerable sixteenth-century versions of vocal polyphony arranged for lute or keyboard, whose existence suggests that performers felt free to arrange in a variety of ways the music they found in printed and manuscript sources.

[25] A modern edition of *Nature ornant* appears in Expert, *La fleur*, pp. 25–8; and also in C. Janequin, *Chansons polyphoniques*, ed. A. T. Merritt and F. Lesure, 6 vols. (Monaco, 1965–71; repr. 1983), v, pp. 191–5.

brief melismas) and the counterpoint is largely note against note, with a few relatively simple imitations among some of the four voices in one or two formally important places – chiefly the fourth line of the two quatrains, and the first line of the first tercet. Moreover, the second quatrain is to be sung to the same music as the first quatrain, and the tenor of the second tercet repeats melodic material from the first tercet. The result is quite formulaic. The simplicity of the music and the amount of formal repetition suggests that the music is merely a vehicle for declaiming the poetry rather than an artful interpretation of a particular set of words. And yet Janequin responded to the rhetoric and prosody of *Nature ornant* in enough detail – by repeating the first line of the sestet, for example, and by repeating clauses and writing half-cadences to reflect poetic caesuras – to make it very difficult to sing his polyphony just as it stands to all fifty-nine of the other sonnets said to be intended for this same music. In spite of the fact that Ronsard (or his musical editor Ambroise de la Porte) claimed that the same music could be re-used, fairly radical editorial intervention would be necessary to adapt the music to all the new words.

Similar questions arise, too, in connection with the equally simple settings of the two odes. Ronsard's *Ode à Michel de l'Hospital*, for example, consists of twenty-four stanzas, each with a strophe, an antistrophe and an epode.[26] A note at the end of the musical supplement to the *Amours* states explicitly that Goudimel's simple setting of the first strophe and of the first epode should be used for all the others. Thus Goudimel's strophe would need to be sung forty-eight times (once for each strophe and once for each antistrophe) and the epode twenty-four times; moreover, the music would need to be modified to fit the inner prosodic details of many of the later stanzas. It may be that the composers were simply not willing to write a music so formulaic that it could be re-used innumerable times, but it is also possible that the music on the page should not be taken very literally as a fixed text. If the music was primarily intended to be sung by a

---

[26] A modern edition of Goudimel's setting of the ode appears in Expert, *La fleur*, pp. 14–20, and in C. Goudimel, *Oeuvres complètes*, XIII–XIV: *Chansons*, ed. P. Pidoux and M. Egan (New York and Basle, 1974–83), XIII, pp. 80–5.

solo singer accompanied by a lute or a guitar, the performers would in any case have needed to arrange the printed text to fit their specific requirements. If we regard the compositions of the musical supplement not as a collection of rigidly fixed texts but as groundplans for a series of performances, it becomes easier to imagine that the performers could adjust the music to make it fit the later stanzas better. Thinking of these compositions as schemas for performance enables us, too, to imagine performances in which the rhetorical skills of the singer and the quality of the poetry could sustain numerous repetitions of the same musical formula, especially if the chief aim was to offer a formal, elaborately declaimed rendition of the poem rather than an artfully worked musical composition.

To musicians then as now, the task set by Ronsard in the supplement to the first book of his *Amours* very probably seemed irreconcilable with a fully expressive music. If the same composition was intended to be sung to sixty different sonnets, the composer can scarcely have written a music highly responsive to a particular set of words. How then can we explain Ronsard's aim? More specifically, where can he have got the idea of sanctioning a set of musical formulas suitable for many different poems of the same formal type? He must have looked to Italy for the model to follow in putting into practice his programme for uniting music and poetry, for nowhere else in the sixteenth century was there so strong a tradition of declaiming narrative as well as lyric poetry to musical formulas. In the fifteenth century, poet improvisers like Pietrobono of Ferrara, Serafino dall'Aquila and others had sung strambotti and other poems in ottava rima to a lute or a *lira da braccio*.[27] Early in the sixteenth

---

[27] On fifteenth- and sixteenth-century musical formulas for declaiming poetry, see N. Pirrotta, 'Early Opera and Aria', *New Looks at Italian Opera: Essays in Honor of Donald J. Grout*, ed. W. W. Austin (Ithaca, NY, 1968), pp. 39–107; republished in Italian as 'Inizio dell'opera e aria', in Pirrotta, *Li due Orfei: da Poliziano a Monteverdi* (Turin, 1969; 2nd rev. edn, 1975), pp. 276–333; translated into English by K. Eales as *Music and Theatre from Poliziano to Monteverdi* (Cambridge, 1982).

On Pietrobono of Ferrara, see L. Lockwood, 'Pietrobono and the Instrumental Tradition of Ferrara in the Fifteenth Century', *Rivista Italiana di Musicologia*, 10 (1975), pp. 115–33, and Lockwood, *Music in Renaissance Ferrara, 1400–1505* (Oxford, 1984), esp. pp. 96–108. On Serafino, see B. Bauer-Formiconi, *Die Strambotti des Serafino dall'Aquila: Studien und Texte zur italienischen Spiel- und Scherzdichtung des ausgehenden 15. Jahrhunderts* (Munich, 1967).

century, the Venetian music printer Ottaviano Petrucci included short schematic compositions in his frottola books, intended for use as groundplans to which to sing any poem of a particular formal type: sonnet, ode, capitolo and so on.[28] And in the later sixteenth century musical anthologies were filled with so-called arias and also with realisations of a number of stock bass patterns derived from informal improvisatory practices.[29] Indeed, it is no exaggeration to claim that Ronsard's whole programme of renovating the French language owes much to Italian models. His goal was very similar to that formulated by Pietro Bembo earlier in the century in his effort to revivify the Italian language, even though Bembo's solution – to purify Italian by returning to older models – produced very different results from Ronsard's goal of enriching and decorating the French language by borrowing words and literary styles from the ancient world, and from various other sources.[30]

Ronsard's debt to Italian ideas doubtless originated in his early association with Jean Dorat and Jean-Antoine de Baïf.[31] Additional support for the hypothesis of a strong Italian influence

[28] See W. F. Prizer, 'The Frottola and the Unwritten Tradition', *Studi Musicali*, 12 (1983), pp. 203–19.

[29] See, for example, the arias in the lutebook of the Florentine courtier and lutenist Cosimo Bottegari (Modena, Biblioteca Estense, MS C 311), published in a modern edition as *The Bottegari Lutebook*, ed. C. MacClintock (Wellesley, MA, 1965). For other arias from the late sixteenth century, see also under 'Aria' in the index of first lines and titles in H. M. Brown, *Instrumental Music Printed Before 1600* (Cambridge, MA, 1965).

[30] On Bembo's goals, see, among other studies, D. Mace, 'Pietro Bembo and the Literary Origins of the Italian Madrigal', *Musical Quarterly*, 55 (1969), pp. 65–86, and M. Feldman, 'Venice and the Madrigal in the Mid-Sixteenth Century' (Ph.D. dissertation, University of Pennsylvania, 1987).

Quite apart from the influence of Italy on the development of the French chanson in the second half of the sixteenth century, we also need to address the question of the diffusion of the French chanson in other countries, a topic not dealt with in the present essay. For some excellent beginnings in this direction, see I. Fenlon, 'La diffusion de la chanson continentale dans les manuscrits anglais'; P. Walls, 'La chanson dans les masques à la cour de Jacques Ier d'Angleterre: "The Music of the King's Peace" '; D. Becker, 'Deux aspects de la chanson polyphonique en Espagne: le chansonnier d'Uppsala et la "Recopilacion" de Juan Vasquez'; I. Bossuyt, 'La chanson française en Allemagne et en Autriche dans la seconde moitié du XVIe siècle'; L. Virágh, 'Les diverses formes de la musique vocale profane en Hongrie au XVIe siècle'; and P. Pozniak, 'Aspects de la chanson en Pologne au XVIe siècle', all in *La chanson à la Renaissance*, ed. Vaccaro, pp. 172–208, 275–303 and 322–46.

[31] F. A. Yates, *The French Academies of the Sixteenth Century* (London, 1947; repr. with foreword by J. B. Trapp, 1988), pp. 1–19.

on Ronsard and the other French poets of the later sixteenth century may come, too, from a closer study of the careers of slightly older poets like Mellin de Saint-Gelais (1491–1558) and Maurice Scève (1501–62).[32] The strong Italianate element in Scève's poetry can, of course, be easily explained by his association with Lyons, home to a large colony of Italian merchants and bankers, and an important centre in France for Italian ideas. The court poet Saint-Gelais also had connections with Lyons (pirated editions of his works appeared there), but the source of his Italianate ideas probably dates from his years as a student of law at the universities of Bologna and Padua. He needs to be studied more closely by musicians, though, because of his unusually strong musical orientation and his fame as an improviser of music to his light and *galans* verse. He certainly patterned his poetry after the Italian strambottists Cariteo, Tebaldeo and Serafino, and he may well have imitated their techniques and styles of musical improvisation.[33] As Barthélemy Aneau writes in his *Quintil*, poets like Saint-Gelais were few and far between, for he 'composes his own lyric verses . . ., sets them to music, sings them, plays them and sounds them on instruments'.[34] He was an exception to the prevailing separation of poets from musicians so much lamented by Ronsard, and his example may partly have inspired Ronsard to conceive of the music for his *Amours* of 1552 as a series of musical formulas, resembling in many ways earlier Italianate models.

If the 1552 *Amours* can be trusted to tell us, Ronsard seems to have had in mind a kind of music that would lightly and discreetly heighten the effect of the poetry without obscuring a listener's understanding of the words. Ronsard's examples, like Tyard's more explicit declarations, seem to imply that the chief function of music is to serve as a handmaiden to poetry, and that music has meaning only from its words. Ronsard obviously

---

[32] On Saint-Gelais, see F. Dobbins, 'Saint-Gelais, Mellin de', *The New Grove Dictionary of Music and Musicians*, ed. S. Sadie, 20 vols. (London, 1980), XVI, pp. 390–1; and D. Stone jr, ed., M. de Saint-Gelais, *Oeuvres poétiques françaises* (Paris, 1993–). On Scève, see V. L. Saulnier, 'Maurice Scève et la musique', *Musique et poésie au XVIe siècle*, ed. Jacquot, pp. 89–103; and D. G. Coleman, *Maurice Scève: Poet of Love: Tradition and Originality* (Cambridge, 1975).

[33] Dobbins, 'Saint-Gelais'.

[34] B. Aneau, *Quintil Horatien* (Lyons, 1556), is quoted in Dobbins, *Music in Renaissance Lyons*, p. 76.

did not want music to compete with his poetry, and as a consequence we can claim with some justice that his plea for a union
between the two was merely a metaphor and nothing more. We
should, moreover, be somewhat sceptical of Ronsard's romantic
claim that all poetry should be sung. Raymond Lebègue points
out that after about 1556 Ronsard generally stopped writing
poetry appropriate for music.[35] His later philosophical, laudatory
and epic hymns, his elegies, his *discours* and the *Franciade* were
never intended for musical setting. Moreover, composers generally
chose his earlier odes, love sonnets and chansons to set to a
relatively elaborate and artful music that did not necessarily
correspond with Ronsard's own ideas about the kind of music
ideally suited to bring his poetry to life.

Ronsard did, on the other hand, continue to write poetry to
be used at court festivities, and much of it was intended to be
sung. The two collections published as *Eclogues et mascarades* and
as *Mascarades, combats et cartels* include much of this occasional
verse.[36] Unfortunately but typically, almost all the music performed on these occasions for the royal court has been lost. Even
so, fragments of French festival music of the later sixteenth
century do survive, and we need to collect and study them, since
they will reveal much about music as an enhancement of royal
magnificence and an element in the idealisation of the monarchy.
From the few fragments that do remain we can fill an important
gap in our knowledge of the role of music in the late Renaissance,
and especially of the way in which it played an important if
supporting role in creating the ideal forms of celebration and
praise. The Parisian publishers Le Roy and Ballard, for example,
issued at least two settings of pieces included in Ronsard's two
festival collections: Nicolas de la Grotte's setting of *Je suis Amour
le grand maistre des dieux* from Ronsard's *Le trophée d'amour à la
comédie de Fontaine-bleau* and Fabrice Marin Caietain's *Le soleil et
le roy* from Ronsard's *Comparaison du soleil et du roy, recitée par deux
joueurs de lyre*.[37] Such pieces could and should be used as the

---

[35] See R. Lebègue, 'Ronsard et la musique', *Musique et poésie au XVIe siècle*, ed. Jacquot,
p. 110.

[36] The two collections are published in a modern edition in, among other places,
Ronsard, *Oeuvres*, ed. Cohen, I, pp. 915–1037.

[37] La Grotte's composition is published in a modern edition in Expert, *La fleur*,
pp. 62–4.

beginning of a wider investigation of the kind of music appropriate for courtly festival music, and hence of the way in which official music supported and celebrated the political structure. In fact, La Grotte created an even more self-effacing polyphony for *Le trophée d'amour* and for his setting of Ronsard's hymn on the victory at Moncontour than his older colleagues had done for the 1552 *Amours*.[38]

It is clear, then, that for Ronsard (and doubtless for the other poets of the Pléiade) music, however important in their world view, was best when it intruded least on the beauty of their words. This humanist strain in late sixteenth-century French music reveals itself, too, in the fashion for single-line melodies without any accompaniment whatsoever – the sorts of melodies collected, for example, in Jehan Chardavoine's *Recueil des plus belles et excellentes chansons en forme de voix de ville* (Paris, 1576), which includes a number of simple melodies to be sung to Ronsard's odes and chansons.[39] The vast repertory of monophonic *voix de villes* and simple *airs* and dancing songs of the mid sixteenth century – the repertory that Daniel Heartz has called a compromise between humanist ideals and musical realities – needs much closer study. Among other things, such a study would reveal the complex relationships between urban or courtly entertainment music (the lightest and most popular musical genres of their day) and the highly serious philosophical and ethical ideas on music of the Pléiade and their successors. Not least, it is possible to trace the dancing song, the *voix de ville* and the simple strophic *air*, alleged to have come into being in the 1570s, at least as far back as the homophonic, strophic

---

[38] La Grotte's setting of Ronsard's hymn is published in a modern edition in Expert, *La fleur*, pp. 56–7.

Models to follow in studying courtly (and other) festivities may be found in the three volumes on *Les fêtes de la Renaissance*, ed. J. Jacquot (Paris, 1956–75), even though few of the essays deal with music.

[39] A selection of Chardavoine's monophonic *voix de villes* are published in a modern edition in Expert, *La fleur*, pp. 74–80; see also the facsimile of the 1576 edition (Geneva, 1980). On the repertory of monophonic melodies, see K. J. Levy, 'Vaudeville, vers mesurés et airs de cour', *Musique et poésie au XVIe siècle*, ed. Jacquot, pp. 185–99; and also D. Heartz, '*Voix de ville*: between Humanist Ideals and Musical Realities', *Words and Music: the Scholar's View: a Medley of Problems and Solutions Compiled in Honor of A. Tillman Merritt*, ed. L. Berman (Cambridge, MA, 1972), pp. 115–35; and Heartz, 'The Chanson in the Humanist Era', *Current Thoughts in Musicology*, ed. J. W. Grubbs (Austin, TX, and London, 1976), pp. 193–230.

dance-like chansons of Jacques Arcadelt published in the 1550s.[40] The foregoing can of course also be considered the pre-history of Jean-Antoine de Baïf's *vers* and *musique mesurés à l'antique*, his realisation of the youthful ideals of Ronsard and Tyard, and especially of Tyard's visionary recommendations about measuring music according to the precepts of the ancient Greeks and Romans, which he hoped would change the ethical behaviour of humankind.[41]

There is yet another connection to be made in studying the simple humanistic music of the later sixteenth century: its relationship with French Protestantism. For there is a curious point of contact between the poets' views of what an ideal music should be and the Protestant view that sacred or devotional texts should be sung to very simple music so that their words might be better understood – not only the Marot translations of the Psalms but also the many *chansons spirituelles*, hymns and other devotional songs that circulated widely in the Protestant world.[42] These simple musical repertories, especially suitable for poets and the devout, have been less closely studied than they should have been because they seem to us so crippling for musicians. But if we are ever to understand the complex interplay of music, poetry, ideas and politics we need to set aside aesthetic criteria, however important they normally are to us, in the effort to comprehend better the entire range of musical activity in sixteenth-century France, as well as its effects and purposes.

[40] For some examples, see J. Arcadelt, *Opera omnia*, ed. A. Seay, 10 vols., Corpus Mensurabilis Musicae 31 (1965–70), VIII, nos. 14, 15, 39, 40, 41, 42, 50, 53, 54, 56, 58, 65, 66, 69, 70, 71, 72, 87, 88, 96 and 98. The most substantial study of this repertory to date is J. O. Whang, 'From *Voix de ville* to *Air de cour*: the Strophic Chanson, c. 1545–1575' (Ph.D. dissertation, University of Pennsylvania, 1981).

[41] On Baïf's *vers et musique mesurés*, see D. P. Walker, 'The Aims of Baïf's Académie de Poésie et de Musique', *Journal of Renaissance and Baroque Music*, 1 (1946), pp. 91–100; Walker, 'The Influence of *Musique mesurée à l'antique*, particularly on the *Airs de cour* of the Early Seventeenth Century', *Musica Disciplina*, 2 (1948), pp. 141–63; Walker and F. Lesure, 'Claude Le Jeune and *Musique mesurée*', *Musica Disciplina*, 3 (1949), pp. 151–70; and Walker, 'Some Aspects and Problems of *Musique mesurée à l'antique*: the Rhythm and Notation of *Musique mesurée*', *Musica Disciplina*, 4 (1950), pp. 163–86.

[42] For some studies of Protestant music in sixteenth-century France, see E. O. Douen, *Clément Marot et le psautier huguenot*, 2 vols. (Paris, 1878–9); M. Cauchie, 'Les psaumes de Janequin', *Mélanges de musicologie offerts à M. Lionel de La Laurencie* (Paris, 1933), pp. 47–56; J. Rollin, 'La musique religieuse protestante française', *Revue Musicale*, nos. 222–3 (1954), pp. 138–56; and P. Pidoux, *Le psautier huguenot du XVIe siècle*, 2 vols. (Basle, 1961).

In truth, there seems to have been a bifurcation in the history of music in the later sixteenth century, a parting of the ways. Despite Ronsard's desire for a closer union between poetry and music, the two were in fact drawing further apart. In defiance of the poets' injunctions to keep it simple, many composers found in the poetry of Ronsard and his contemporaries a fertile source of musical invention through which they could continue to develop the already rich French tradition of polyphonic song. They wrote chansons quite opposed, or at least indifferent, to the strong ethical and philosophical programme of the poets and intellectuals. For this group of musicians, by far the best represented of Margaret McGowan's ideal forms was surely the idealisation of feminine beauty, for which Ronsard's love poetry was ideally suited.

Who were these musicians, what did they write, and how did they match their music to the rhetoric of the poets of the Pléiade? A convenient starting point for a consideration of the musical scene in France after 1550 must surely be with the composers of Ronsard's 1552 *Amours*: Certon, Janequin and Goudimel. We badly need studies of the late works of Janequin and Certon, and of Jacques Arcadelt as well, if we are to understand the transition from the chansons published by Pierre Attaingnant of Paris during the second quarter of the sixteenth century – chansons that Ronsard would probably have characterised as those dominated by settings of Clément Marot's poetry – to the newer styles of mid century.[43]

Another way to study the later chansons of Arcadelt, Certon and Janequin would be to concentrate on precisely the questions

---

[43] Although Arcadelt has been studied as a madrigalist, scholars have ignored his chansons. A. Agnel, 'Les chansons polyphoniques de Pierre Certon' (Ph.D. dissertation, University of Paris, 1970), the work most likely to shed light on the chansons of the 1550s, has not been available to me. On Goudimel, see Egan-Buffet, *Les chansons de Claude Goudimel*. On Janequin, the series of articles by F. Lesure – 'Clément Janequin: recherches sur sa vie et sur son oeuvre', *Musica Disciplina*, 5 (1951), pp. 157–93; (with P. Roudié) 'Clément Janequin, chantre de François Ier (1531)', *Revue de Musicologie*, 43–4 (1959), pp. 193–8; and (with P. Roudié) 'La jeunesse bordelaise de Clément Janequin', *Revue de Musicologie*, 49 (1963), pp. 172–83 – remain our chief source of information on the composer and his music. J.-C. Margolin, 'L'expression de la culture populaire dans les chansons de Clément Janequin', *La chanson à la Renaissance*, ed. Vaccaro, pp. 120–38, offers a useful view of one aspect of Janequin's oeuvre.

raised above. Did they write a self-effacing sort of music that merely allowed the poetry to be declaimed, or did they continue and enrich their earlier styles? Did they manipulate purely musical elements, in other words – melody, harmony, texture and rhythm – in an effort to offer an interpretation of a poem, analysing by means of their music either the prosody of the poetry, or its rhetoric, or even its meaning? Or were they capable of writing a kind of music that did not interfere with the poetry and yet interpreted it musically in a rich and complex way? Only by asking such questions will we be able to chart the dimensions of the later sixteenth-century French chanson, setting up an opposition between a music in the service of the poets and a music in the service of the musicians, with all the possible permutations between those two extremes.

A preliminary look at those of Certon's later chansons recently published by Jane Bernstein suggests that in fact the two poles coexisted in composers' works.[44] The settings of odes by Mellin de Saint-Gelais and others in the *Premier livre de chansons . . . par M. Pierre Certon*, published by Le Roy and Ballard in 1552, involve a simpler sort of music than he had ever written earlier. Certon added to Saint-Gelais's multistrophic poems extremely simple music for the first stanza. In almost all these chansons, for example, the music for the first couplet (or the first line) is repeated for the second couplet (or second line), and all the voices move homorhythmically. The formulaic music supplied by Certon was intended to be sung for all the other stanzas of the poem, and the music could easily be arranged for solo voice and lute. Certon's modest music does little more than allow a heightened declamation of the poem.

Appendix 2 includes all the poems of Ronsard published in musical settings between 1552, the year of the first book of *Amours*, and 1566, the year that saw the appearance in print of the first volume of chansons with Ronsard's name in the title – a publication marking the beginning of a decade of intense preoccupation with Ronsard by French musicians. The list is taken from Thibault and Perceau's bibliography of musical

---

[44]   P. Certon, *Complete Chansons Published by Le Roy and Ballard*, ed. J. A. Bernstein, The Sixteenth-Century Chanson 6 (New York, 1990).

settings of Ronsard's poetry.[45] Certon's three Ronsard settings from those years differ markedly in style from his simple settings of Saint-Gelais's odes.[46] In *Si je t'assaux*, for example, the words 'des alarmes' at the end of the first quatrain trigger a long and elaborate section of fast declamatory 'alarm music', individual words and phrases are singled out for special emphasis, and Certon did not repeat any musical phrases in a formally significant way. Likewise in *Las! pour vous trop aymer* the music was fashioned to emphasise particular words and phrases, for example the last line, which is set as a peroration that takes up more than half the entire chanson. Even in *Je suis un demi-dieu*, where the same music is set to several different lines of poetry, Certon responded to particular sets of words. In none of these pieces could the music be repeated for subsequent strophes or for poems in similar form. They all do more than offer a heightened declamation of the poem: they offer an artfully organised musical reading of the poem; they interpret it.

A comparison of three settings of the same poem, *Je ne veux plus que chanter de tristesse* (all listed in Appendix 2), also reveals the coexistence of strikingly different attitudes of composers towards their texts in the 1550s and 60s. (It should be noted that *Je ne veux plus* appears as a poem in twenty quatrains in Ronsard's *Nouvelle continuation des Amours* of 1556, but it was published as early as 1543 in an anthology of anonymous poetry and so its attribution to Ronsard is not secure.)[47] All we know about François Roussel is that he worked for much of his career in Italy. His 1559 setting of *Je ne veux plus* is as formulaic as any of Certon's odes.[48] Roussel composed simple homophonic music for a single quatrain, music capable of being sung to all twenty stanzas. The French provincial composer Pierre Clereau, one of

---

[45] G. Thibault and L. Perceau, *Bibliographie des poésies de P. de Ronsard mises en musique au XVIe siècle* (Paris, 1941).

[46] The three chansons by Certon appear in Bernstein, pp. 143–6, 94–7 and 90–3.

[47] See O. de Lassus, *Sämtliche Werke*, xiv: *Kompositionen mit französischem Text*, ii, ed. H. Leuchtmann (Wiesbaden, 1981), p. xxv, for the information that the poem was published in *Recueil de vray poesie française* (Paris, 1543). See also Ronsard, *Oeuvres*, ed. Laumonier, i, p. 137 and vii, p. 186, where the poem is published and its sources noted.

[48] Modern edition in F. Roussel, *Opera omnia*, ed. G. Garden, 5 vols., Corpus Mensurabilis Musicae 83 (1980–2), v, pp. 6–7.

the earliest to set a number of Ronsard's poems to music, included two quatrains of the poem in his chanson, in a style slightly more complex than that of Certon's odes and in a manner not so different from the examples in the musical supplement to the 1552 *Amours*.[49] Clereau reworked the music of the first couplet, for instance, to serve for the second couplet, and the first and fourth lines of the second quatrain (the rhyming lines) also share similar melodic material. And yet he changed the texture and rhythmic pace of the music to match the rhetoric of the poem, and it is inconceivable that his chanson could have been sung to any other stanzas of the poem. Lassus's setting is the most selfconsciously artistic of the three, without any significant formal repetition and with highly sophisticated and nuanced control of the texture, the pace and the typically rich harmonies.[50] It, too, is a response to a particular set of words, rather than a formula capable of setting various sets of words.

There is, in short, no easy answer to my initial question about the place of music in the view of French intellectuals and connoisseurs in the late sixteenth century. Serving both as exemplification of the Platonic world order and also as a powerful adjunct to rhetoric, music played a central role, as Margaret McGowan has shown us, in at least three of her four paradigms of ideal form: the triumphal and dance-like modes and the depiction of *la belle forme*. I have not mentioned painting at all, for music as an abstract non-verbal art seems to have had little direct contact with painting in the way that poetry did. Music was an indispensable handmaiden to poetry. Ronsard and his colleagues, consciously or not, supposed that music was the servant of the poetry and that it took all its meaning from the words. That attitude may have been quite common in both France and Italy in the sixteenth century, even though we have come to associate it with Monteverdi's apparently revolutionary manifesto explaining and defending his second practice. The history of the musical settings of lyric poetry in the late sixteenth century, however, needs also to be studied independently of the

---

[49] Modern edition in The Sixteenth-Century Chanson 7, ed. J. A. Bernstein (New York, 1988), pp. 99–101.
[50] Modern edition in Lassus, *Kompositionen mit französischem Text*, II, ed. Leuchtmann, pp. 88–91.

history of poetry, for musicians did not all follow the dictates of the poets. However stimulating the dialogue between poetry and music, and however influential the poets in determining the nature of music, composers also drew on other sources for their inspiration – the rich tradition of earlier French song, for instance, and the inherent possibilities of elaborate polyphony to gloss and analyse a poem.

II: COMPOSERS AND GENRES

Music scholars need to make many more exploratory comparisons of settings by different composers of the same texts, like my brief and superficial examination of the settings of *Je ne veux plus que chanter* by Roussel, Clereau and Lassus, in order to clarify the continuum of possibilities available to French composers in the second half of the sixteenth century. We should also begin to look systematically at the chansons printed by each of the French music publishers of the second half of the sixteenth century and study their production as selfconsciously formed repertories, beginning with the men who could rightly have claimed to be the foremost music publishers of France, the firm of Le Roy and Ballard in Paris. Appendixes 3–5 offer conspectuses of the composers whose chansons they printed during the 1550s, 1560s and 1570s respectively.[51] From this long list of composers, some of them very well known and some almost completely unknown, it will be possible eventually to build a picture of the nature of the chanson as seen in Paris in the second half of the sixteenth century and to understand better the extent to which composers followed the poets' dictates, whether completely, partly or not at all.

Le Roy and Ballard were not the only music publishers working in Paris. Thibault and Lesure, for example, published a bibli-

---

[51] Appendixes 3–5 are derived from the information in F. Lesure and G. Thibault, *Bibliographie des éditions d'Adrian Le Roy et Robert Ballard (1551–1598)* (Paris, 1955). For a bibliography of all the chansons published in the sixteenth century, see H. Daschner, *Die gedruckten mehrstimmigen Chansons von 1500–1600: literarische Quellen und Bibliographie* (Bonn, 1962). For a bibliography of the sources of poetic texts, see F. Lachèvre, *Bibliographie des recueils collectifs de poésies du XVIe siècle* (Paris, 1922). The best overview of French secular music in the second half of the sixteenth century remains F. Lesure, *Musicians and Poets of the French Renaissance* (New York, 1955).

ography of the volumes of music published by Nicolas du Chemin between 1549 and 1576.[52] Michel Fezandat printed music between 1551 and 1558.[53] There were doubtless other music publishers active in Paris during the second half of the sixteenth century whose names and achievements could easily be documented.[54] In addition to listing the volumes these men published, we also need to begin to hear and study the music they made available, examining individual pieces carefully in an effort to illuminate their meanings, and projecting those meanings against the larger screen of the complete surviving works of their composers, and of the works by other composers writing at the same time.

We should also study the music issued by individual publishers as repertories, basing our work on the assumption that particular firms either shaped taste or reflected the interests and preoccupations of the segment of the population that commissioned and performed the music. In making a selection from the music available publishers were doubtless influenced by various factors. Discovering the special interests of particular publishers can help to clarify the nature of the repertory that has come down to us, and hence the place of music in the general culture of the time. We can and should ask a series of questions about the volumes produced by each firm, beginning with the simplest and most prosaic: whose music did they publish? Who were their regular composers? Who chose the music, and who edited it? What were the editorial policies of each firm, and how did they differ in their practices from other publishers? For whom were they publishing? Who bought their books, and who played and sang from them? Did particular publishers concentrate on the achievements of individuals, or did they attempt to offer what seemed to them a comprehensive (or partial) view of the chansons of their time? Did they publish only one kind of chanson by the composers whose works they made available to a larger public? In short, why did various publishers issue precisely what they did, and

---

[52] F. Lesure and G. Thibault, 'Bibliographie des éditions musicales publiées par Nicolas du Chemin (1549–1576)', *Annales Musicologiques*, 1 (1953), pp. 269–373.

[53] On Fezandat, see F. Dobbins, 'Fezandat, Michel', *The New Grove Dictionary*, VI, p. 519.

[54] See, for example, P. Renouard, *Imprimeurs parisiens* (Paris, 1898), and D. Heartz, 'Parisian Music Publishing under Henri II', *Musical Quarterly*, 46 (1960), pp. 448–67.

what can we learn about the basic assumptions and prejudices of French sixteenth-century society by asking about the policies of particular publishers?

We need to ask such questions not only about the publishers in the French capital but also about those in the provinces, especially in Lyons, the second city of France. Samuel Pogue has published a bibliography of the works of Jacques Moderne, for example, and we should begin to study the music he published in greater detail than has been done up to now.[55] In studying the music of Lyons, we must heed Frank Dobbins's cautions against thinking too simplistically of a Lyonnais school of composers.[56] Moderne published the work of a variety of composers, some chiefly active in Lyons (though whether they therefore constitute a Lyonnais school is a more complicated question) and some working in other provincial cities, at various distances from Lyons, as well as Italo-French composers, Protestant composers, and so on. It will be no easy task to separate the various traditions represented by Moderne's (and indeed earlier by Attaingnant's) composers, for we know almost nothing about many of them. Even so relatively prolific a composer as P. de Villiers, whose works appear both in Attaingnant's and in Moderne's anthologies, and who may have taught at the Collège de la Trinité in Lyons, remains a mysterious figure (we do not even know his first name for certain).[57] And yet it may legitimately be claimed that he, along with the Italian Francesco de Layolle, were the principal composers of secular music in Lyons in the 1530s, if only because they are among the best-represented composers in Moderne's anthologies.[58] It may even be that our view of that city's music should centre on those two figures.

Moderne was not the only person who published music in Lyons in the second half of the sixteenth century. The smaller firms are now much better known than the smaller Parisian publishers, thanks to Laurent Guillo's accounts of their careers

[55] S. Pogue, *Jacques Moderne: Lyons Music Printer of the Sixteenth Century* (Geneva, 1969).

[56] Dobbins, *Music in Renaissance Lyons*, pp. 173–4.

[57] See Dobbins, *Music in Renaissance Lyons*, pp. 185–8. A selection of chansons by Villiers appears in L. E. Miller, ed., *Thirty-Six Chansons by French Provincial Composers (1529–1550)* (Madison, WI, 1981), where the composer's first name is given as Pierre.

[58] Layolle's music is published in F. A. D'Accone, ed., *Music of the Florentine Renaissance*, Corpus Mensurabilis Musicae 32/iii–vi (1969–73).

in his book on music printing in Lyons.[59] He lists and describes the activities of printers, publishers and booksellers: Godefroy and Marcellin Beringen; Macé Bonhomme; Michel du Bois; Robert Granjon (the most important publisher of chansons in Lyons after Moderne); Simon Gorlier; Antoine Vincent (publisher of the Genevan Psalter); Antoine Cercia; Thomas de Straton; Jean de Tournes; Clément Baudin and Gasparo Fiorino; Charles Pesnot and Barthélemy Vincent (who worked either in Lyons or in Geneva); and Jean Pillehotte. The music they published should also be studied, not so much as collections of masterpieces as for the insight they can give into the character of the society that produced them.

In dividing French music publishers between those in Paris and those in Lyons, I have had recourse to one of the basic metaphors of musicological study: the metaphor of the centre and the periphery. This paradigm corresponds remarkably well, of course, to the realities of French cultural life, then as now, with its capital city and centralised government. In fact, secular music in France can conveniently be studied in terms of a centre and its peripheries not only in real geographical terms – what various composers were writing in all the cities of France – but also in a more figurative sense: who were the most important, the best or the most influential composers, and who were their followers, and those musicians who seem less important to us, whether because they wrote so little, had so little influence on their contemporaries or lived in a small town, or for some other reason. Writing history in this way may not be completely defensible intellectually, but there are strong pragmatic reasons for maintaining the fiction that we can and should differentiate between the more and the less important musicians, for we shall be less able to conceptualise the music of late sixteenth-century France clearly if we become mired in treating on an absolutely equal footing the hundreds of composers whose works appear in anthologies.

I would even argue that the impression Anglo-American musicologists have that French music of the second half of the

---

[59]   L. Guillo, *Les éditions musicales de la Renaissance Lyonnaise* (Paris, 1991); see also Dobbins, *Music in Renaissance Lyons*, chapter 4: 'Music Copied and Printed in Lyons', pp. 134–72.

sixteenth century has not been much studied comes at least
partly from the fact that we cannot readily identify a central
tradition, or the most 'important' composers. From the mass of
chanson composers known to us, we have not yet identified those
whom we should regard, or who were seen by their contemporaries, as being the most significant. In addressing that question,
we should perhaps consult the tastes of the Parisian publishers
of the time. In 1570, Nicolas du Chemin published *Les meslanges
de Maistre Pierre Certon*, the only volume called 'meslanges' that
he published during his career of more than twenty years.[60] In
the same year, Le Roy and Ballard published a *meslange* of music
by Orlande de Lassus as well as the complete works of the court
composer Guillaume Costeley, in a volume titled *Musique de
Guillaume Costeley, organiste ordinaire et vallet de chambre, du treschretien
et tresinvincible Roy de France, Charles IX*. In 1586, the same firm
issued the *Meslanges de la musique de Clau[de] Le Jeune*.[61] In order

[60]   Certon's *Meslanges* is described and its contents listed in Lesure and Thibault, 'Bibliographie des éditions musicales publiées par Nicolas du Chemin', pp. 343–5. Perhaps
the three volumes of music by Josquin and the four by Janequin also published by
Du Chemin should be included in the list of large, commemorative editions, although
they are not called 'meslanges'. On that question, see I. His, 'Les *Mélanges* musicaux
au XVIe et au début du XVIIe siècle', *Nouvelle Revue du Seizième Siècle*, 8 (1990), pp.
95–110. In any case, both Du Chemin and Le Roy and Ballard seem to make
distinctions between large, commemorative editions and volumes that contain a
particular segment of one composer's works; and they also distinguish between books
of newer or more current chansons, and collective editions (for example, the *livres de
recueil* in Du Chemin's case) that mostly reprint the best or most successful chansons
from their previous anthologies or from the past.
        The importance of these *mélanges* has become clear to me in discussions with Kate
van Orden, at the time of writing a graduate student at the University of Chicago
working on a dissertation on poetry and music in France in the second half of the
sixteenth century. Her ideas inform a good many parts of the present essay, and I
am grateful to her for sharing them with me.
[61]   The chansons of Lassus, including those in the 1570 *meslange*, are published in a
modern edition in Lassus, *Sämtliche Werke*, XII, XIV and XVI, ed. Leuchtmann (1981–
2). On his chansons, see W. Boetticher, *Orlando di Lasso und seine Zeit, 1532–1594*
(Kassel and Basle, 1958); J. Bernstein, 'Lassus in English Sources: Two Chansons
Recovered', *Journal of the American Musicological Society*, 27 (1974), pp. 315–25;
F. Dobbins, 'Lassus – Borrower or Lender: the Chansons', *Revue Belge de Musicologie*,
39–40 (1985–6), pp. 101–57; and J.-M. Vaccaro, 'Roland de Lassus, les luthistes et
la chanson', *ibid.*, pp. 158–74. Costeley's chansons are published in modern editions
in G. Costeley, *Musique*, ed. H. Expert, Les Maîtres Musiciens de la Renaissance
Française 3, 18 and 19 (Paris, 1896–1903; repr. New York, n.d.); Costeley, *Selected
Chansons*, ed. J. A. Bernstein, The Sixteenth-Century Chanson 8 (New York, 1989),
and in I. Godt, 'Guillaume Costeley: Life and Works' (Ph.D. dissertation, New York
University, 1969). The chansons of Le Jeune are published in a modern edition in
Le Jeune, *Mélanges*, ed. H. Expert, Les Maîtres Musiciens de la Renaissance Française,
16 (Paris, 1903; repr. New York, 1965); Le Jeune, *Le printemps*, ed. Expert, *ibid.* 12–

to gain an even better idea of what the Parisian publishers of the late sixteenth century supposed appropriate for large retrospective, commemorative editions, we must also add the *Livre de meslanges, contenant six vingtz chansons des plus rares, et plus industrieuses qui se trouvent, soit des autheurs antiques, soit des plus memorables de nostre temps*, first published by Le Roy and Ballard in 1560 and reprinted in 1572.[62] This and the volumes dedicated to Lassus and Le Jeune are the only anthologies Le Roy and Ballard called 'meslanges'.

Taken together, these five volumes would appear to stake out a possible 'centre' for the history of the chanson in the second half of the sixteenth century. The choice of composers to commemorate reflects the opinions of at least some Parisians as to what was 'plus memorable' – most important, most interesting, or at least most noteworthy – in the 1550s, 60s and 70s. Du Chemin evidently supposed Pierre Certon, a slightly older figure, to be the only composer worthy of a commemorative edition; and Le Roy and Ballard chose the court composer Costeley and the foreigner Lassus (plus all the old and new composers whose works apear in the 1560 *Meslanges*) to embody all that was best in French music in the 1550s and 60s, and Claude Le Jeune to represent the same for the 1570s and early 80s. Even though it is not entirely clear whose views such choices reflect (is it possible, for example, that Adrian Le Roy was really the most important taste maker in Paris during those decades, or were his selections strongly influenced by the court, the musical leaders of the city, the editor for his firm, or his circle of friends?), these five large retrospective editions may properly serve as the starting point for thinking about ways to shape our view of the history of the chanson in Paris in the second half of the sixteenth century.

Following Du Chemin and Le Roy and Ballard, we should probably conclude that the music of Pierre Certon (as well as

14 (Paris, 1900–01; repr. New York, 1963); Le Jeune, *Complete Unpublished Chansons*, ed. J. A. Bernstein, The Sixteenth-Century Chanson 16–17 (New York, 1989–90); and Le Jeune, *Airs of 1608*, ed. D. P. Walker and F. Lesure, 4 vols., AIM Miscellanea 1–4 (Rome, 1951–9). See also I. His, 'Les *Mélanges* de Claude Le Jeune (Anvers: Plantin, 1585): transcription et étude critique' (Ph.D. dissertation, University of Tours, 1990).

[62] For a modern edition of the collection, see Jacobs, ed., *Le Roy & Ballard's 1572 Mellange*.

that by Clément Janequin and Jacques Arcadelt) will tell us a great deal about the transition from the Parisian chanson of the 1530s and 40s, reflected in the anthologies published by Pierre Attaingnant, to that of the 1550s and 60s, of which we have as yet only the crudest of views. In order to refine those views, Le Roy and Ballard seem to tell us, we should look in the first place at the chansons by the favourite court composer, Costeley, whose complete works were issued in the year he went into semi-retirement, never, so far as we know, to write (or at least never to publish) another composition; and also at the chansons of Lassus, whose prominence in the publications of Le Roy and Ballard is puzzling only in so far as he was one of the most widely circulated and most influential composers of chansons even though he was never resident in France, and therefore neither took part in any musical or artistic activities in the French capital city nor engaged in those intellectual debates that presumably shaped the character of the chanson. To these two composers, evidently regarded in their time as major figures, we should perhaps add the Protestant Claude Goudimel, killed at the St Bartholomew's Day massacre in 1572, if only because in his earlier years he played so important a role as taste maker in his capacity as proofreader and eventually partner of Nicolas du Chemin.[63] The picture of musical activity in Paris can then be filled out by taking into account the *Meslanges* of 1560 and 1572, that gigantic collection which presumably reflects the publisher's view of what constitutes the best and most representative music of his time and before, and can therefore be regarded as a central document in our attempts to understand the music that was written, performed and highly valued in Paris in the later sixteenth century. Finally, Le Roy and Ballard send us to Claude Le Jeune to understand what they thought was the best music of the 1570s and early 80s. Constructing a history of the chanson from these five central anthologies will have the salutary effect, among others, of placing previous discussions of *musique mesurée*

---

[63] The chansons of Goudimel are published in a modern edition in Goudimel, *Oeuvres complètes*, ed. Pidoux and Egan, XIII–XIV. On his chansons, see M. Egan[-Buffet], 'Problèmes d'interprétation rythmique dans les chansons de Claude Goudimel', *La chanson à la Renaissance*, ed. Vaccaro, pp. 139–56; and Egan-Buffet, *Les chansons de Claude Goudimel*.

à l'antique in a larger and therefore less isolated context. In seeing how Costeley, Lassus and their contemporaries reacted to the poets' views of how music should be ordered, we shall understand better just how important *musique mesurée* was in musical circles and thus be better able to assess its proper place in the history of music in France.

The metaphor of the centre and its periphery has, as I have said, a more literal geographical significance as well as its figurative power to persuade us to distinguish between more and less important musicians. We need also to extend our studies of the differences between music in Paris and in Lyons, Toulouse and other French cities. Toulouse, for example, had been an important cultural centre long before the sixteenth century, and it continued to be important in the sixteenth century. Yet its intellectual and musical life has hardly been studied.[64] We should know more about Toulouse not least because it was doubtless the centre for the musical activities of Anthoine de Bertrand, a figure who raises questions about the very idea of studying the past, even the French past, in terms of a centre and its periphery. In my opinion, Bertrand was one of the very best composers writing chansons in late sixteenth-century France.[65] To dismiss him merely as a provincial composer is to marginalise the importance of his achievements and the quality of his work. Yet we shall surely understand him better, and be better able to assess his special qualities, if we can do so against the background of the preoccupations and concerns of the circle of poets and musicians active in Toulouse in the sixteenth century. Moreover, studying the music composed and performed in France outside Paris is

[64] For a brief sketch of musical life in Toulouse, with helpful indications of subjects for further study, see F. Dobbins, 'Toulouse', *The New Grove Dictionary*, XIX, pp. 92–3.
[65] On Bertrand, see J.-M. Vaccaro, 'Musique et poésie à l'époque de la Pléiade: Anthoine de Bertrand 1540–1581' (master's thesis, University of Poitiers, 1965); Vaccaro, 'Le livre d'airs spirituels d'Anthoine de Bertrand', *Revue de Musicologie*, 56 (1970), pp. 35–53; Vaccaro, 'Les préfaces d'Anthoine de Bertrand', *Revue de Musicologie*, 74 (1988), pp. 221–36; Vaccaro, 'Anthoine de Bertrand: *Las! pour vous trop aymer*', *Models of Musical Analysis: Music before 1600*, ed. M. Everist (Oxford, 1992), pp. 175–207; G. Thibault, 'Anthoine de Bertrand, musicien de Ronsard, et ses amis toulousains', *Mélanges offerts à M. Abel Lefranc* (Paris, 1936), pp. 282–300; J. Brooks, '"Ses Amours et les miennes tout ensemble": la structure cyclique du *Premier livre* d'Anthoine de Bertrand', *Revue de Musicologie*, 74 (1988), pp. 201–20; Brooks, 'French Chanson Collections', esp. pp. 204–72.

valuable in itself in revealing the richness and diversity of musical life at that time.

In addition, we should study much more intensively than we have the relationship between the composers of Paris, Lyons and Toulouse, and those working in francophone Netherlands. The music published in Antwerp and Louvain – above all by Tylman Susato and Pierre Phalèse, but also by less prolific publishers like Hubert Waelrant – needs to be taken into account in any comprehensive view of the chanson in the second half of the sixteenth century.[66] We must begin to refine our crude generalisations about the differences between the Parisian and the Netherlands chanson, generalisations based on insufficient study of at least partly unlike things. There is doubtless a kernel of truth in the simplistic idea that Netherlands chansons, with their emphasis on imitative counterpoint, more closely resemble motets than do the texturally simpler, more supple but more homophonic Parisian chansons, whether written in 1530 or 1560. But we have hardly begun to understand either the musical diversity of the settings of French lyric poetry issued in the Netherlands or their dependence on earlier French traditions.

Attempting to survey the vast production of chansons in the second half of the sixteenth century is clearly a mammoth task. To make any sense of this great mass of material we have to ask stylistic and formal questions, not just about the composers' attitudes towards poetry, and whether or not musicians took account of the ideas of Ronsard, Tyard and the other members of the Pléiade, but also about genres, compositional techniques and style.[67] Scholars should refine their techniques for assessing the musical impact of individual pieces, and they should inquire about the way individual pieces fit into the complete works of various composers, how the work of one composer relates to that of others, and how one sort of repertory relates to another.

[66] Susato's publications are listed and described in U. Meissner, *Der Antwerpener Notendrucker Tylman Susato*, 2 vols. (Berlin, 1967). See also K. Forney, 'Tielman Susato, Sixteenth-Century Music Printer: an Archival and Typographical Investigation' (Ph.D. dissertation, University of Kentucky, 1978). The publications of Phalèse's firm before 1578 are listed and described in H. Vanhulst, *Catalogue des éditions de musique publiées à Louvain par Pierre Phalèse et ses fils, 1545–1578* (Brussels, 1990). Timothy McTaggart is currently completing a dissertation for the University of Chicago on the chansons published by Waelrant and Laet.

[67] For an exemplary genre study, see C. S. Adams, 'Some Aspects of the Chanson for Three Voices during the Sixteenth Century', *Acta Musicologica*, 49 (1977), pp. 91–114.

Scholars interested in French music of the late Renaissance need, among other things, to join the current discussions about the way Renaissance composers conceived of pitch relationships, and how we should therefore conceive of them. Clearly, for example, Le Jeune in his series of long and elaborate settings of the Psalms, published as the *Dodecacorde* in 1598, followed the system of twelve modes established by Glarean and Zarlino.[68] But what does that mean? Which French composers made the change and which stayed with the older eight-mode system, and when did the orientation of French composers begin to change? Can we use French music of the late sixteenth century to test Harold Powers's thesis that modality is post-compositional and not prescriptive, not a part of the actual technique of composing?[69] Can we, in short, illuminate the nature of sixteenth-century tonality by studying the ways French composers used and thought about the modal systems that were the principal conceptual tools of sixteenth-century theorists writing about the organisation of pitches? Was there a consensus about the higher meaning of modality and its relationship with the ancient world, so that we can identify a specifically French attitude, for example, towards the theory of modal affect? Can we, finally, see that the way composers conceived of pitch relationships is connected in one way or another with the way they viewed the nature of music in general? Can we, in short, relate theories of modality to wider theories about the nature of systems and ideas about world order, and thus to the history of ideas in the sixteenth century?

Not least of all, we need to think rather more than we have about the various genres of chanson in the late sixteenth century. Can we identify important differences between chansons by dividing them into those written for the royal court, those written for

---

[68]   C. Le Jeune, *Dodécacorde, comprising Twelve Psalms of David Set to Music according to the Twelve Modes*, 3 vols., ed. A. H. Heider, Recent Researches in the Music of the Renaissance 74–6 (Madison, WI, 1988).

[69]   See H. Powers, 'Tonal Types and Modal Categories in Renaissance Polyphony', *Journal of the American Musicological Society*, 34 (1981), pp. 428–70. For some attempts to address these questions, see U. Hertin, *Die Tonarten in der französischen Chanson des 16. Jahrhunderts: Janequin, Sermisy, Costeley, Bertrand* (Munich, 1974); H. M. Brown, 'Theory and Practice in the Sixteenth Century: Preliminary Notes on Attaingnant's Modally Ordered Chansonniers', *Essays in Musicology: a Tribute to Alvin Johnson*, ed. L. Lockwood and E. Roesner (Philadelphia, 1990), pp. 75–100; C. S. Adams, 'The Early Chanson Anthologies Published by Pierre Attaingnant (1528–1530)', *Journal of Musicology*, 5 (1987), pp. 527–48.

aristocratic salons in the capital city and elsewhere, those intended for urban middle-class entertainment, and those written for provincial circles? Should we further distinguish between songs intended for courtly dramatic or semi-dramatic festivities, songs for performance by professionals before an audience of cultivated amateurs, and songs intended primarily for performance either by amateurs or by professionals? Or is it more meaningful to group musical settings of lyric poetry according to their poetic form and style, or their geographical origin, separating the music into settings of poetry arranged in tercets, quatrains, cinquains and so on, or into settings of sonnets or strophic poems, or of Petrarchan or non-Petrarchan love lyrics, or is it more sensible merely to divide music into that from Paris, Lyons, Toulouse and other places?

Even relatively simple settings of strophic poems deserve to be more carefully studied for what they tell us about one important genre of chanson. In the first place, many musical anthologies from the 1530s on include settings of single strophes from poems that we know from literary sources to have had many strophes. We have scarcely even asked the question whether such settings, by Claudin de Sermisy and others, were meant to be repeated for all the other strophes of the poem, or whether they were understood to have been intended only for a single strophe. Such songs differ markedly from those simple songs, many in dance rhythms, that appear in the works of Sandrin, Arcadelt and others in the 1550s.[70] The publishers of those strophic songs included all or most of the strophes with the music, and it is clear that the music was intended to be repeated for each new strophe. Kenneth Levy and others have already noted that such strophic songs were called *voix de villes* or *vaudevilles* earlier in the century and came to be called *airs de cour* after 1571.[71] But were *airs de cour* really exactly the same as *vaudevilles* and simply called by a different name? Was there as much continuity as previous scholarship has suggested? And if so, what exactly are the implications of the term *air de cour*? Did members of the royal court adopt a music originally conceived as urban middle-class song,

---

[70]   For examples, see note 40 above.
[71]   See note 39 above.

and, if so, when and why? Or was the resemblance between the two kinds of song more or less accidental and not indicative of any real historical connection? Whatever the answers, scholars should explore these questions further, in the effort to clarify questions of genre.

Many strophic songs appear to be dancing songs, which is to say they consist of repeated rhythmic patterns associated with particular kinds of dance. Does that mean people actually danced to them while they were being sung, or were they merely stylised dances, having lost all association with social or theatrical dancing? The same question needs to be asked, too, about the instrumental dances published in great quantities in the late sixteenth and early seventeenth centuries.[72] The dance has always played a more important role in France than in other countries, and it is time we acknowledged that fact by incorporating dance music more directly into our view of the history of secular music in general. Not least of all, we should make a greater effort to connect surviving dances with their place in particular *ballets de cour*. Indeed, the *ballet de cour*, as well studied as it has been as a cultural phenomenon, needs more attention from musicians.[73] In our continuing effort to link the history of music more closely with the history of ideas, for example, we need to take more account of the *ballet de cour* and its music for what we can learn about the way French courtiers conceived of a world order, how they celebrated kings and princes, and how they reinterpreted the ancient world in accordance with their own concerns in the sixteenth century.

III: POETRY FOR MUSIC: POETIC AND MUSICAL TRADITIONS

We should never consider French music in isolation from poetry or dance. The three are inseparable, for in France music has

---

[72] The best introduction to French instrumental dances is J.-M. Vaccaro, *La musique de luth en France au XVIe siècle* (Paris, 1981). For a bibliography including French instrumental dances of the sixteenth century see Brown, *Instrumental Music*.

[73] Recent studies of the *ballet de cour* include M. M. McGowan, *L'art du ballet de cour en France, 1581–1643* (Paris, 1963); M.-F. Christout, *Le ballet de cour de Louis XIV, 1643–1672* (Paris, 1967); and P. Bonniffet, *Un ballet démasqué: l'union de la musique au verbe dans 'Le printans' de Jean-Antoine de Baïf et Claude Le Jeune* (Paris and Geneva, 1988).

always been allied more closely than in other countries with literary ideas, in the later sixteenth century as at other times. One important way to study chansons, therefore, involves asking questions about the poetry composers chose to set. What kinds of poem appear in anthologies of music, and what kinds do not? Can we infer from the choices made by composers what their criteria were for selecting particular poems or poetic genres? Can we ever know what they understood to be poetry for music? It seems appropriate to begin with questions about chansons set to poems by members of the Pléiade, since they presumably wrote the best of the new kinds of lyrics in the second half of the sixteenth century. To study the musical settings of their poetry should therefore reveal to us the layer of songs in the anthologies that reflects the latest fashions, the most modern attitudes, and the greatest innovations. I have already suggested a few ways of approaching the chansons that set Ronsard's poetry, and have listed in Appendix 2 the Ronsard poems set to music between 1550 and 1566. The bibliography of Thibault and Perceau makes all the other Ronsard settings from the sixteenth century easily available.[74] In studying and interpreting this information we may begin to understand whether composers approached the challenge of writing music for the newest kind of poetry differently from the way they thought about older or lesser poems. Do the Ronsard settings, and settings of poems by other membes of the Pléiade, differ in kind from settings of anonymous poems, occasional poems or popular poems? Were the composers who set Ronsard especially closely allied with him and his friends? Do their settings of Ronsard's poems therefore represent choices dictated at least partly by the poet's own advice? One of the directions in which we should move, in short, is towards defining more closely the difference between the music allied with the newest poetry, self-consciously promulgated as examples of the way in which the French language should be enriched and ennobled, and songs that set an older-fashioned or a different kind of lyric.

We have already seen, for example, that Certon composed the music for the odes of Mellin de Saint-Gelais and others in a different style from the one he had used earlier for his chansons

---

[74] Thibault and Perceau, *Bibliographie des poésies de P. de Ronsard.*

from the 1530s and 40s; and his style presumably changed again when he began setting the new poetry of the 1550s. Moreover, research into the musical settings of the *vers mesurés* of Baïf, one of the few relatively well-studied corners of French music history in the late sixteenth century, has revealed that composers conscientiously created a kind of music that embodied the poet's ideas about prosody.[75] We should begin to ask also whether and how composers set the works of Du Bellay, Belleau, Jodelle and Tyard, and whether or not they adopted a particular attitude towards them.[76] Did their settings fulfil or frustrate the aspirations of the poets, and did they differ in significant ways from settings by other poets?

In short, we need to begin to classify the kinds of chanson composers wrote in an attempt to explain the great diversity of musical styles to be found in late sixteenth-century anthologies. Some chansons use more imitation than others, some incorporate borrowed material, some are metrically freer than others, and some are graceful and more or less homorhythmic while others are rhythmically foursquare and highly contrapuntal. The explanation of these differences will almost certainly have some literary implications. Certain musical styles were associated with particular literary genres. The reason for only two of Costeley's *airs* (*Heureux qui d'un soc laboureur* and *Il n'est trespas plus glorieux*) displaying a surprising degree of metrical freedom doubtless relates to the kinds of poem he chose.[77] Similarly, the enormous diversity in Lassus's chansons can be attributed in some degree to his choice of poems. Lassus borrowed Lupi's melody for *Susanne un jour* at least partly because it had become traditional to base *chansons spirituelles* on previously composed melodies. In its metrically free, homorhythmic texture, Lassus's setting of Baïf's well-known *Une puce j'ai dedans l'oreille* comes as close to being *musique mesurée* as anything the composer ever wrote. And the foursquare rhythms and the kind of imitation he used in *Et d'ou*

---

[75] For studies of Baïf and his circle, see note 41 above.
[76] For a beginning in this direction, see F. Dobbins, 'Les madrigalistes français et la Pléiade' and J.-P. Ouvrard, 'La chanson française du XVIe siècle: lecture du texte poétique', *La chanson à la Renaissance*, ed. Vaccaro, pp. 157–71 and 106–19.
[77] Modern editions of the two chansons appear in Costeley, *Selected Chansons*, ed. Bernstein, pp. 65–7 and 68–9.

venez vous reflect the fact that the poem tells an amusing popular story. These three examples, taken from a single volume of his complete works, demonstrate obvious ways in which poetic choice dictated musical style.[78] It would be less easy to say what differences in kind there are between his settings of anonymous older poems on the one hand, and poems by Clément Marot and Ronsard on the other. The attempt would be worth making, though, partly to account for Lassus's popularity in France given his evident predilection for the older poetry of Marot and his contemporaries, but mainly in order to try to bring together the various strands in the history of the chanson in the attempt to offer an intelligent and intelligible conspectus of Lassus's compositional virtuosity, and indeed an explanation for the enormous diversity in musical styles in the works of all chanson composers in the second half of the sixteenth century.

Most anthologies of music published during the century, in France as well as in Italy, include more anonymous poems than ones attributed to named poets (whether famous or little known). Even though it is impossible to identify the poets of many of the chanson texts, we must try to classify the anonymous poetry composers chose to set and even ask – though our answers will be highly speculative – why the poetry remained anonymous. Many songs were composed to quatrains, cinquains and huitains, short lyric poems of a sort that must have seemed old-fashioned to members of the Pléiade. This phenomenon requires explanation. Does it signify a rift between the élitist avant garde and the remainder of the music-loving public (whoever they were)? Or did the poetry of the Pléiade circulate among a relatively small group, so that songs on old-fashioned texts met the needs of most musicians? Was it for social reasons that so many song texts remained anonymous, whether because aristocratic poets did not wish to reveal their identities or because composers set poetry by their friends and colleagues? By discovering which attributed poems the anonymous ones most resemble, we can begin to establish their place in literary history and thus under-

---

[78] All three appear in Lassus, *Kompositionen mit französischem Text*, II. On *Susanne un jour*, see K. J. Levy, '"Susanne un jour": the History of a 16th Century Chanson', *Annales Musicologiques*, 1 (1953), pp. 375–408.

stand better the poetic choices composers made and hence the
correlation between music and poetry.

Many of the poems set to music in the anthologies published
by Le Roy and Ballard (and other French publishers) in the
1550s and 60s can be found in earlier anthologies of poetry. *La
fleur de poésie françoyse* of 1543, for example, contains a large
number of poems from the French literary past, many of them
the kinds Ronsard would surely have dismissed as barbaric or
at least very old-fashioned.[79] Many of them resemble in style
and content the poems of Clément Marot, or even those of his
father Jean, others belong to a more popular tradition of French
poetry for the entertainment of the urban populace.

The presence of so many older poems among those set by
musicians in the 1550s and later signals a strong interest on the
part of French cultural leaders in past traditions. That Le Roy
and Ballard published music by many older composers in their
anthologies also indicates a desire to cultivate the past which
has been little noted in the musicological literature to date.
Indeed, the fascination with the music of the early sixteenth
century on the part of French publishers from the 1550s onwards
is a topic that cries out for investigation. Scholars have been
inclined to single out Josquin des Prez as an exceptional case in
music history because his music began to be reissued thirty and
more years after his death.[80] In fact, he was by no means unique
among composers of chansons. Appendix 6 lists those musicians
whose works were published by Le Roy and Ballard in the
Melanges of 1560 and 1572.[81] The list reveals the number of
musicians represented who died about 1560 or even well before
that date, along with some composers, like Nicolas and Fourmen-

---

[79] *La fleur de poésie françoyse: recueil joyeulx contenant plusieurs huictains, dixains, quatrains,
chansons & aultres dictez de diverses matières, mis en nottes musicalles par plusieurs autheurs*
(Paris: Alain Lotrian, 1543). The volume was republished in a modern edition in
Raretés bibliographiques . . . pour une société de bibliophiles (Paris, 1864). The title suggests
that the collection was made by selecting texts that had already been set to music
(mostly from Attaingnant's anthologies of polyphonic song). I am grateful to Kate
van Orden for pointing out the importance of this particular collection.

[80] See, for example, W. Kirsch, 'Josquin's Motets in the German Tradition', *Josquin des
Prez*, ed. E. E. Lowinsky in collaboration with B. J. Blackburn (London, 1976), pp.
261–78. Hirsch does not claim, however, that the revival of Josquin's music is unique.

[81] Appendix 6 is derived from Lesure and Thibault, *Bibliographie des éditions d'Adrian Le
Roy et Robert Ballard*, pp. 91–4 and 156–9.

tin, who may have been older (but about whom virtually nothing is known).

In short, Parisian musical circles in the 1550s, 60s and 70s cultivated early music to an unprecedented extent, so far as we know. The survival, or revival, of this older French tradition should be not only documented but also interpreted and explained. What did the past mean to publishers, musicians and their audiences? Were they merely emulating their immediate predecessors, thereby indicating their intention of continuing to work in a tradition upheld in the immediate past? Were they making explicitly anti-Ronsard statements in directing their attention to earlier poems and earlier music? Or were they in fact supporting Ronsard's aims of returning to the ancient world? Is it possible that in the absence of antique Greek and Roman models, French composers of the 1560s and 70s used Josquin, Sermisy and others as examples of an ancient music worth emulating? Certainly they knew and used musical material from the past: among other things, composers' penchant for basing new chansons on older models needs much closer attention.

Le Roy and Ballard and their contemporaries not only published older French music, and new settings of old French poems, they also issued a substantial amount of music influenced by Italian traditions and practices. This Italian presence in France manifested itself in at least three ways: some composers followed the dictates of Italian theorists, some emulated Italianate techniques of composition and performance and, more prosaically, some actually set Italian texts. Moreover, the poets of the Pléiade were deeply influenced by Italian models – Petrarchism infuses the sonnets of Ronsard, for example – and their Italianisms doubtless affected the composers they knew who set their poems to music.[82] Each of these Italianate strands in the history of the chanson needs closer investigation in the attempt to take account of all the complex layers in the history of the chanson in the second half of the sixteenth century, and to begin to understand the ways in which pan-European musical ideas penetrated French musical circles.

---

[82] On the question of Italian influence and Petrarchism, see, among other studies, H. Weber, *La création poétique au XVIe siècle en France* (Paris, 1955), esp. pp. 12–22 and 231–6.

In their experiments with the chromatic genus, Guillaume Costeley and Anthoine de Bertrand attempted to put into practice the theories of Nicola Vicentino,[83] and Bertrand and Claude Le Jeune followed the treatises of Heinrich Glarean and Gioseffo Zarlino in ordering their collections of compositions modally.[84] Clearly, then, some French composers had read the Italian theorists and accepted their teachings. Through what channels did the Italian theorists reach French composers? Which composers continued to think in terms of the eight-mode system, and which in terms of the newer twelve modes? When did the French interest in Italian theories begin, and did they spread throughout France or circulate only in isolated circles? What contact, in short, did French composers actually have with Italian musical life?

We have already seen that Ronsard was probably emulating Italian practices in commissioning 'neutral' formulaic settings of the sonnets in the 1552 *Amours*, settings that were intended to be used to sing any one of a large group of poems in the same poetic form. Odes based on ancient Greek models, and certain kinds of newly written French poems, were also clothed in simple musical garb, almost certainly in emulation of Italian improvisers.[85] Mellin de Saint-Gelais was not the only French poet said to have written music for his own poetry and then performed it: Maurice Scève was also well known as a musical and poetic improviser,[86] and it may be that he, too, modelled himself on earlier Italian poet musicians. How did these French poets come into contact with Italian models, and how close were their imitations? Most important, how did the simple music that resulted compare – what was its connection – with French dancing songs, vaudevilles and *airs de cour*, those simple strophic songs that

---

[83] On Costeley's chromatic chanson, see K. J. Levy, 'Costeley's Chromatic Chanson', *Annales Musicologiques*, 3 (1955), pp. 213–63; and C. Dahlhaus, 'Zu Costeleys chromatischer Chanson', *Die Musikforschung*, 16 (1963), pp. 253–65.

[84] Le Jeune's modally ordered motets are published in a modern edition in Le Jeune, *Dodécacorde*, ed. Heider. On modal ordering in Bertrand's chansons, see Brooks, ' "Ses amours et les miennes tout ensemble" '.

[85] On the literary tradition of imitating Greek odes, see A. Delboulle, *Anacréon et les poèmes anacréontiques: texte grec avec les traductions et imitations des poètes du XVIe siècle* (Geneva, 1970); and P. Rosenmeyer, *The Poetics of Imitation: Anacreon and the Anacreontic Tradition* (New York, 1992).

[86] A fact not noted in Coleman, *Maurice Scève*.

played so large a role in French musical life of the late sixteenth century?

Quite apart from presumed Italian influences discernible in the theoretical assumptions of French composers, or their emulation of Italian traditions, some French composers also set Italian poetry to music. And Italian music was by no means unknown in late sixteenth-century France; Appendix 7, which lists all the songs in Italian published by Le Roy and Ballard between 1554 and 1598,[87] makes clear that the fashion for Italian music in France concentrated on the lighter poetic forms – villanellas, *moresche* and the chanson-like madrigals of the generation of Arcadelt and Festa – rather than on the virtuoso madrigals being developed at that time in the most cultivated musical circles of the northern Italian courts. Much of the Italian music in French anthologies came directly from Italy or from musicians who had lived and worked there. In addition to the few madrigals of Arcadelt, Festa, Rore and Vicentino, for example, Le Roy and Ballard published a good many of the lighter Italian pieces by Lassus, who had received most of his musical education in or near Naples. They also issued music by Italian musicians employed in France – Fabrice Marin Caietain, and the two members of the Vecoli family, Lucchese musicians who spent most of their careers as musicians in Lyons, Paris and Savoy – as well as home-grown Italian music by composers who never went to France: a volume of anonymous villanellas and a book of madrigals by Luca Marenzio, the virtuoso madrigalist who received the greatest acclaim outside Italy. Le Roy and Ballard's publications reveal, too, that a certain number of French composers who, so far as we know, never went to Italy – Jean de Castro, Pierre Clereau, Claude Le Jeune and Guillaume Tessier – also set Italian poems, a phenomenon that demands an explanation. Perhaps these latter composers were emulating Lassus, the most widely published chanson composer of the 1560s and 70s; perhaps there was a greater vogue for foreign fashions than has been hitherto supposed; or perhaps Catherine de' Medici's presence at the French royal court had a decisive impact on the country's musical life. Whatever the

---

[87] Appendix 7 is derived from Lesure and Thibault, *Bibliographie des éditions d'Adrian Le Roy et Robert Ballard.*

explanation, the villanellas and simple madrigals by native Italians, Italian-trained foreigners and Frenchmen who never left home must be taken into account in any analysis of the state of secular music in France in the late sixteenth century.

In sum, music scholars should begin to concentrate their attention on the various poetic traditions that made up the rich mix of chansons circulating in France in the second half of the sixteenth century. A leading group of composers set poetry in the newest styles, reflecting current debates about the nature of the French language and the subject matter and models appropriate for lyric poetry. Some of the same composers, however, also wrote songs on poems that had already been in circulation for several decades, or on new poems that reflected older styles and conventions. Some even set poems in Italian, mostly villanellas and other lighter forms. Music publishers did not issue only music that followed the latest fashions: they also published collections that include substantial amounts of 'early music', chansons by composers of previous generations; French publishers appear to have cultivated early music to a much greater degree than their counterparts in Italy. We shall not understand the period unless we take all these diverse strands into account.

IV: TOWARDS A HISTORY AND AN ANTHROPOLOGY OF THE FRENCH CHANSON

French music of the second half of the sixteenth century should be studied in a social as well as an intellectual context. It is essential that we discover the ways in which chansons were used, and who used them, and that we determine who the greatest patrons of music were, and what their strategies of patronage, so that we can know who paid for the creation of chansons, and who therefore might most have influenced their poetic content, their musical character and their style. In short, we need to begin to write an anthropology of the chanson. We can uncover one important aspect of the way music was used and who paid for it, for example, by writing histories of the chanson royal reign by royal reign, in addition to studying the chanson decade by decade from the composers', poets' and publishers' points of view.

In the first place, of course, we should find out how different
kings influenced or affected music, by asking, for example, how
interested they were in music, whether they cultivated or neglected their composers, and whether their musical establishments
were larger or smaller than those of their predecessors and
successors. We must also attempt to discover less tangible aspects
of the relationship between the royal court and official French
culture. Did the royal court make taste, or were the king and
his courtiers so bound by longstanding conventions that they
merely followed traditions in what they did and how they did
it? Did the king or one or more of his courtiers actually suggest
poems or musical details to composers, and did any of these
upper-class amateurs ever perform with their professional
musicians? Did the king and his courtiers take an active personal
interest in the musical activities they sponsored? For example,
does Janequin's dedication to the queen, Catherine de' Medici,
of his settings of Marot's translations of the Psalms imply that
she (as well as the king's mistress, Diane de Poitiers) sang the
psalms in French and encouraged their composition, or was she
merely the passive recipient of a gift from a loyal courtier?[88]
Does the establishment of the Académie de Poésie et de Musique
under Charles IX reflect the tastes and active interests of the
king and his courtiers, or did they merely tolerate its existence?
And did the attitude towards Baïf and his theories change when
the Académie du Palais was founded under Henri III?[89]

After the death of François I in 1547, Henri II (reigned 1547–
59) came to the throne.[90] The official royal musical establishment
flourished during the twelve years of his rule. Claudin de Sermisy
directed his chapel choir; Pierre Certon served as master of the
choirboys at the Ste Chapelle; and the Italian lute virtuoso

---

[88] Janequin's psalms, for which only a single bass partbook survives, are listed and
described in Lesure and Thibault, *Bibliographie des éditions d'Adrian Le Roy et Robert
Ballard*, pp. 81–3.

[89] See Yates, *The French Academies*, pp. 1–35.

[90] For very brief sketches of music in the reigns of Henri II, Charles IX, Henri III
and Henri IV, see I. Cazeaux, *French Music in the Fifteenth and Sixteenth Centuries*
(Oxford, 1975), chapter 1: 'Royal Courts and Music', pp. 9–32. The information in
the following paragraphs devoted to each reign has been assembled from standard
reference books. Except for Cazeaux, few music scholars have tried to characterise
the state of music under each of the French kings in the second half of the sixteenth
century.

Alberto da Ripa performed at court, eventually being appointed a *valet de chambre*. During Henri's reign, Pierre Sandrin and Clément Janequin were given the probably honorary title of 'compositeur de musique de la chapelle du Roy', the former in 1547, the latter in 1557, the first musicians to be so named (Certon was appointed 'compositeur' in 1567, and Le Jeune in 1598). Although Henri's mistress, Diane de Poitiers, pretended to great austerity as a widow, she was in fact keenly interested in music. She played the lute and keyboard instruments and sang. Henri's wife, Catherine de' Medici, who had her own chapel, loved music and dance and played an important role as patron and instigator of court festivities, especially during her years as regent for her sons Charles IX and Henri III. Her involvement with the organisation of various court entertainments has been fairly well studied, but never from the musical side. Catherine was an important patron of music whose role in courtly musical activities deserves to be given more attention. Henri died in 1559, but his successor, his young son François II, ruled for only a year (1559–60); he died at the age of sixteen.

François's brother Charles IX (reigned 1560–74) remained under the strong influence of their mother, the regent Catherine de' Medici, for many years. It was during his reign that she began to play such an active part in sponsoring court spectacles. The king himself was also evidently musical, for he sometimes joined his choristers to sing tenor or discant parts at Mass (in this activity, according to Brantôme, he was imitating his late father Henri II).[91] Both Nicolas Millot and Eustache du Caurroy directed his chapel choir and Guillaume le Boulanger, seigneur de Vaumesnil, served as lutenist at the court.[92] Charles was the king who tried unsuccessfully to lure Lassus to Paris. Indeed,

[91] Brantôme is quoted in A. Verchaly, 'Desportes et la musique', *Annales Musicologiques*, 2 (1954), p. 276.

[92] The music of Du Caurroy is in the process of being published in modern edition in E. du Caurroy, *Oeuvres complètes*, ed. B. Pidoux, 1 vol. to date (Brooklyn, 1975–). The chansons of Millot originally published by Le Roy and Ballard are available in a modern edition in *Chansons issued by Le Roi and Ballard: Nicolas Millot, Marchandy, Nicolas de Marle, Thomas Champion ('Mithou'), Pierre Moulu, Jean Mouton, Pagnier, Hilaire Penet, Claude Petit Jehan*, ed. J. A. Bernstein, The Sixteenth-Century Chanson 19 (New York, 1991). For the two surviving pieces by Vaumesnil, see *Oeuvres de Vaumesnil, Edinthon, Perrichon, Rael, Montbuysson, La Grotte, Saman, La Barre*, ed. A. Souris, M. Rollin and J.-M. Vaccaro (Paris, 1974).

Lassus and the court organist Costeley enjoyed their greatest vogue in French musical circles during the reigns of Charles IX and Henri III. Charles also demonstrated his interest in cultural activities by granting letters patent to Jean-Antoine de Baïf in 1571 for his first Académie de Poésie et de Musique.

In spite of these activities, though, court music under Charles IX (and Henri III) may have lacked the vitality of previous reigns because of the religious wars which began in 1562 and lasted until resolved under Henri IV in 1598. It was during Charles's reign, for example, that Protestants were massacred in Paris and the provinces on St Bartholomew's Day 1572, an event that cost the life of the composer Goudimel among many others. Quite apart from the disruption to musical life caused by war, the Protestants disapproved of elaborate music on religious principle. The predilection of the reformers for restricting music to simple settings of psalms and devotional songs – a phenomenon probably not altogether unrelated to the evident French penchant for simple strophic songs – surely influenced the shape of French music in the last quarter and more of the sixteenth century. And the nature and intensity of patronage, at court, in the capital city, and in various provincial towns, must have been affected by the religious wars.[93] It could hardly have been possible for a lively and vital musical life to continue when important composers like Goudimel and Le Jeune were forced to live difficult and dangerous lives because of their religious beliefs.

The religious wars continued under the rule of Charles's brother Henry III (reigned 1574–89), the last of the Valois line. A weak and irresolute king, Henri was nevertheless deeply religious. Driven by the ideals of the Counter-Reformation, he encouraged the formation of a religious academy in Vincennes. But his court also continued to sponsor secular poetry and music. Philippe Desportes began to supplement Ronsard as the favourite poet of musicians.[94] And Henri allowed Baïf to organise a second academy, the so-called Académie du Palais, which numbered among its members some of the most distinguished intellectuals

---

[93] For a beginning in this direction, see G. Pau, 'De l'usage de la chanson spirituelle par les Jésuites au temps de la Contre-Reforme', *La chanson à la Renaissance*, ed. Vaccaro, pp. 15–34.

[94] See Verchaly, 'Desportes', pp. 271–345.

of the time. These included not only Baïf and his musical collaborator Joachim Thibault de Courville (whose newly invented neo-classical lyre and its musical capabilities merit further investigation), but also Ronsard, the classicising Toulousain poet Guy du Faur de Pibrac (who helped steer the academy away from music and towards philosophy and rhetoric and whose poetry was set to music by Guillaume Boni, Jean Planson, Lassus and others), Pontus de Tyard and the Huguenot poet Agrippa d'Aubigné. There were several women members, too, including the king's sister Marguerite de Valois and the highly cultivated and influential Claude-Catherine de Clermont, Comtesse and, later, Duchesse de Retz, whose salon in Paris became an important meeting place for artists and intellectuals. Indeed, Henri's reign served as the focus of Frances Yates's seminal study on French academies of the sixteenth century.[95] On the other hand, there seem to have been few composers of true distinction in royal service during his years on the throne. Du Caurroy continued to direct the chapel, and Nicolas de la Grotte served as organist. Henri's reign should not, however, be dismissed as a completely fallow time for music, for, among other things, the famous *Balet comique de la royne*, regarded as the first *ballet de cour*, took place in 1581, devised by Balthasar de Beaujoyeulx, the Italian ballet master and violinist at court, probably from ideas emanating from Baïf's academy.[96] Some, though not all, of the music was published in a volume commemorating the event; the edition does not include the battle piece commissioned for the ballet from Le Jeune and La Grotte.

With the accession of Henri IV (reigned 1589–1610) a new era in French history began. The religious wars finally ended, political recognition was granted to the Huguenots by the Edict of Nantes in 1598, and eventually peace and prosperity returned to France. Among various reforms designed to improve the management of the country and of his court, Henri reorganised his

---

[95] On the Académie du Palais, see Yates, *The French Academies*.

[96] Facsimiles of the 1582 commemorative edition have been published as B. de Beauioyeulx, *Balet comique de la royne 1582*, ed. G. A. Caula (Turin, 1962), and, more recently, with an introduction by M. McGowan, as *Le balet comique by Balthazar de Beaujoyeulx 1581*, Medieval and Renaissance Texts and Studies 6 (Binghamton, NY, 1982). On the *balet comique*, see also F. A. Yates, 'Poésie et musique dans les "Magnificences" au mariage du duc de Joyeuse', *Musique et poésie au XVIe siècle*, ed. Jacquot, pp. 241–64.

musical establishment. The Protestant Claude Le Jeune was appointed 'compositeur du roi' in 1598 and succeeded on his death in 1600 by Pierre Guédron, who had served as the director of the king's chamber singers. But the revitalisation of the royal music under Henri IV really belongs to the following period of French musical history.

These brief sketches of the reigns of successive French kings between 1547 and 1589 name only a few of the official musicians and relate only a few of the more prominent and better-known events. Before we can begin to understand the nature of music and musical life in late sixteenth-century France we need more detailed chronicles of the musical events that took place and the people who shaped them during the reigns of Henri II, Charles IX, Henri III and Henri IV. More important, music scholars should endeavour to find out the nature of the music created for each king and the extent to which it was dictated by official policy, intellectual and artistic debate or personal inclination. A clear picture of the character of the music, and the institutional apparatus and cultural politics that created and supported it, could then serve as a useful point of comparison for study of the chansons by musicians not employed in the official establishment: the music of men like Jacques Mauduit, aristocrat, royal secretary and registrar in the judiciary but with no place in the official court musical establishment; Claude Le Jeune, whose official recognition by the court had to wait until the last two years of his life; and the many other Parisian and provincial composers outside the immediate circle of king and courtiers.

Many French aristocrats employed musicians: Fabrice Marin Caietain held a position as *maître de chapelle* to Henri, Duke of Guise; Pierre Clereau spent a part of his career working for René de Lorraine, Marquis d'Elbeuf; Le Jeune enjoyed the protection of a group of Huguenot noblemen and eventually became master of choirboys at the court of François, Duke of Anjou, the brother of Henri III, and La Grotte worked for the same duke.[97] Many other French musicians of the period are known to have served in the households and courts of the nobility. We know little

---

[97] The examples in this paragraph have all been taken from the articles on each composer in *The New Grove Dictionary*.

about such musical establishments in France or any other country during the sixteenth century. Music at cathedrals, royal courts, the courts in Italian and German city-states, and at the Vatican have been relatively well studied.[98] We do not know, however, what typically constituted the musical establishment of a lesser member of the nobility, a cardinal, or any of the cultural élite who possessed relatively little political power and yet felt the urge to support musicians.

Nor do we yet know enough about Parisian musical life to begin to understand the cultural politics of the capital city during the later sixteenth century. Was there, for example, a significant difference between the music commissioned and performed by and for the king and his more or less peripatetic court on the one hand, and that cultivated by the city's music-loving aristocracy on the other? In whose houses was music performed? Was music specially commissioned for performance at private salons? When a Parisian intellectual like Mme de Retz was said to be influential, what precisely does that mean? How did she or her friends affect the nature of the poetry and music being created by the members of the Pléiade and composers like Costeley who frequented her salon? Adrian Le Roy claimed to be her hereditary retainer. Does that mean that the choice of music to be published and the decision as to which composers to honour were determined partly by his indebtedness to his patroness? Was her salon an extension of the court, or in competition with it?[99]

One point of contact between the rich bourgeoisie of France and the aristocratic musical establishment doubtless came through the musical contest held each year at Evreux: the *puy de musique* established there about 1570 in honour of St Cecilia.[100]

---

[98] For some examples relating to French institutions before 1550, see S. Bonime, 'Anne de Bretagne (1477–1514) and Music: an Archival Study' (Ph.D. dissertation, Bryn Mawr College, 1975); R. Freedman, 'Music, Musicians, and the House of Lorraine during the First Half of the Sixteenth Century' (Ph.D. dissertation, University of Pennsylvania, 1987); C. Wright, *Music and Ceremony at Notre Dame of Paris, 500–1550* (Cambridge, 1989); and A. W. Robertson, *The Service-Books of the Royal Abbey of Saint-Denis* (Oxford, 1991). Comparable studies of the music associated with various French institutions in the second half of the sixteenth century have yet to be made.

[99] See J. Brooks, 'La comtesse de Retz et l'air de cour des années 1570', *Le concert des voix et des instruments à la Renaissance*, ed. J.-M. Vaccaro (Paris, 1994).

[100] T. Bonnin and A. Chassant, *Puy de musique érigé à Evreux, en l'honneur de madame sainte Cecile* (Evreux, 1837).

Prizes were awarded for the best compositions in various categories (chansons, motets etc.), and they were regularly given to the most distinguished composers in France. Research should be done to discover, for example, whether this competition was unique, how it was judged, and how important it was in establishing the reputation and careers of particular composers.

Not least of all, in beginning to try to understand French music of the late sixteenth century, we must expand our vision beyond the music that is the subject of this essay: the music of the cultural élite. We should also study the music associated with other layers of society: urban street songs, popular music, peasant music and so on. Such studies are obviously difficult to undertake because the music has been almost entirely lost. Some clues as to the nature of urban popular music do, however, exist in the form of single sheets, pamphlets and larger books containing the poems (but not the music) of the songs circulating on the streets of Paris and other French cities.[101] Many such songs were sung to dance tunes or upper-class chansons that survive in printed books and manuscripts; and there may well be indirect reflections of popular (or at least urban lower-class) culture in some of the anthologies printed by Le Roy and Ballard, Moderne and the other French publishers of the sixteenth century. We may have to be content, however, with reading at second hand about the music of peasants and itinerant minstrels, for those repertories would seem to be completely lost. In any case, it is no easy task to distinguish today the various social strata of music from the distant past. And yet we should attempt to do so in order to understand the way various traditions of music interconnect and reflect current concerns at any given time, and in order to place particular pieces and repertories in their true historical context.

In sum, there are many tasks to carry out before we can claim to begin to understand much about French secular music in the second half of the sixteenth century. Not all the questions I have posed can ever be answered. I would stress first and foremost

[101] B. Jeffery, ed., *Chanson Verse of the Early Renaissance*, 2 vols. (London, 1971–6), reprints in modern edition the contents of all such songbooks published up to the 1540s. A comparable edition of later songbooks, or at least a comprehensive study of such anthologies, would be an invaluable aid to study.

that we cannot hope to understand the music of this period unless and until we begin to understand the poetry, and the ideas that led to its creation. We need to find out what poets thought about music as well as what musicians thought about poets and poetry. We must try to discover how and why Ronsard and his fellow members of the Pléiade worked with certain composers, and whether or not the composers believed in and tried to carry out Ronsard's and Tyard's ideas about the nature of poetry and the relationship between poetry and music. Above all, we need to explain the bewildering diversity of the French chanson, a slightly paradoxical statement in view of my suspicion that this repertory has been neglected by the Anglo-American scholarly community because it has seemed to them too uniform and too simple.

It may be that we have been looking at French music through Italianate spectacles, searching for a highly expressive music whose composers were inclined to violate traditional musical rules of decorum, melodic grace and counterpoint in the effort to write a music that embodies the meaning of the poetry it sets. Instead, we should be looking for uniquely French ways of thinking about prosody and rhetoric – even equating correct prosody with deeply serious moral issues – and about more subtle relationships between music and literary ideas. We should try to learn more about the connection of the chanson repertory with dance. We should consider more carefully than we have in the past possible ways of creating a music that supports and enhances the text and yet allows the words to be clearly heard; and we should contrast the musical solutions whereby that task is accomplished with the old-fashioned idea, also current in late sixteenth-century France, that a song can be composed in such a way that it clothes (and even clarifies) the text without weakening or destroying the musical fabric. We have hardly yet begun to explore the riches of fifty years of French music.

University of Chicago

APPENDIX I

Works of French Renaissance theory[102]

1. Anon., *L'art et l'instruction de bien dancer* (Paris: Michel de Toulouse [1490])
2. Anon., *L'art, science & practique de plaine musique tresutile, profitable, & familiere, nouvellement composee en françoys: moyennant laquelle ung chascun pourra comprendre, practiquer, & scavoir par soy mesmes, & parvenir a grand cognoissance & perfection en ladicte musique* (Paris: widow of Jehan Trepperel [1502])
3. Anon., *Utilissime musicales regules cunctis pernecessarie planicantus simplicis contrapuncti rerum factarum tonorum seu organorum blualium et artis accentuandi tam speculative practice novissime impresse* (Paris: Jean Petit, 1512)
4. Anon., *Livre plaisant et très utile pour apprendre a faire et ordonner toutes tablatures hors le discant dont et par lesquelles l'on peut facilement et legierement aprendre a jouer sur les manicordion, luc, et flutes* (Antwerp: Guillaume Vosterman, 1529)
5. Anon., *Utilissimum gregoriane psalmodie enchiridion tonorum artem et regulas aperte demonstrans tractus de arte accentuandi epistolas et evangilias metrice et prosaice a pluribus extractus . . .* (Paris: D. Maheu [1530])
6. Anon., *S'ensuyvent plusieurs basses dances tant communes que incommunes: comme on pourra veoyr cy dedans* (Lyons: Jacques Moderne, [1535])
7. Anon., *Des chansons reduictz en tablature de lut à deux, trois et quatre parties, avecq une briefve et familière introduction pour entendre par soy mesmes à jouer dudict lut, livre premier* (Louvain: Pierre Phalèse, 1545)
8. Anon. [Des Périers, Jacques Peletier du Mans, Élie Vinet], *Discours non plus mélancolique que divers, de choses mesmement qui appartiennent à notre France: & à la fin la manière de bien & justement entoucher les lucs & guiternes* (Poitiers: Enguilbert de Marnef, 1557 [1556])
9. Anon., *La main harmonique, ou les principes de musique antique et moderne, et les propriétés que la moderne reçoit des sept planettes* (Paris: Nicolas du Chemin, 1571)
10. Anon., *Traicté de musique contenant une théorique succinte pour méthodiquement pratiquer la composition* (Paris: Adrian Le Roy and Robert Ballard, 1583)

---

[102] Editor's note: this list has been revised after Howard Mayer Brown's original by Philippe Vendrix.

11. Angleberme, Jean Pyrrhus, *Index opuscolorum Pyrrhi Anglebermei . . . Sermo de musica et saltatione ex Luciano festivissimus* (Paris [Orléans]: J. Hoys [A. Boucard], 1517)

12. Arbeau, Thoinot, *Orchésographie et traité en forme de dialogue par lequel toutes personnes peuvent facilement apprendre et practiquer l'honneste exercice des dances* (Langres: Jehan Des Près, [1588])

13. Arena, Antonius de, *Antonius de Arena provincialis de bragardissima villa de Soleriis ad suos compagnones studiantes qui sunt persona friantes bassas dansas de novo bragarditur in gallanti stillo compositas* (Lyons: Claude Nourry, 1528)

14. Basanier, Martin, *Plusieurs beaux secrets touchant la théorie et la pratique de la musique* (Paris: 1584) [lost]

15. Bernard, Emery, *Brieve et facile méthode pour apprendre à chanter en musique* (Paris, 1541) [lost]

16. Blockland (de Montfort), Cornelius, *Instruction fort facile pour apprendre la musique practique, sans aucune gamme, ou la main, jusques aujourd'huy tant accoustumée de plusieurs musiciens* (Lyons: Jean de Tournes, 1573)

17. Boiseul, Jean, *Traité contre les danses* (La Rochelle: heirs of Hierosme Haultin, 1606)

18. Boulenger, Jules Cesar, *De theatro ludisque scenicis libri duo* (Troyes: Pierre Chevillot, 1603)

19. Bourgeois, Loys, *Le droict chemin de musique avec la manière de chanter les pseaumes . . .* (Geneva: [Jean Girard], 1550)

20. Caus, Salomon de, *Institution harmonique divisée en deux parties: en la première sont montrées les proportions des intervalles harmoniques, et en la deuxiesme les compositions d'icelles* (Frankfurt: Jan Norton, 1615)

21. Caus, Salomon de, *Les raisons des forces mouvantes avec diverses machines tant utilles que plaisantes . . . livre troisiesme traitant de la fabrique des orgues* (Frankfurt: Jan Norton, 1615)

22. Champier, Symphorien, *Symphoriani Champerii, philosophi ac medici ingenio eruditioneque summi viri libri VII de dialectica, rhetorica, geometria, arithmetica, astronomia, musica, philosophia naturali . . .* (Basle: Heinrich Petri, 1537)

23. Coyssard, Michel, *Discours de l'utilité que toute personne tire de chanter en la doctrine chrestienne, et ailleurs, les hymnes, et chansons spirituelles en vulgaire: et du mal qu'apportent les lascives, et hérétiques, controuvées de Sathan* (Tournon: Claude Michel, 1596)

24. Dandin, Laurent, *Instruction pour apprendre à chanter à quatre parties, selon le plain chant, les Pseaumes, et Cantiques ensemble les Antiphones, et*

Pneumes, qui se chantent ordinairement aux églises suyvant les huict tons usitez en icelles (Caen: Bénédic Macé, 1582)

25. Daneau, Lambert, *Traité des danses, auquel est amplement resolue la question,à sçavoir s'il est permis aux chrestiens de danser* (s.l., 1579)

26. Daneau, Lambert, *De saltationibus et choreis, pius et eruditus tractatus, quo quidem illas inter christianos ferendas non esse demonstratur ex gallico auctoris* (Lyons: Jean Berjon, 1581)

27. Du Faur de Saint-Jorry, Pierre, *De re athletica ludisque veterum gymnicis, musicis, atque circensibus spicilegiorum tractatus, tribus libris comprehensi, opus tessellatum, nunc primum in lucem editum* (Lyons: Franciscus Faber, 1592)

28. Finé, Oronce, *Très brève et familière introduction pour entendre et apprendre par soy mesmes à jouer toutes chansons reduictes en la tablature de luth* (Paris: Pierre Attaingnant, 1529)

29. Finé, Oronce, *Epithoma musice instrumentalis ad omnimodum hemispherii seu luthine atque theoricam et praticam* (Paris: Pierre Attaingnant, 1530)

30. Gerson, Jean Charlier, *Tertia pars operum Johannis de Gerson doctoris christianissimi* (Strasbourg, 1488)

31. Gregoire, Pierre, *SYNTAXEΩN artis mirabilis, alter tomus, in quo omnium scientiarum et artium tradita est epitome, unde facilius istius artis studiosus, de omnibus propositis, possit rationes et ornamenta rarissima proferre* (Lyons: Ant. Gryphius, 1576)

32. Guerson, Guillaume, *Utilissime musicales regulae cunctis summopere necessarie plani cantus simplicis contrapuncti rerum factarum tonorum et artis accentuandi tam exemplariter quam practice par magistrum . . .* (Paris: Michel de Toulouse, [1495])

33. Guilliaud, Maximilien, *Rudiments de musique practicque, reduits en deux briefs traictez, le premier contenant les preceptes de la plaine, l'autre de la figuree* (Paris: Nicolas du Chemin, 1554)

34. Guyot, Jean, *Minervalia Ioan. Guidonii, Castiiletani in quibus scientiae praeconium, atque ignorantiae socordia, consideratur, artium liberalium in musicen de certation lepida appingitur* (Maastricht: Jan Baethen, 1554)

35. Hesdin, Jérôme, *Regles communes de plain chant avecques la fin des tons tant reguliers que irreguliers nottée, pour bien cognoistre de quel ton est le chant que l'on chantera, et aussi pour bien scavoir et seurement hault ou bas entonner toutes sortes de plain chant, lesquelles regles ont esté baillées par mestre . . .* (Avignon: Jehann de Channey, [1530])

36. Jambe de Fer, Philibert, *Epitome musical des tons, sons et accordz, es voix humaines, fleustes d'Alleman, fleustes à neuf trous, violes, & violons: item, un petit devis des accordz de musique par forme de dialogue interrogatoire &*

responsif entre deux interlocuteurs, P. et I. (Lyons: Michel du Bois, 1556)

37. Julien, Pierre, *Le vrai chemin pour apprendre à chanter toute sorte de musique* (Lyons, 1570) [lost]

38. Lefèvre d'Etaples, Jacques, *In hoc opere contenta: arithmetica decem libris demonstrata, musica libris demonstrata quattuor, epitome in libros arithmeticos diui Seuerini Boetij, rithminachie ludus qui et pugna numerorum appellatur* (Paris: Johann Higman and Wolfgang Hopyl, 1496).

39. Le Gendre, Jean, *Briefve introduction en la musique, tant au plein-chant que choses faictes* (Paris: Pierre Attaingnant, 1554) [lost]

40. Le Munerat, Jean, *Martirologium (explicit:) simul et antiqua atque nova regula canonica seu ecclesiastica, cum tractatu de concordia grammatice et musice in ecclesiastico officio* (Paris: Guy Marchant, 1490)

41. Le Roy, Adrien, *Instruction de partir toute musique des huit divers tons en tablature de luth* (Paris, 1557)

42. Le Roy, Adrien, *Brève et facile instruction pour apprendre la tablature, à bien accorder, conduire et disposer la main sur le cistre* (Paris: Adrien LeRoy and Robert Ballard, 1565)

43. Maillart, Pierre, *Les tons ou discours sur les modes de musique et les tons de l'église, et la distinction entre iceux, . . . divisez en deux parties; ausquelles a esté adjoustée la troisième, par ledict autheur, en laquelle se traicte des premiers éléments et fondements de la musique* (Tournai: Charles Martin, 1610)

44. Martin, Claude, *Claudii Martini Colchensis elementorum musices practicae pars prior, libros duobus absoluta, nunc primùm in lucem aedita* (Paris: Nicolas du Chemin, 1550)

45. Martin, Claude, *Institution musicale, non moins brève que facile, suffisante pour apprendre à chanter ce, qui ha cours aiour-d'huy entre les musiciens: extraicte de la première partie des Elémens de musique practique de Claude Martin, et par luy mesmes abregée* (Paris: Nicolas du Chemin, 1556)

46. Mauburne, Jean, *Rosetum exercitiorum spiritualium et sacrarum meditationum, in quo etiam habetur materia predicabilis per totius anni circulum* (Paris: J. Petit and J. C. Scabeler, 1510) [1st edn, Zwolle: Peter van Os, 1494]

47. Menehou, Michel de, *Nouvelle instruction familière en laquelle sont contenues les difficultés de la musique, avecques le nombre des concordances, & accords: ensemble la maniere d'en user, tant à deux, à trois, à quatre, qu'à cinq parties: nouvellement composée* (Paris: Nicolas du Chemin, 1558)

48. Paradin, Guillaume, *Le blason des dances* (Beaujeu: for J. and P. Garils, 1556)

49. Postel, Guillaume, *Musices ex theorica ad praxim aptatae compendium à Guilielmo Postello ex variis authoribus collectum* (Paris: Guillaume Cavellat, 1552)

50. Rivault, David de, *L'art d'embellir tiré du sens de ce sacré paradoxe ... estendu en toute sorte de beauté, et és moyens de faire que le corps retire en effet son embellissement des belles qualitez de l'ame* (Paris: Julien Bertault, 1608)

51. Telin, Guillaume, *Bref sommaire des sept vertus, sept ars libéraulx, sept ars de poésie, sept ars méchaniques, des philozophies, des quinze ars magicques: La louenge de musique* (Paris: Galliot du Pré, 1533)

52. Tuccaro, Archange, *Trois dialogues de l'exercice de sauter, et voltiger en l'air, avec des figures qui servent à la parfaicte demonstration et intelligence dudict art* (Paris: Claude de Monstr'oeil, 1599)

53. Tyard, Pontus de, *Solitaire second, ou prose de la musique* (Lyons: Jean de Tournes, 1555)

54. Varenius, Alanus, *Dialogus de harmonia, et de harmoniae elementis* (Paris: Robert Etienne, 1503) [lost]

55. Vigenère, Blaise de, *Les images ou tableaux de platte-peinture de Philostrate lemmien, sophiste grec, mis en françois par Blaise de Vigenère avec des argumens et annotations sur chacun d'iceux* (Paris: Nicolas Chesneau, 1578)

56. Wollick, Nicolaus, *Enchiridion musices de gregoriana et figurativa atque contrapuncto simplici percommode tractans, omnibus cantu oblectantibus perutile et necessarium* (Paris: Jehan Petit and François Regnault, 1509)

57. Yssandon, Jean, *Traité de la musique pratique, divisé en deux parties: contenant en bref les règles et préceptes d'icelles, ensemble les tables musicales, avec divers exemples pour plus facile intelligence de l'art, le tout extraict de plusieurs auteurs latins et mis en langue françoise* (Paris: Adrian Le Roy and Robert Ballard, 1582)

APPENDIX 2

Musical settings of Ronsard's poetry published between 1550 and
1566
(excluding the musical supplement to the 1552 *Amours*)[103]

Arcadelt
Mais de quoy sert le desirer (12)
Blancher
Tais-toi, babillarde arondelle (6)
Certon
Je suis un demi dieu quand assis vis-à-vis (10, 11)
Las! pour vous trop aymer (12)
Si je t'assaux, Amour, dieu qui m'es trop cognu (7)
Clereau
Comme un qui prend une coupe (13)
Comment au departir, l'adieu pourrois-je dire (14)
De peu de bien on vit honestement (13)
D'un gosier machelaurier (13)
Je ne veux plus que chanter de tristesse (14)
La lune est coustumiere (13)
Le comble de son scavoir (13)
Mais de quoy sert le desirer (14)
Nature ornant la dame qui devoit (14)
O dieux que j'ay de plaisir (13)
Qui voudra voir dedans une jeunesse (14)
Ton nom que mon vers dira (13)
Durand
Corydon, verse sans fin dedans mon verre du vin (6)
Du Tertre
La terre les eaux (15)
Entraigues
Que dis-tu, que fais-tu, pensive tortorelle (15, 18)

---

[103] Numbers in parentheses refer to volumes listed in G. Thibault and L. Perceau,
Bibliographie des poésies de P. de Ronsard mises en musique au XVIe siècle (Paris, 1941).
The sources of the poems in Ronsard and their forms are identified in J. Brooks,
'French Chanson Collections on the Texts of Pierre de Ronsard, 1570–1580' (Ph.D.
dissertation, Catholic University of America, 1990), pp. 8–10.

Gardane

Que dy-tu, que fais-tu, pensive tortorelle (17)

Goudimel

Amour quiconqu'ait dit que le ciel fut ton pere (6)

Bon jour, mon coeur, bon jour, ma douce vie (12)

Celui qui n'ayme est malheureux (20)

Certes mon oeil fut trop adventureux (24)

Du jour que je fu amoureux (20)

Il me semble que la journée (20)

Marie qui vouldroit vostre beau nom tourner (5)

Plus tu cognois que je brusle pour toy (15, 18)

Prenes mon cueur, dame, prenes mon cueur (8)

Tu me fais mourir de me dire (20)

Une jeune pucelette (11)

Janequin

Pourquoi tournes-vous vos yeux (10, 11)

Bel aubepin verdissant (10, 24)

Lassus

Bon jour, mon coeur, bon jour, ma douce vie (26)

Je ne veux plus que chanter de tristesse (27)

La terre les eaux va beuvant (27)

Rendz-moy mon coeur (18)

Millot

Bel aubepin verdissant (12)

Plus tu cognois que je brusle pour toy (10, 11)

Nicolas

Quand je te veux raconter (19)

Roussel

Je ne veux plus que chanter de tristesse (16)

APPENDIX 3

Chanson composers published by Le Roy and Ballard between 1551
and 1559[104]

Arcadelt (7bis, 8, 11, 12, 13, 14, 20, 21, 35, 37, *53, 58, 60, 63, 65)
Beaulieu (8)
Besancourt (60)
Bichenet (7bis)
Bonard (14)
Boyvin (2, 11, 65)
Cadeac (11)
Cartier (*34)
Certon (*3, 7bis, 8, 11, 12, 14, 17, *17 bis, 19, 20, 21, 37, 58, 60, 62, 65)
Ciron (8)
Clereau (*56, *61)
Costeley (62)
Crecquillon (7bis)
De Bussy (7bis, 8, 11, 12, 13, 14, 35, 64, 65)
Delafont (11, 62)
Desbordes (62)
Du Buisson (60)
Du Tertre (7bis, 37, 63)
Ebran (64)
Entraigues (7bis, 12, 13, 21, 35, 63)
Festa, Costanzo (11)
Fourmentin (60, 62)
Gerould (7bis)

Godard (7bis, 8, 60)
Gombert (11)
Gosse (17)
Goudimel (20, *32, *33, 37, *54, 58, 60, 63, 64)
Grouzy (19, 20, 58)
Herissant (8, 19, 62)
Jacotin (17, 20, 58)
Jacquet (17)
Janequin (*18 ter, 19, 20, 21, 37, *48, *55, *57, 58, 62)
Lassus (63, 64)
Le Roy (*5, 12, 14, 21, *22)
Leschenet (13, 35, 37)
Lupi (11)
Maillard (1, 7bis, 11, 12, 17, 20, 58)
Millot (37, 60, 64)
Mithou (12, 20)
Mornable (8)
Moulu (20, 58)
Nicolas (58, 62, 63)
Pagnier (8)
Passereau (17)
Penet (37)
Richafort (17)
Rore (37, 65)
Roussel (64)
Sandrin (1, 11, 17, 20, 58, 65)

---

[104] Numbers in parentheses refer to volumes inventoried in F. Lesure and G. Thibault, *Bibliographie des éditions d'Adrian Le Roy et Robert Ballard (1551–1598)* (Paris, 1955). An asterisk before a number indicates that the volume was devoted exclusively to chansons by the composer concerned. I have included lute and guitar songs, *chansons spirituelles*, and both psalm settings and other devotional works in French. Reprints of volumes are not listed.

Santerre (19, 21)
Sermisy (1, 11, 17)
Touteau (21)
Vassal (17)

Villefont (7bis)
Villiers (8, 11, 17, 19)
Vulfran (60)

APPENDIX 4

Chanson composers published by Le Roy and Ballard between 1560 and 1569[105]

Arcadelt (68, 71, 72, 73, 74, 75, 91, 104, 105, 106, 107, 120, 121, 122, 124, 129, 134, 135)
Belin (*68 bis)
Benedictus (68)
Bercoy (138)
Besancourt (72)
Boyvin (129)
Briault (138)
Cadeac (129)
Certon (68, 72, 73, 75, 79, *86, 87, 108, 121, 122, 129, 134, 135)
Chevalier (128)
Clemens non Papa (68)
Clereau (*116, *117, *118)
Costeley (79, 107, 108, 128, 138)
Crecquillon (68, 92, 129, 135)
De Bussy (71, 72, 73, 120, 121, 122, 129)
Delafont (79)
Desbordes (79)
Du Buisson (134)
Ebran (106)
Entraigues (74, 105, 134)
Festa (129)
Fourmentin (68, 79, 135)

Gardane (68, 70)
Godard (68, 72, 121, 135)
Gombert (129)
Gosse (91)
Goudimel (*66, *69, 74, *77, *78, 79, *79 bis, *84, *102, 104, 105, *112, *114, *115, 134, 135)
Grouzy (104, 106, 128)
Hesdin (129)
Jacotin (91, 129, 134)
Jacquet (91)
Janequin (91, 92, 104, 134)
Josquin (68)
La Grotte (*132, 138)
La Rue (68)
Lassus (68, 74, 75, 105, 106, 107, 108, *109, 124, 128, 138)
Lebrun (68)
Le Jeune (*85)
Le Roy (76?, *78 bis, 87, *93, 111)
Leschenet (68)
Lupi (91)
Maillard (68, 71, 72, 73, 91, 120, 121, 122, 129, 134)
Marchandy (128)

[105] For key, see note 104 above.

Millot (*119, 128, 135, 138)
Mithou (104)
Monte (128)
Mornable (72, 121)
Moulu (68, 134)
Mouton (68)
Nicolas (68, 75, 79, 87, 104, 105, 106, 124)
Passereau (91)
Pathie (Rogier) (91, 92, 129)
Petit Jehan (138)
Phinot (68)
Richafort (68, 91)

Ripa (*80)
Rore (107)
Rouince (106)
Rousee (68)
Roussel (68)
Sandrin (129)
Sermisy (68)
Touteau (79, 104)
Vassal (91)
Verdelot (68)
Villiers (70, 91)
Willaert (*67, 68)

APPENDIX 5

Chanson composers published by Le Roy and Ballard between 1570 and 1579[106]

Arcadelt (165, *169, 174, 188, 220, 221)
Benedictus (165)
Bertrand (143, *195, *211, *212, 223)
Besancourt (174)
Boni (*196, *197)
Caietain (*152, *197 bis, *214)
Castro (142, *184)
Certon (158, 165, 174, 177, 220)
Clemens non Papa (165)
Clereau (142, *185)
Conseil (219)
Cornet (165)
Costeley (*139, 177, 222, 227)
Crecquillon (165, 218)
De Bussy (143, 174, 188, 218, 219, 221, 223)

Delafont (177, 222)
Desbordes (177, 222)
Du Buisson (219)
Entraigues (220)
Ferrabosco (i) (165)
Fevin (218, 219)
Fourmentin (165, 177, 222)
Gardane (165, 217)
Gascongne (219, 219 bis)
Godard (165, 174)
Gombert (165)
Gosse (158)
Goudimel (165, 177, 188)
Grouzy (188, 221)
Hauville (165)
Hesdin (218, 219)
Jacotin (158, 220)
Jacquet (158)

---

[106] For key, see note 104 above.

Janequin (174, 177, 188, 219, 220, 222)
Josquin (165, 219, 219 bis)
La Grotte (*140, *162)
Le Heurteur (219)
La Rue (165)
Lassus (*141, 142, 143, *153, *199, *199 bis, 207, 223, 227)
Leblanc (217, 219, *232, *233)
Lebrun (165)
Le Jeune (165, 207)
Le Roy (154, *171)
Leschenet (165)
Lupi (165)
Maillard (142, 158, 165, 174, 220)
Maletty (*215, *216)
Marle (158)
Meldaert (142)
Millot (142, 143, 165, 188, 218, 219, 221, 223, 227)
Monte (142, 165, *187, 207)
Moulu (165, 218, 220)
Mouton (165, 219 bis)

Nicolas (165, 177, 218, 222)
Passereau (158)
Penet (188, 218)
Petit Jehan (227)
Phinot (165)
Regnard (*234)
Rennes (218)
Renvoisy (*172)
Richafort (158, 165, 219, 220)
Rore (165, 188, 207)
Rousee (165)
Roussel (143, 165, *203, 221, 223)
Santerre (188)
Sermisy (158, 218, 219)
Strige (Striggio) (165)
Touteau (177, 222)
Vassal (158)
Verdelot (165)
Verius (220, 227)
Vicentino (165)
Villiers (158, 217, 219)
Wilder (165)
Willaert (165, 219 bis)

APPENDIX 6

Composers included in Le Roy and Ballard's *Mellanges* of 1560 and 1572[107]

A. alphabetically by composer

Arcadelt (1505?–68)
Benedictus (Appenzeller?) (c. 1480/88 – after 1558)
Certon (d. 1572)

Clemens non Papa (c. 1510/15–55/56)
[Cornet] (c. 1530–82)
Crecquillon (c. 1480/1500–1557?)

---

[107] Names in square brackets are those of composers newly added for the 1572 edition. All dates are taken from *The New Grove Dictionary*.

[Ferrabosco, Alfonso (i)] (1543–88)
Fourmentin (dates unknown)
Gardane (1509–69)
Godard (*fl.* 1536–60)
[Goudimel] (1514/20–72)
[Hauville] (*fl. c.* 1553 – *c.* 1572)
Josquin (*c.* 1440–1521)
La Rue (*c.* 1460–1518)
Lassus (1532–94)
Lebrun (*fl. c.* 1498–1513)
[Le Jeune] (1528/30–1600)
Leschenet (d. *c.* 1603)
[Lupi] (*c.* 1506–39)
Maillard (*fl. c.* 1538–70)
[Millot] (*fl.* 1556–86)

[Monte] (1521–1603)
Moulu (*c.* 1480/90 – *c.* 1550)
Mouton (*c.* 1459–1522)
Nicolas (possibly Guillaume Nicolas, *fl. c.* 1533)
Phinot (*c.* 1510 – *c.* 1555)
Richafort (*c.* 1480 – *c.* 1547)
[Rore] (1515/16–65)
Rousee (*fl.* 1534–60)
Roussel (*c.* 1510 – after 1577)
Sermisy (*c.* 1490–1562)
[Strige] (Striggio) (*c.* 1540–92)
Verdelot (1470/80 – before 1552)
[Vicentino] (1511 – *c.* 1576)
[Wilder] (*c.* 1500–53)
Willaert (*c.* 1490–1562)

B. *chronologically*
(by date of death or latest documentation)

Lebrun (*fl. c.* 1498–1513)
La Rue (*c.* 1460–1518)
Josquin (*c.* 1440–1521)
Mouton (*c.* 1459–1522)
Nicolas (possibly Guillaume Nicolas, *fl. c.* 1533)
[Lupi] (*c.* 1506–39)
Richafort (*c.* 1480 – *c.* 1547)
Moulu (*c.* 1480/90 – *c.* 1550)
Verdelot (1470/80 – before 1552)
[Wilder] (*c.* 1500–53)
Phinot (*c.* 1510 – *c.* 1555)
Clemens non Papa (*c.* 1510/15–55/56)
Crecquillon (*c.* 1480/1500–1557?)
Benedictus (Appenzeller?) (*c.* 1480/88 – after 1558)
Godard (*fl.* 1536–60)
Rousee (*fl.* 1534–60)
Sermisy (*c.* 1490–1562)

Willaert (*c.* 1490–1562)
[Rore] (1515/16–65)
Arcadelt (1505?–68)
Gardane (1509–69)
Maillard (*fl. c.* 1538–70)
Certon (d. 1572)
[Goudimel] (1514/20–72)
[Hauville] (*fl. c.* 1553 – *c.* 1572)
[Vicentino] (1511 – *c.* 1576)
Roussel (*c.* 1510 – after 1577)
[Cornet] (*c.* 1530–82)
[Millot] (*fl.* 1556–86)
[Ferrabosco, Alfonso (i)] (1543–88)
[Strige] (Striggio) (*c.* 1540–92)
Lassus (1532–94)
[Le Jeune] (1528/30–1600)
Leschenet (d. *c.* 1603)
[Monte] (1521–1603)
Fourmentin (dates unknown)

APPENDIX 7

Settings of Italian poetry published by Le Roy and Ballard between
1554 and 1598
(excluding music for lute and guitar)[108]

11. *Premier recueil de chansons* (1554; later editions 129 and 183): includes
O passi sparsi by Costanzo Festa

13. *Tiers livre de chansons* (1554; later edition 35): includes *La pastorella
mia* by Arcadelt (omitted in later editions 71, 120 and 173)

56. Pierre Clereau, *Premier livre de chansons tant francoises qu'italiennes* (1559;
later edition with different title 116; Italian pieces omitted in 185):
includes 5 compositions with Italian text

61. Pierre Clereau, *Dixiesme livre de chansons tant francoises, qu'italiennes*
(1559; later edition 89; Italian pieces omitted in 142, 189 and 261):
includes 3 compositions with Italian text

91. *Second recueil des recueils* (1564): includes *Quand'io pens'al martire* by
Arcadelt (omitted in later edition 158)

107. Orlande de Lassus, *Sesieme livre de chansons* (1565; later editions
125, 144, 179, 193, 226 and 235): includes *Non mi togl'il mio ben*.
Two later editions (269 and 303) also include Rore's *Ancor che col
partire*

109. Lassus, *Dixhuictieme livre de chansons* (1565; later editions 127, 146,
181, 200 and 244): includes 6 *napolitaines*

110. *Il primo libro di villanelle alla napolitana* (1565): contains 23 compositions, all with Italian text

141. *Mellange d'Orlande de Lassus* (1570): includes *I vo piangendo* and, in
later editions (199 and 279), 6 other madrigals

165. *Mellange de chansons* (1572): includes *Passa la nave mia* by Don.
Nicollo [Vicentino]

169. Jacques Arcadelt, *Chansons a troys parties* (1573): includes *La pastorella
mia*

214. Fabrice Marin Caietain, *Second livre d'airs, chansons, villanelles napolitaines & espagnolles* (1578): includes 8 villanellas

---

[108] Numbers refer to volumes inventoried in Lesure and Thibault, *Bibliographie des éditions
d'Adrian Le Roy et Robert Ballard*.

227. *Vingtieme livre de chansons* (1578): includes *Que d'altra montagna ombra* by Lassus

238. Jean de Castro, *Second livres de chansons, madrigalz et motetz a trois parties* (1580): includes 4 madrigals

243. Lassus, *Libro de villanelle, moresche, et altre canzoni* (1581): contains 23 compositions, all with Italian text

254. G. Thessier, *Premier livre d'airs tant francois, italien, qu'espagnol* (1582; other editions 255 and 271): includes 9 compositions in Spanish and Italian

268. Lassus, *Continuation du mellange* (1584; later editions 312 and 317): includes 6 villanellas and 19 madrigals

280. Claude Le Jeune, *Meslanges* (1586; later edition 292): includes 37 compositions with Italian text

282. Regolo Vecoli, *Il secondo libro de madrigali* (1586): a first volume, published by Clément Baudin in Lyons in 1577, contains 29 madrigals

294. Pietro Vecoli, *Il primo libro de madrigali a sei voci* (1587): contains 21 madrigals

318. *Airs de court* (1597): includes one *air* with Italian text

319. Luca Marenzio, *Madrigali a quatro voci* (1598): contains 29 madrigals

.

Early Music History (1994) Volume 13

JEANICE BROOKS

RONSARD, THE LYRIC SONNET AND THE LATE SIXTEENTH-CENTURY CHANSON*

Music was an important metaphor for Ronsard, and references to music and musical instruments are frequently found in his poetry. His writings about music are few, however. In his article '*Ut musica poesis*: Music and Poetry in France in the Late Sixteenth Century' Howard Brown has referred to two of the most explicit examples of such writing: the preface to Le Roy and Ballard's *Livre de meslanges* (1560) and the passage from Ronsard's *Abbregé de l'art poëtique françois* (1565) on the desirability of union between poetry and music. Such passages are important in illuminating poets' attitudes towards music and in demonstrating ways in which the relationship between text and music could be conceptualised in the sixteenth century. They are frustratingly vague, however, about how the poets' ideals should be achieved, and they leave many practical questions unanswered. Did poets have any influence on composers' choices of texts? Did movements in poetic circles ever affect the pitches or rhythms of musical settings – that is, could poets influence the way music sounded?

Brown has also touched upon Ronsard's remarks in the *Abbregé* about the structural requirements of poetry to be set to music. Ronsard follows Sebillet in claiming that poetry with shorter verses, especially if the strophes are heterometric, is better suited to music,[1] comments that should be read in the light of distinctions between aria and recitative verse in opera and other sung

---

* I would like to thank Dr John O'Brien for reading an earlier version of this study and for his many helpful suggestions.

[1] T. Sebillet, *Art poétique françois*, ed. F. Gaiffe, rev. F. Goyet (Paris, 1988), p. 147. The standard edition of Ronsard's poetry is the *Oeuvres complètes*, ed. P. Laumonier, rev. and completed by I. Silver and R. Lebègue, 20 vols. (Paris, 1914–75), hereafter referred to as L. This passage from the *Abbregé* is found in L xiv, p. 27.

entertainments in Italy and France later in the century. His other recommendations have to do with the rhythmic structure of poetry for music: the concepts of strophic regularity and alternation of rhyme. It is on these passages that I would like to concentrate, in an effort to understand what Ronsard meant when he said his poetry was 'mesurée à la lyre', to determine whether his ideas had an effect on composers' choices of text and whether their musical settings were affected by his regulation of these aspects of the structure of the poetry. My goal is to offer some ideas in response to Brown's paper and to open some possible avenues for further inquiry.

RONSARD'S POETRY 'MESURÉE À LA LYRE'

The earliest mention of music in Ronsard's prose has to do with the rhythmic requirements of poetry intended to be set to music. In the preface to the *Quatre premiers livres des odes* (1550), speaking of one of his odes which had been published in 1547 in a collection of poetry by Jacques Peletier du Mans, Ronsard admits that 'Il est certain que telle ode est imparfaite, pour n'estre mesurée, ne propre à la lire'.[2] He does not specify what he means by 'mesurée'; but upon examining the ode ('Quand je seroy si heureux de choisir', subtitled 'Ode non mesurée' in his works from 1560 onwards) we find that the rhythmic structure defined by the first strophe of the poem, including its pattern of masculine and feminine rhyme, is not used for the succeeding strophes.[3] Since a verse ending in feminine rhyme has one more syllable than one ending in masculine rhyme, the absence of strophic regularity means that the strophes cannot all be sung to the same music without some adjustment of rhythm or text underlay. At this early stage, the 'measured' structure of the poetry is separated from its 'suitability' (or not) for the lyre in Ronsard's phrase; later on, as we shall see, these two aspects are conflated in his expression 'mesuré à la lyre'.

Ronsard came to consider strophic irregularity a defect, although it was frequently found in his earliest poetry. He began

---

[2] L I, p. 44.
[3] L I, p. 3. See also the facsimile of Peletier's collection in *Les oeuvres poétiques de Jacques Peletier du Mans*, ed. M. Françon (Rochecorbon, 1958), pp. 258–60.

showing his first odes to Peletier in 1543, and Peletier later wrote in his *Art poëtique* (1555) that the poems were not 'mesurées a la Lire, comme il à bien sù fere depuis'. Peletier further pointed out that although Ronsard was the first to use the term 'mesurée à la Lire' to describe strophic regularity, the principle had sometimes been observed by other poets before him, most importantly Clément Marot.[4] The problematic relationship of the Pléiade with Marot's work is well known; while rejecting his poetry in principle and attempting to award his position of leading poet to Ronsard, Pléiade poets (and particularly Ronsard) in fact adopted many of the older poet's practices. Marot's example certainly played an important role in Ronsard's adoption of strophic regularity, and Marot is mentioned in virtually every account of the development of the technique by writers on both sides of the contemporary aesthetic debate between the Pléiade poets and the *marotiques*.

For Ronsard, as for a number of other poets and literary theorists of the period, the idea of strophic regularity was associated with the principle of regular alternation of masculine and feminine rhyme. In Ronsard's strophic poems from the end of 1547, not only do all the strophes follow the same rhythmic pattern, but these patterns also involve alternating masculine and feminine rhyme. Furthermore, the alternation of rhyme could be observed in poems that were not strophic (for example, in *rimes plates*), and by 1550 even his non-strophic poetry featured alternating masculine and feminine rhyme.[5] Ronsard's 'mesurée à la lyre' refers to two related techniques: strophic regularity with alternating rhyme in strophic poems, and alternating rhyme in non-strophic poems. It does not concern any specific musical practice involving a lyre or any other instrument, but refers to

---

[4] *L'art poëtique*, ed. A. Boulanger (Paris, 1930), pp. 172–6. See also L I, pp. xxxviii–xxxix.

[5] L I, p. xxix. Laumonier discusses in detail Ronsard's adoption of strophic regularity and alternating rhyme in *Ronsard poète lyrique*, 2nd edn (Paris, 1923), pp. 673–85. I do not intend to discuss here the gendered discourse implied by the practice of alternating rhyme, except to mention that the combination of 'masculine' and 'feminine' verse in equal parts meshes well with the androgynous ideal of the Platonist atmosphere in which Ronsard worked; the use of alternation in verse intended for music thus takes on a particular significance, as music was thought of as the sounding image of the ideal represented by the harmony of the spheres.

the rhythmic requirements for poetry in lyric genres – that is, poems appropriate for singing, in the broadest sense.

In Ronsard's writings as well as in other contemporary accounts, the observation of strophic regularity and alternation of masculine and feminine rhyme were directly related to the purpose of the poem and whether or not it was meant to be set to music. As Brown has remarked, Ronsard, in the *Abbregé*, instructed the beginning poet to observe the alternation of rhyme and strophic regularity and made the connection between these techniques and musical setting explicit:

Apres, à l'imitation de quelqu'un de ce temps, tu feras tes vers masculins & foeminins tant qu'il te sera possible, pour estre plus propres à la Musique ... Si de fortune tu as composé les deux premiers vers masculins, tu feras les deux autres foeminins, & paracheveras de mesme mesure le reste de ton Elegie ou Chanson, afin que les Musiciens les puissent plus facilement accorder.[6]

Ronsard's most important predecessor in this respect again seems to have been Marot. Etienne Pasquier notes:

Je ne passeray soubs silence, ce que j'ay observé en Clément Marot. Car aux Poëmes qu'il estimoit ne devoir estre chantez, comme Epistres, Elegies, Dialogues, Pastorales, Tombeaux, Epigrammes, Complaintes, Traduction des deux premiers livres de la Metamorphose, il ne garda jamais l'ordre de la rime masculine & feminine. Mais en ceux qu'il estimoit devoir, ou pouvoir tomber soubs la musique, comme estoient ses Chansons, & les cinquante Pseaumes de David, par luy mis en François, il se donna bien garde d'en user de mesme façon, ains sur l'ordre par luy pris au premier couplet, tous les autres furent de mesme cadence, voire que le premier couplet estant, ou tout masculin, ou tout feminin, tous les autres sont aussi de mesme.[7]

---

[6] 'Then, following the example of someone of our time, you will make your verses masculine and feminine as well as you can, so that they are more appropriate for music ... If by chance you have made the first two verses masculine, you will make the next two feminine, and you will complete the rest of your elegy or chanson in the same measure, so that musicians can set them more easily.' L xiv, p. 9.

[7] 'I will not fail to mention what I have observed in [the works of] Clément Marot. For in poems which he thought should not be sung, such as epistles, elegies, dialogues, pastorales, *tombeaux*, epigrams, *complaintes*, or his translation of the first two books of the *Metamorphoses*, he never kept the order of masculine and feminine rhyme. But in those poems which he thought should be, or might be, set to music, as in his chansons and psalms of David (which he translated into French), he was very careful to follow the pattern he established in the first strophe in all of the other strophes, even if the first strophe was entirely masculine or entirely feminine.' Pasquier's statement that Marot sometimes followed the rule of strophic regularity without observing the alternation of rhyme is made in language implying that this is excep-

Pasquier goes on to observe that Ronsard's contemporary Etienne Jodelle rarely followed the rules of strophic regularity and alternation of rhyme in his plays, except in the choruses, where they were scrupulously observed. And another Pléiade poet provides yet more evidence that alternating rhyme and strophic regularity were generally regarded as desirable for poetry intended for music. In the famous manifesto of the Pléiade, the *Deffence et illustration de la langue francoyse* (1549), Joachim du Bellay commented:

Il y en a qui fort supersticieusement entremeslent les vers masculins avecques les feminins, comme on peut voir aux Pseaumes traduictz par Marot. Ce qu'il a observé (comme je croy) afin que plus facilement on les peust chanter sans varier la musique, pour la diversité des mesures qui se trouverroint à la fin des vers.[8]

Unlike Ronsard, however, Du Bellay apparently made a distinction between 'lyric poetry' and 'poetry for singing', for in the preface of his *Vers lyriques* (1549) he says:

Je n'ay (Lecteur) entremellé fort superstitieusement les vers masculins avecque les feminins comme on use en ces vaudevilles et chansons qui se chantent d'un mesme chant par tous les couplets, craignant de contreindre et gehinner ma diction par l'observation de telles choses.[9]

Du Bellay was aware that alternation and strophic regularity were considered necessary for lyric poetry but chose not to observe the principles because of the poetic constraint they imposed; he was later condemned for this by Pasquier.[10] Du Bellay closes the preface to the *Vers lyriques* by noting that in four odes in the collection, he had, however, followed the rules

---

tional ('*voire que le premier couplet estant, ou tout masculin, ou tout feminin*'; my emphasis). *Recherches de la France*, in *Oeuvres d'Estienne Pasquier* (Amsterdam [Trévoux], 1723), I, col. 714. For information on the numerous earlier editions of the *Recherches de la France* see D. Thickett, *Bibliographie des oeuvres d'Estienne Pasquier* (Geneva, 1956), pp. 32–44.

8 'There are those who most scrupulously alternate the masculine and feminine verses, as may be seen in the psalm translations of Marot. He did this (I believe) so that the psalms could be sung more easily without varying the music, for the diversity of measures found at the ends of verses.' J. du Bellay, *La deffence et illustration de la langue francoyse*, ed. H. Chamard (Paris, 1948; repr. 1970), pp. 164–5.

9 'I have not (Reader) alternated scrupulously the masculine and feminine verses in the way one does for those vaudevilles and songs which use the same music for every strophe, fearing that the observation of such practices would constrain and inconvenience my diction.' *Oeuvres poétiques*, ed. H. Chamard (Paris, 1912; repr. 1983), III, p. 3.

10 *Recherches*, I, col. 713.

of alternation and strophic regularity despite this constraint. Ironically (given his scorn for 'ces vaudevilles et chansons'), one of these four regularly constructed odes, the *Chant du desespéré* ('La Parque si terrible'), became associated with a tune which became one of the most frequently used *timbres* of the late sixteenth century. The tune, sometimes called 'le chant de La Parque', is indicated in innumerable anthologies of chanson texts as a *timbre* for new poems and appears with Du Bellay's text and notated music in Jean Chardavoine's 1576 collection of popular *voix de ville*.[11]

Ronsard's writings show that he wanted his poetry to be set to music, and that he believed that strophic regularity and alternation of masculine and feminine rhyme should be observed in verse which was meant to be sung. He was not alone in this belief, which seems to have been shared by many of his contemporaries. The association of music with certain kinds of poetry fed in turn into mid sixteenth-century concerns about genre; this preoccupation is manifest in treatises on both sides of the contemporary aesthetic debate (in both Sebillet and Du Bellay, for example). Ronsard's ambitions to recreate the aesthetic of classical poetry in French, and particularly his aspirations to become a French equivalent of Horace and Pindar, meant that the siting of his own works in the lyric genres took on a special importance. Although French poets before Ronsard experimented with alternating rhyme and strophic regularity, Ronsard was the first to practise both consistently, and his example was highly influential on later poets. In this context it is worth noting that the increasing popularity of the strophic *air de cour* in the second half of the sixteenth century coincides with the adoption of these techniques for lyric poetry and a generally greater interest in strophic lyric verse on the part of leading poets.[12]

---

[11] 'La Parque si terrible' is included in Chamard's edition of the *Vers lyriques*, pp. 37–9. On other settings of Du Bellay, see F. Dobbins, 'Joachim Du Bellay et la musique de son temps', *Du Bellay: actes du Colloque international d'Angers du 26 au 29 mai 1989* (Angers, 1990), pp. 587–605. On Chardavoine's *Le recueil des plus belles et excellentes chansons en forme de voix de ville* (Paris, 1576; facsimile ed. Geneva, 1980), see A. Verchaly, 'Le recueil authentique des chansons de Jehan Chardavoine (1576)', *Revue de Musicologie*, 49 (1963), pp. 203–19.

[12] On the absence of strophic regularity in earlier poems and the questions this raises in the context of the chanson and *voix de ville*, see J. O. Whang, 'From *Voix de ville* to *Air de cour*: the Strophic Chanson, c. 1545–1575' (Ph.D. dissertation, University of Pennsylvania, 1981), pp. 62–6.

THE 'AMOURS' AND THE SONNET AS A LYRIC GENRE

Ronsard's innovation was not the invention of the principles of strophic regularity and alternation of masculine and feminine rhyme for poetry which was to be sung, but his systematic application of the principles to a relatively new genre, the sonnet. His first published sonnet cycle, the *Amours* of 1552, contains sonnets using a limited number of rhyme schemes featuring alternating masculine and feminine rhyme. Laumonier has identified the four patterns which account for the bulk of the collection:

> I: 2(fmmf) m2 m2 f2 m3 m3 f2
> II: 2(mffm) f2 f2 m2 f3 f3 m2
> III: 2(fmmf) m2 m2 f2 m3 f2 m3
> IV: 2(mffm) f2 f2 m2 f3 m2 f3[13]

The volume was provided with the famous musical supplement containing settings of nine poems (six sonnets, a chanson and two odes) by four musicians: Claude Goudimel, Clément Janequin, Pierre Certon and Marc-Antoine Muret. The supplement was furnished with a separate preface, signed by Ambroise de la Porte (son of the printer), and instructions specifying that the sonnet settings were to be used as formulas for the singing of the other sonnets in the book with the same structure. The type I setting can be used for 92 poems, type II for 59, type III for 14 and type IV for 3. Eight sonnets are not provided with any musical setting; all eight adhere to a fifth type of rhyme scheme in which alternation of masculine and feminine rhyme between the quatrains and the sestet is not observed.

Although Ronsard apparently wrote his sonnets as he did in order that they might be set to music, he may not have been the originator of the project of publishing a supplement in which his aims are put into practice. That the preface to the supplement is signed by La Porte rather than Ronsard himself is enough to cast some doubt on the extent of the poet's involvement. He probably participated to some degree, however, even if only in choosing the poems to be set and soliciting the aid of musicians whom he knew at court. He must have approved of the supplement, as otherwise it is unlikely that he would have agreed

---

[13] L IV, p. xvii.

---

to its publication with his volume of poetry. In the preface, La Porte borrows Ronsard's phrase 'mesuré à la lyre' to refer to alternating rhyme. He specifies that Ronsard was the first to 'measure to the lyre' his sonnets, 'ce que nous n'avions encore apperceu avoir esté faict de tous ceux qui se sont exercités *en tel genre d'escrire*' (my emphasis).[14]

In 1552 the sonnet was still a relatively new form in French poetry. It was apparently introduced by Marot, and several of his contemporaries (including Saint-Gelais, Scève and Peletier) wrote a few sonnets, although not all of them were in print by mid century. By 1548, however, the form had become popular enough for Sebillet to feel obliged to include a short chapter on it in his *Art poétique*, and in the few years before the publication of Ronsard's *Amours* the Pléiade poets who were to make the sonnet one of their primary vehicles of expression had already begun to publish collections of them. Du Bellay's path-breaking sonnet cycle *L'Olive* was first printed in 1549; and Tyard's *Erreurs amoureuses* (1550) and *Continuation des erreurs* (1551) and Des Aut-elz's *Repos de plus grand travail* (1550) contain numerous sonnets among epigrams and chansons. None of these poets applied the formulas used by Ronsard for the *Amours* (*L'Olive*, for example, contains over sixty different combinations of rhyme schemes and patterns of masculine and feminine rhyme, including many without regular alternation[15]). None indicated in any way that they intended their sonnets to be set to music.

The sonnet is never mentioned among poems appropriate for musical setting in theoretical discussions from before the appearance of Ronsard's *Amours*. The issue of music usually arises in the definition of the chanson or the ode, or in the context of the battle between the Pléiade poets and the *marotiques* over whether there was a difference between the two. Pasquier, in his list of poems by Marot cited above, does not include the sonnet as a type of poem for which Marot envisaged musical setting (although he does not specifically exclude it either). Sebillet's mention of music in the *Art poétique* is made in the section of the treatise

---

[14] 'which we have never seen done before by anyone engaging in this genre of writing'; L IV, p. 189. Laumonier reproduces the entire supplement in facsimile on pp. 189–250.

[15] L IV, p. xvi.

dealing with the chanson and ode; in his section on the sonnet there is no question of musical setting.[16] Guillaume des Autelz mentions odes 'mesurées à la lyre' in defending Saint-Gelais against Du Bellay, but does not say anything about 'measuring' sonnets.[17] Du Bellay seems to include the sonnet among the lyric genres in a passage from the *Deffence*: 'Sonne moy des beaux sonnetz, non moins docte que plaisante invention Italienne, conforme de nom à l'ode, & differente d'elle seulement pource que le sonnet a certains vers reiglez & limitez, & l'ode peut courir par toutes manieres de vers librement'.[18] But, as we have seen, he did not necessarily equate 'lyric' and 'appropriate for singing', and at least one contemporary critic believed the sonnets of his *Olive* completely unsuitable for music. In the *Quintil Horatien*, Barthélemy Aneau responded to Du Bellay's attack in the *Deffence* on the poems of Saint-Gelais: 'Et si elles [the chansons of Saint Gelais] peuvent estre sonnées à la lyre (commes elles sont), meritent le nom de vers lyriques, myeux que les bayes de ton *Olive* ne la suyte, qui ne furent onques chantées, ni sonnées, & à peine estre le pourroient'.[19] Except for Aneau (who was talking about one specific group of sonnets, not the form in general), literary theorists do not actually describe the sonnet as inappropriate for music. But neither do they include it among the lyric genres with the chanson and the ode, which most writers, like Aneau, still defined by association with the actual practice of music.[20]

---

[16] Sebillet, *Art poétique*, pp. 115–18.

[17] *Replique aux furieuses defenses de Louis Meigret* (1550), cited in Du Bellay, *Deffence*, ed. Chamard, p. 115n.

[18] 'Sound for me those beautiful sonnets, no less learned than agreeable Italian invention, conforming to the ode in name, and differing from it only in that the sonnet has rules and limits on certain verses, and the ode may flow freely through all manner of verses'; Du Bellay, *Deffence*, ed. Chamard, pp. 120–1.

[19] 'And if they can be sounded to the lyre (as they are), they merit the name of lyric verses, more than the fruits of your *Olive* and the rest, which were never sung, or sounded, and scarcely could be either.' See Du Bellay, *Deffence*, ed. Chamard, p. 115n. The entire text of the *Quintil Horatien* (Lyons, 1550) is reproduced in the notes of Chamard's edition.

[20] Du Bellay is a notable exception; he seems to lean towards a more modern definition of 'lyric', separating a musical aesthetic (created by poetic style and subject matter) from the practice of singing poetry. Ronsard, like many of his contemporaries (see for example Sebillet's *Art poétique*, pp. 146–52), evokes the classical meaning of 'lyric' as describing poetry for singing. For a short outline of the changing meanings of 'lyric' see J. Myers and M. Simms, *The Longman Dictionary of Poetic Terms* (New York and London, 1989), pp. 171–2.

The 1552 *Amours* and its supplement can thus be read as a statement about the nature and purpose of the sonnet. The application of the rules concerning strophic regularity and the alternation of rhyme, and the inclusion of sample musical settings, clearly place the sonnet with the ode among the lyric genres, legitimising the new form by association with those (like the ode) whose prestige and classical pedigree were already established. In other words, Ronsard was, I think, concerned less with demonstrating what kind of music he thought was appropriate for poetry than with what kind of poetry was appropriate for music. Looking to the *Amours* supplement for explicit information about his musical vision would therefore seem to be fraught with problems. In this I disagree with Brown's statement, 'Presumably, these pieces were added . . . to demonstrate precisely the kind of music Ronsard had in mind in arguing for the union of music and poetry'.

Ronsard's clear definition of the sonnet as a lyric poem suited to musical setting probably did have an effect on some composers, however, influencing their choice of poems if not the style in which they set them. The early indecision about how to regard the new form before the publication of the *Amours* seems to have been reflected in musical circles. Although sonnets had already become popular in Italy as texts for music, chanson composers were slow to adopt them, and very few musical settings of sonnets were printed in France before Ronsard's *Amours*. Jean-Pierre Ouvrard has identified only four such settings: Arcadelt's *Au temps heureux* (Saint-Gelais; *RISM* 1539[16]); Boyvin's *Mort sans soleil* (Marot; 1547[9]); Janequin's *Mais en quel ciel* (1549[21]); and Gentian's *O foible esprit* (Du Bellay; 1549[22]).[21]

After the *Amours*, sonnets were increasingly used as song texts, taking their place beside the chansons and odes that had always been considered appropriate for musical setting. The sonnet's growing popularity with composers was probably at least partly due to this encouragement from Ronsard, the most influential poet of his generation and one who had working relationships with a number of musicians. The change in composers' practice

---

[21] J.-P. Ouvrard, 'Le sonnet ronsardien en musique: du *Supplément* de 1552 à 1580', *Revue de Musicologie*, 74 (1988), pp. 149–64, on pp. 158–9.

was not universal or immediate, as Ouvrard has observed;[22] nevertheless, for some it represents an important characteristic of their work and may indicate that they were particularly receptive to ideas propounded in literary circles. This is especially true of some of the chanson collections of the 1570s featuring settings of Ronsard: Jean de Castro's *Chansons, odes et sonetz de Pierre Ronsard* (1576), Philippe de Monte's *Sonetz de P. de Ronsard* (1575), and especially Guillaume Boni's two books of *Sonetz de P. de Ronsard* (1576), Jean de Maletty's two volumes of *Amours de P. de Ronsard* (probably 1578) and Anthoine de Bertrand's two books of *Amours de P. de Ronsard* (1576 and 1578). The southern French composers Bertrand, Boni and Maletty in fact concentrated almost exclusively on settings of sonnets by Ronsard and focused particularly on the *Amours*. Their collections can thus be seen as positive responses to the invitation Ronsard issued in 1552.

Much work remains to be done on how the sonnet was adapted to French musical practice in the late sixteenth century, building on the preliminary studies of Jean-Pierre Ouvrard. Questions that need to be addressed include the relationships between poetic and musical form and the impact of Italian models on both texts and music. More research is needed on the number and kinds of sonnet settings after 1550, not only for the sonnets of Ronsard (a task facilitated by Thibault and Perceau's index of sixteenth-century Ronsard settings[23]) but also for sonnets by other poets who followed Ronsard's example.

MUSICAL SETTING AND THE STRUCTURE OF THE 'AMOURS'

After publication of the *Amours*, alternation of masculine and feminine rhyme in the sonnet became standard, and Ronsard's regulation of its rhythmic structure was instrumental in the development of the French sonnet.[24] As many scholars have

---

[22] *Ibid.*, pp. 149–50.
[23] G. Thibault and L. Perceau, *Bibliographie des poésies de P. de Ronsard mises en musique au XVIe siècle* (Paris, 1941).
[24] French poets had been experimenting with alternating rhyme since the fourteenth century, but as L. E. Kastner observes, it required a poet of Ronsard's authority to elevate what had been an option into a rule, not only for sonnets but for many other

pointed out, if the *Amours* poems were written as they were because the poet wished them to be set to music, then music indirectly influenced the history of French poetry to a significant extent. It seems clear that the *Amours* had no such profound impact on the subsequent development of musical style. It was probably more important than has been claimed, however, particularly in the context of musical rhythm and text setting.

The limitation of the number of rhyme schemes and rhythmic patterns in the *Amours* is the result of the application of the principle of strophic regularity to an entire collection of poems rather than to the strophes of a single poem. The goal, put into practice in the supplement, seems to have been to permit the same music to be used for a large number of poems. As Brown has pointed out, the obvious historical precedent is the practice of singing sonnets (among other kinds of poems) using melodic formulas, with the accompaniment of lute or *lira da braccio*, popular in Italy in the early part of the century. Ronsard may have had some such practice in mind when he wrote in the preface to the 1550 *Odes*: '& ferai encores revenir (si je puis) l'usage de la lire aujourd'huy resuscitée en Italie, laquelle lire seule doit & peut animer les vers, et leur donner le juste poix de leur gravité'.[25] The experiment of the *Amours* does not seem to have been successful in fostering such practices in France. A few traces of sonnets being sung to formulas remain (Caietain's 'air pour chanter tous sonnets', and some sonnets in Claude Pontoux's *Gélodacrye*, for example), but on the whole the French response seems to have been unenthusiastic.[26]

Did the other important feature of the *Amours* sonnets, the alternation of masculine and feminine rhyme, have more impact

kinds of poetry as well. *A History of French Versification* (Oxford, 1903), pp. 63–5. See also Pasquier, *Recherches*, i, cols. 713–14, and P. de Laudon, *L'art poétique français* (1597), ed. J. Dedieu (Toulouse, 1909; repr. Geneva, 1969), pp. 95–6, for evidence of the influence of Ronsard's example.

25 L i, p. 48. Ronsard may have been using the lyre as a metaphor (as he does when referring to poetry 'mesurée à la lire') rather than referring to an actual instrument, however.

26 F. M. Caietain's four-voice sonnet-singing formula was published in his collection *Airs mis en musique à quatre parties* (Paris, 1576); interestingly, the sonnet used as a model (*Hé, Dieu du ciel*) is by Ronsard. On Pontoux's *Gélodacrye* (also 1576), see Ouvrard, 'Le sonnet ronsardien', p. 152.

on the musical setting of the poetry? Some scholars have asserted that it had none at all. According to Brian Jeffery:

the alternation of masculine and feminine endings on which the whole grouping of sonnets depends, however significant it may be for the poetry, is quite simply not important when it comes to musical settings. [note] The doubtful reader should simply compare the cadences in 'Nature ornant' with those in 'Qui vouldra voir' [both given musical settings in the supplement], whose line endings are different, and he will find no essential differences.[27]

It seems unlikely, however, that not only Ronsard but many literary theorists of the sixteenth century would advocate the alternation of rhyme for poems intended for musical setting if the issue was entirely irrelevant. Perhaps it is less important that only four rhyme schemes were used for the bulk of the *Amours* than that all four have alternating rhyme. Comparing settings of *Nature ornant* and *Qui vouldra voir* with each other yields no real insights, since both feature the alternation of masculine and feminine rhyme, although in different combinations. A more profitable approach, one which may shed some light on why poets thought alternation was important, could be to compare settings of Ronsard with settings of poems in which there is no alternation of rhyme.

In Janequin's *Nature ornant* from the *Amours* supplement, verse endings are clearly audible. The piece is written in the tradition of the 'Parisian' chanson, a line-by-line setting in a treble-dominated texture primarily of strict or animated homophony, with a few lightly imitative passages. In verses with feminine endings, closings of two basic varieties are used. One type, in which the penultimate syllable falls on a beat and the final unstressed syllable does not, can be seen in bars 6, 29 (Tenor), 32, 37 (Contra) and 41 of the modern edition of the pieces (see Example 1).[28] In the other type, the final syllable falls on a beat, but the

---

27 'The Idea of Music in Ronsard's Poetry', *Ronsard the Poet*, ed. T. Cave (London, 1973), pp. 209–39, on p. 212.

28 Bar numbers refer to C. Janequin, *Chansons polyphoniques*, ed. A. T. Merritt and F. Lesure, v (Monaco, 1969), pp. 191–5. *Nature ornant* is also included in *La fleur des musiciens de P. de Ronsard*, ed. H. Expert (Paris, 1923; repr. New York, 1965), pp. 25–8. The former edition reduces the original note values by half; the latter retains the original note values but transposes the song up a third from its original tonality.

Example 1. Clément Janequin, *Nature ornant*, bars 5–6 and 31–2

stressed penultimate sylable is still accented in some way, by
rhythmic expansion, a melisma or a dissonant suspension, as in
bars 8–9, 13–14, 24–5, 28–9 and 37–8 (see Example 2). Feminine-
ending verses provided the composer with two alternatives: the
possibility of a strong-beat ending, with resulting rhythmic
closure, or of a weak-beat ending that permitted greater rhythmic
continuity.[29]

---

[29]   The closings discussed here are rhythmic, and need to be understood separately from
the contrapuntal phenomenon of a cadence, since the harmonic resolution may not

Example 2. Clément Janequin, *Nature ornant*, bars 8–9

In cadences of verses with masculine endings, the final (stressed) syllable always falls on a beat, as in bars 4, 18, 21, 35, 44 and 48 (Example 3). Some of the endings resemble the second type of feminine-ending closing, although there is not as much emphasis on the penultimate syllable, but the first type of feminine-ending close is never used for masculine-ending verses. In other words, masculine-ending verses do not permit the same flexibility of rhythmic treatment as feminine-ending verses. This is an obvious consequence of text setting in music which closely follows the stress patterns of the words. A similar practice was advocated by Stoquerus for composers setting Latin texts; he emphasised the importance of the stress of the final word of a phrase and the necessity of distinguishing between final words in which the penultimate syllable is accented and those in which the final syllable receives the accent. Similar rules for Latin text setting were advocated by Lanfranco and Zarlino.[30]

coincide with the pronunciation of the final syllable of a verse (particularly in verses with feminine endings). In some traditional common-practice harmony, 'feminine cadences' are those in which harmonic resolution occurs on a weak beat, and 'masculine cadences' resolve on a strong beat; using this sort of terminology the second variety of feminine-ending close I have described would often count as a 'masculine cadence' when harmonic resolution occurred in conjunction with the final syllable of the verse.

30   A. C. Rotola, S.J., 'Gaspar Stoquerus, "De musica verbali": Critical Edition, Trans-

Example 3. Clément Janequin, *Nature ornant*, bars 20–1

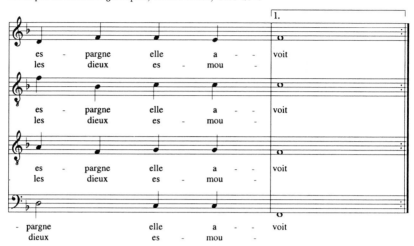

Although no similar commentary dealing with text setting in French exists, there is abundant evidence testifying that at least some French composers were increasingly concerned with accurate reflection of textual stress in their music. The most extreme manifestation of this trend is without doubt the activities of Jean-Antoine de Baïf's Académie de Poésie et de Musique, which influenced or attracted the collaboration of several composers, including Claude Le Jeune, Joachim Thibault de Courville, Jacques Mauduit and eventually Eustache du Caurroy. Fabrice Marin Caietain, in the preface to his *Airs mis en musique . . . sur les poesies de P. de Ronsard* (1576), claimed that he had given his music to Beaulieu and Courville so that they might correct any errors in text setting that he as a foreigner might have unwittingly made in setting French. Anthoine de Bertrand, in the preface to his first book of *Amours de P. de Ronsard* (1576), apologised for errors in text setting that might be apparent in these early chansons, and said that in his later music he had paid more attention to the correct stress of the words.[31]

lation and Commentary' (Ph.D. dissertation, Catholic University of America, 1984), pp. 252–8.

[31] For evidence of similar concern on the part of Jean de Castro, see my article 'Jean

The alternation of masculine and feminine rhyme in Ronsard's sonnets as well as in his other lyric poems means that composers are never obliged to write more than two masculine- or feminine-ending cadences in a row, allowing for some variety and flexibility in the rhythmic placement of verse endings. In Janequin's *Nature ornant*, for example, the regular appearance of feminine endings created the possibility of combining two verses into a larger rhythmic unit or of separating them more forcefully, depending on the type of rhythmic closure the composer chose and the degree of harmonic cadential reinforcement used. Du Bellay implies that this is the reason for observing the rule of alternation when he says that Marot wrote his psalm translations in alternating rhyme for the 'diversité de mesures qui se trouverroint à la fin des vers'.

This diversity was not always characteristic of earlier chanson verse. The well-known *Tant que vivray*, for example, begins with six verses with masculine endings:

> Tant que vivray en aage florissant,
> Je serviray d'amours le roy puissant,
> En fais, en ditz, en chansons, et accordz.
> Par plusieurs fois m'a tenu languissant:
> Mais apres deul m'a faict rejoyssant:
> Car j'ay l'amour de la belle au gent corps.[32]

In Sermisy's setting of the poem, each verse end falls on a beat, and each time there is a distinct break in rhythmic continuity (Example 4). Whereas earlier in the century this sort of static rhythm apparently had not posed problems for poets or for musicians (it is by no means the only such example in Marot's work), the evidence of the poetic sources indicates that by 1550 it was considered less desirable than regular rhythmic patterns of greater variety.

Even after the *Amours* Ronsard still sometimes wrote poems without alternating rhyme, and composers set them as they did

---

de Castro, the Pense Partbooks and Musical Culture in Sixteenth-Century Lyons', *Early Music History*, 11 (1992), pp. 91–149, esp. pp. 124–6.

[32] Text drawn from C. de Sermisy, *Opera omnia*, ed. G. Allaire and I. Cazeaux, Corpus Mensurabilis Musicae 52/IV (Rome, 1974), p. 99. In the same volume there are many other texts which feature long series of a single type of rhyme, by Marot as well as other poets; see, for example, *Secourez moy*, *Si j'ay du bien* and *Rigueur me tient*.

Example 4. Claudin de Sermisy, *Tant que vivray*, bars 1–12

the poems with stricter versification. They also continued to set popular older poems in which there was no alternating rhyme, although notably the use of older poems is more characteristic of Netherlandish composers, who tended to write in an imitative texture which de-emphasises verse endings. The conclusion to be drawn is that poems without alternating rhyme were not absolutely wrong but simply less desirable than those with regular alternation, in both their spoken and their musical form.

In music with carefully overlapped seams, a large amount of imitative writing or extensively fragmented text setting, the alternation of verse endings probably did not affect the sound of the music to a significant degree. The issue is of importance only in chansons featuring syllabic text setting, a rate of declamation fast enough for the verse structure to be heard, and clearly audible verses and verse endings. In other words, verse ending patterns were particularly important for music such as that of Bertrand and Boni or of composers of *airs*. Comparison of Bertrand's setting of *Nature ornant* with that of Janequin, for example, shows that Bertrand rhythmically differentiated the masculine and feminine verse endings as carefully as did the older composer. The resulting balanced rhythmic flow is characteristic of Bertrand's settings of Ronsard, as well as of many of the chansons of Boni (see, for example, the latter's setting of *Son chef est d'or* for an especially clear example of audible verse endings).[33] Jane Ozenberger Whang has pointed out that Pierre Clereau, a composer with strong connections to Pléiade poets, wrote *airs* whose 'natural continuity' (as opposed to the 'stop-and-go' character she associates with the earlier strophic song repertory of Certon and Arcadelt) is in part created by Clereau's sensitive treatment of feminine endings.[34]

Ronsard was a poet particularly concerned with the rhythmic qualities of his work. In the *Abbregé* he emphasises the role of the poet's ear, and it is a commonplace of criticism of his poetry

---

[33] Bertrand's *Nature ornant* in modern edition can be found in Monuments de la Musique Française au Temps de la Renaissance, ed. H. Expert (Paris, 1924–30; repr. New York, n.d.), v, pp. 68–71. *Son chef est d'or* is included in Boni, *Sonetz de P. de Ronsard*, ed. F. Dobbins (Paris, 1987), pp. 68–71.

[34] Whang, 'From *Voix de ville* to *Air de cour*', pp. 205–6. Clereau's music has been edited in J. A. Bernstein, The Sixteenth-Century Chanson 7 (New York, 1988).

that even in his poems of less than outstanding imagery or inspiration rhythmic flaws are very rare. His experiments with rhythm influenced generations of poets and profoundly affected the sound of French poetry. It seems logical to assume that any such change in the aural qualities of poetry should have some effect on music in which composers attempted to reproduce those qualities. What effect this was, and how extensive, can be determined only by a full-scale study of text setting in the sixteenth-century chanson. Any such study would of course be hampered by the scarcity of contemporary treatises on text setting, and particularly by the absence of any detailed commentary on the subject in French, which poses problems not encountered in setting Latin or Italian. But a careful examination of the repertory from before and after about 1550 may show that the rhythmic patterns of the chanson were affected by the standardisation of the rule of alternating rhyme; if this is indeed the case, then Ronsard's 1552 *Amours* will be seen as a landmark in the history of the chanson, not only for the musical supplement it contains but for the step it represents in the regulation of poetic rhythm.

University of Southampton

Early Music History (1994) Volume 13

FRANK DOBBINS

MUSIC IN FRENCH THEATRE OF THE LATE SIXTEENTH CENTURY

In his first major published monograph, *Music in the French Secular Theater, 1400–1550* (Cambridge, MA, 1963), Howard Mayer Brown skilfully plotted the development of musical practices in the traditions of farces, *sotties*, moralities and monologues until the middle of the sixteenth century, by which time the 'influence of works from the ancient world and from Italy' had turned the 'current of educated opinion . . . against the older French forms'. Thus he chose to terminate his study just as the new forms of neo-classical comedy, tragedy, tragicomedy and pastorale were emerging, although he did allude fleetingly to the Protestant dramas of Louis des Masures in citing one of three *cantiques* from the *Bergerie spirituelle* (Geneva, 1566) as one of his two examples of 'new music for the stage'.[1] Des Masures's play is only one of a number of dramatic or quasi-dramatic pieces published with music as well as spoken text during the period 1550–1600, reflecting a fashion for new music specifically composed for the theatre. In the present paper I propose to examine this considerable repertory, which has largely escaped the attention of modern scholars.[2]

ANEAU'S NATIVITY PLAYS AND THE *NOËL*

While the practice of citing as *timbres* appropriate popular chansons (some of which may be identified from extant polyphonic

---

[1]   The other was a four-voice motet composed by Jean Vrancken for a Flemish miracle play copied in a manuscript dating from 1565–6 (p. 44).

[2]   The following articles consider the role of music in tragedy and comedy but cite no notated music: R. Lebègue, 'Les représentations dramatiques à la cour des Valois', *Les fêtes de la Renaissance*, ed. J. Jacquot (Paris, 1956), pp. 85–90; H. Purkis, 'Choeurs chantés ou parlés dans la tragédie française au XVIe siècle', *Bibliothèque d'Humanisme*

settings) survives in mysteries and farces performed throughout the sixteenth century, it is rarely found in the new Protestant or humanist dramas and seems to have declined even in more traditional genres. A notable example of change occurs in the work of the Lyonnais Barthélemy Aneau, principal of the Collège de la Trinité at Lyons between 1540 and 1561. In 1539 Aneau published his *Chant natal contenant sept noels, ung chant pastourel et ung chant royal avec un mystere de la nativité par personnages, composez en imitation verbale et musicale de diverses chansons* (Lyons: S. Gryphe, 1539). This is a sequence of clearly identified contrafacta of secular chansons and dances, most of which survive in polyphonic settings by Aneau's friend P. de Villiers, Francesco de Layolle and others, many of them printed in Lyons and Paris around the same time.[3] It would be a relatively easy matter to present this work today as a Nativity play with music for two, three or four voices (and/or instruments) reconstructed from the versions published in various chanson collections around that time. But we could not be absolutely certain that a performance by the pupils and staff of the Collège de la Trinité would have used exactly the same music, simple and appropriate as it may be.

However, there can be no doubt about a second sequence of Christmas verses which Aneau published twenty years later under the title *Genethliac: noel musical et historial de la conception, & nativité de nostre Seigneur Jesus Christ, par vers & chants divers* (Lyons: G. Beringen, 1559).[4] As explained in its Preface, this publication includes new music that was composed along with the words in 1558. With much of the verse arranged in dialogue, a dramatic performance is again conceivable, even if the Preface suggests, perhaps for commercial reasons, a domestic performance in accordance with the traditional custom of people 'singing carols at Christmas time in their houses within the family with their wives, children and servants'. In the *Genethliac* three- or four-part music is provided for seventeen scenes or 'chants' and a conclud-

---

et Renaissance, 22 (1960), pp. 294–30; H. Purkis, 'Les intermèdes à la cour de France au XVIe siècle', *ibid.*, 20 (1958) pp. 296–309.

[3] The texts and their musical models are discussed in F. Dobbins, *Music in Renaissance Lyons* (Oxford, 1992), pp. 60–4.

[4] The only surviving copy (Paris, Bibliothèque Nationale, Rés. 85, Conservatoire 30029) contains the Cantus and Tenor parts of the music. The Altus and Bassus parts must have been printed in a separate volume.

CANTVS, & TENOR.

GENETHLIAC

NOEL MVSICAL ET HISTO-
rial de la Conception, & Natiuité de noſtre ſei-
gneur IESVS CHRIST, par vers & chants diuers,
entreſemez & illuſtrez des nobles noms Royaux,
& Principaux, anagrammatizez en diuerſes ſenten-
ces, ſoubz myſtique alluſion aux perſonnes diui-
nes, & humaines.

CHANT ROYAL POVR
chanter à l'acclamation des Roys.

AIGLOGVE SIBYLLINE DE VERGIL',
prophetiſant l'enfantement de la Vierge, & Natiuité
du Filz diuin. Traduicte en decaſyl-
labes François.

La Muſe aſſiſe au chef du Tertre
Coronné d'eternel rameau,
Par chants fait reſonner la lettre
Signée en la Foy de l'Aneau.

A' LYON,
PAR GODEFROY BERINGEN,
M. D. LIX.
Auec Priuilege du Roy, pour cinq ans.

Figure 1   Title page of Barthélemy Aneau, *Genethliac* (Lyons: G. Beringen, 1559).
(Reproduced by permission of Paris, Bibliothèque Nationale)

ing *Eclogue*. The composers of the last two *chants* are named as D[idier] Lupi [Second] and C[laude] Goudimel; the preceding pieces remain unattributed, although the first line of a quatrain printed on the title page may indicate that they were written by [Estienne] Du Tertre, just as the final line identifies Aneau as the author of the verse (Figure 1).

The verse employs varied rhyme and metre in the manner of contemporary *noëls*[5] and relates, mostly in dialogue, the Annunciation, Visitation, Adoration and other episodes in the Nativity story. The musical settings are fairly simple and include the first one or two strophes with the rest appended below. They are mostly syllabic with occasional brief melismas at the cadences; all but one are in duple metre, although the first, fourth and tenth *chants* have sections in triple or compound metre; the shepherds' branle (Chant ix) is in compound metre throughout. As in the contemporary French chanson and psalm, the musical forms are lucid and are subjected to varied repetition, with cadences that faithfully respect the prosody (*coupes* and rhyme). The main melodic interest lies in the Tenor voice, with the Cantus often proceeding in imitation or in parallel sixths (see Figure 2).[6] Some of the melodies (e.g. those of the seventh, eighth and ninth *chants*) have a folk-like simplicity, and the music is predominantly homophonic, although the first, third and thirteenth *chants* have imitative openings.[7]

PROTESTANT DRAMA AND THE *CANTIQUE*

1548, the first year of Henri II's reign, saw not only the Paris Parliament's ban on the Confrères de la Passion and the

---

[5] Like those of the Le Mans schoolmaster François Briand (1512), the Angers organist Jean Daniel (c. 1520–40) and the Savoyard poet Nicolas Martin (1555), all of whom were closely connected with the theatre. Briand's *Noelz nouvaulx* (1512) includes four *nöels* for two voices that were connected with four Advent plays in the same collection.

[6] The melodic predominance of the Tenor part is underlined by monophonic collections like the anonymous *Fleur de noels* (Lyons 1535); cf. J. Babelon, *Recueil des livres anciens* (Paris, 1914, I, pp. 369–404) which prints ten Tenors. It is also reflected in the two-voice pieces from the *Noels nouveaulx* of François Briand (Le Mans, 1512; repr. Le Mans, 1904).

[7] For a facsimile of the first *chant* and description of the others see Dobbins, *Music in Renaissance Lyons*, pp. 67–71. The final piece, 'Genethliac ou Chant Natal, Aiglogue quatrieme, extraict des vers de la Sibylle Cumane', is reprinted in C. Goudimel, *Oeuvres complètes*, ed. P. Pidoux and others, XIII (Boston, 1974), no. 71, pp. 262–7.

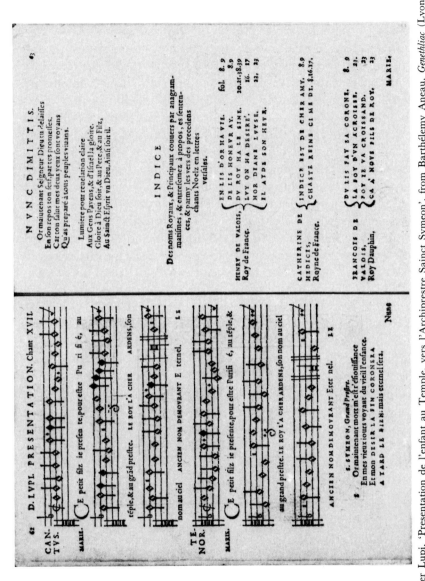

Figure 2 Didier Lupi, 'Presentation de l'enfant au Temple, vers l'Archiprestre Sainct Symeon', from Barthélemy Aneau, *Genethliac* (Lyons: G. Beringen, 1559), pp. 62–3, Chant XVII. (Reproduced by permission of Paris, Bibliothèque Nationale)

89

consequent decline of the traditional mysteries and miracle plays,[8] but also the performance at Lyons of one of the recent Italian tragicomedies (Bibbiena's *Calandria*) with elaborate musical *intermedi* written by Luigi Alamanni and set to music by Piero Mannucci.[9] Around the time that the new humanist generation were seeking to revive classical theatre with neo-Latin tragedies (by Buchanan and Muret), translations (by Sebillet, La Péruse, Toutain) and imitations (by Jodelle, La Taille, Grévin), the Calvinists in Geneva and Lausanne were discovering the propaganda value of biblical drama in simple language with elements of classical form. Théodore de Bèze's *Abraham sacrifiant* (Geneva, 1550), which has been described as the 'first tragedy in French that is not a translation from the ancients',[10] accords an important role to music, including a shepherds' chorus which participates in the dialogue as well as singing two *cantiques*. However, none of the many surviving printed editions[11] includes the music for these choruses or for the two 'pauses' which divide the play into three parts.

The first of the new Protestant 'dramas' to be published with the music was *La desconfiture de Goliath* by Joachim de Coignac, a pastor from Berry, who followed Calvin to Switzerland. His short 'tragédie' was printed by Adam and Jean Riverez in Geneva in 1551, with a dedication to King Edward VI of England, the new David who would champion the Protestant cause against the Roman church represented here by Goliath.[12] The play, based closely on an incident described in the Bible (1 Samuel xvii), still resembles the old *mystères* in its multiplicity of characters (twenty – excluding the chorus of Daughters of Israel), its stage action, its lack of Aristotelian unities, its simple, direct language

---

[8] The Confrères continued to present secular pieces (e.g. *La destruction de Troye*), romances (*Huon de Bordeaux* and *Griseldis*) and moralities until 1598. The Basochiens and Enfants sans Souci associations also continued their activities intermittently until 1580.

[9] Cf. Dobbins, pp. 111–16.

[10] R. Lebègue, *La tragédie religieuse en France* (Paris, 1929), p. 318.

[11] Originally written for a speech-day performance, Bèze's *Abraham* was revived many times by both amateur and professional troupes in the course of the next 100 years, while other Protestant plays (e.g. those of Jean de la Taille, Pierre Heyns and Gérard de Vivre) and even some humanist ones (e.g. those of George Buchanan, Marc-Antoine de Muret and Georgius Macropedius) were clearly written for schools or colleges. Cf. Lebègue, *La tragédie religieuse*, pp. 312–18 and 507–13.

[12] London, British Library C.65.a.11.

Example 1. 'Cantique des filles d'Israel', from Joachim de Coignac, *La desconfiture de Goliath* (Geneva, 1551), p. 68 (composer unknown)

with botched verse in short metre and its division into episodes by *pauses*, which might have been occupied by instrumental music. Much of David's part consists of short sermons and prayers and includes the recommendation for singing psalms and *cantiques* 'in a language understood by all'. A final lengthy prayer intoned by a chorus of 'Filles d'Israel' culminates in a *cantique* comprising thirteen five-line strophes, of which the first is set below a single Tenor part (see Example 1), followed by the play's moral quoted from the Bible (Judges v.31): 'So let all thine enemies perish, o Lord: but let them that love him be as the sun when he goes forth in his might.'

This music could hardly be simpler or more symmetrical: the five seven-syllable lines with alternating feminine and masculine rhymes are treated syllabically with no melisma, while each line is divided by a *semibrevis* rest; the first and last phrases cadence in the tonic (transposed Dorian mode), the second and third on the dominant and the fourth on the mediant (relative major). The composer is not identified and the tune may well be rhythmically adapted from some pre-existent sacred or secular melody, like many of those that Loys Bourgeois adapted for the Huguenot Psalter.[13]

The proselytising and polemical intention of Calvinist drama was underlined during the next two decades by the publication

---

[13] Its melodic outline is similar to that noted in P. Pidoux, *Le Psautier Huguenot* (Basle, 1962), I, p. 128, Pseaume 144b.

in Geneva of a number of plays including similar prayers and canticles with notated music by the same (anonymous) composers and printers who enjoyed such popular success with the contemporary Huguenot psalms.[14]

Coignac's *Goliath* represents a satirical, anti-papal genre, which modifies a venerable tradition found in moralities and indeed some mystery plays of the fifteenth century. Another example is found in Jaques Bienvenu's 'comedie apocalyptique' *Le triomphe de Jesus Christ* (Geneva: J. Bonnefoy, 1562),[15] which offers a French verse translation of John Foxe's *Christus triumphans* (Basle: J. Oporin, 1556), a 'comedy' in six acts drawing on events throughout human history and a vast cast of allegorical characters to depict the Pope as the agent of Satan. Bienvenu finds a role for music in the concluding 'Chant nuptial' whose brief heterometric strophes are set anonymously for four voices in the simplest homophonic manner of the Huguenot psalms of Loys Bourgeois and Claude Goudimel (Example 2). Bienvenu's *Comedie du monde malade* (Geneva: J. Crespin, 1568),[16] a morality 'recited' by its allegorical characters (Truth, Peace, Deceit and War) during the celebrations for the alliance between the municipalities of Berne and Geneva, also includes a concluding *cantique* set for four voices in similar style. *Cantiques* were again sung or recited by the chorus of Babylonians and by the three brothers cast into a furnace by Nebuchadnezzar in a *Tragi-comedie* (s.l., 1561)[17] by Antoine de la Croix, a gentleman in the service of Antoine de Bourbon, King of Navarre (see also below, p. 110).

The singing of canticles in Protestant drama was thus well established by 1566 when François Perrin of Geneva printed the three *tragédies sainctes* of Louis des Masures,[18] who expanded the

---

[14] Continuing the didactic tradition of liturgical drama and mystery plays, singing seems to have endowed some performances with the character of religious services; the metrical and melodic simplicity of this music may even suggest the participation of the audience or congregation.

[15] London, British Library C.47.e.17.

[16] Geneva, Bibliothèque Publique et Universitaire Rés. Hf. 2204.

[17] Paris, Bibliothèque Nationale Rés. p.Yc 1198 (2). Like the biblical dramas of Bèze, Coignac, Des Masures and Lecocq, this play was divided by *pauses* which may have been occupied by instrumental music.

[18] Des Masures was born in Tournai around 1515 and spent much of his career in Lorraine, where he translated the *Aeneid*, published at different stages in Paris (1547) and Lyons (1552 and 1560). After returning in 1549 from Rome, where he enjoyed the protection of Cardinal Jean du Bellay, he converted to Protestantism; although

theme of Coignac's tragedy into a trilogy representing the combat, triumph and flight of David. The three tragedies resemble Coignac's *Goliath* in their kinship with the *mystère* tradition (juxtaposed scenes and action broken by *pauses*) as well as in their edifying proselytism; but they are also indebted to classical models for their increased psychological drama and characterisation resulting from a smaller cast and a greater temporal unity. The role of music is increased to include eleven *cantiques*, all printed in four parts (Cantus and Tenor on left-hand pages with Altus and Bassus opposite). These are mostly choruses representing the Israelites (the three 'Cantiques à danser de la trouppe' in *David triomphant* alternate lines or couplets between the *Trouppe* and *Demi trouppe*). Other *cantiques* were sung by David, for example, the three in *David fugitif* and three of the five in *David combattant* (the first being for Isai and David and the second for 'La trouppe d'Israel'). In each case the text of the first strophe is placed below the music in all four voice parts and the remaining stanzas are appended after the music. In accordance with the Calvinist psalm performance practice, the plays do not mention instruments, although they may have played during the dividing *pauses*.

Most of the *cantiques* are composed strictly in the manner of the simple homophonic four-voice settings of the Genevan Psalter, published a few years earlier. They are consistently set in duple metre (¢), although the phrase lengths vary from three to eight semibreves in line with the alternating poetic metre ranging from three to ten syllables (plus feminine rhymes).[19] The voices have few melismas (small groups of passing notes mostly in cadential

he translated twenty psalms for Duke Jean de Lorraine (published in Lyons in 1557, with a further six added for an edition which appeared in Lyons in 1564), as well as composing an *Eclogue spirituelle* for the son of Duke Charles de Lorraine (published Geneva, 1566), he was eventually compelled to flee Lorraine and settled first in Metz (1562) before moving on to Alsace, Strasbourg (1567) and finally Basle (1572). On 3 May 1563 the Geneva town council granted him a privilege to publish 'quelques comédies de David' and three years later issued a new privilege to reprint 'certaines tragédies de David qu'il a déjà imprimées'. Perrin's edition of 1566 and Gabriel Cartier's Genevan edition of 1583 also include both the *Eclogue spirituelle* and the *Bergerie spirituelle*, which are omitted from the editions of Nicolas Soolmans (Antwerp, 1582) and Mamert Patisson (Paris, 1587 and 1597).

19 A few *cantiques* ('A Dieu au souverain Dieu', 'O Seigneur eternel' and 'Au grand Dieu veinqueur' from *David combattant*, and 'Dieu tout puissant' from *David fugitif*) are isometric but extend some cadences and introduce anacrusis to vary the phrase symmetry a little.

Example 2. 'Chant nuptial', from Jaques Bienvenu, *Le triomphe de Jesus Christ* (Geneva, 1562), fols. T5ᵛ–6 (composer unknown)

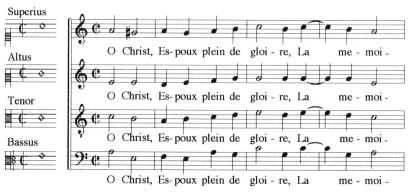

extensions) to disturb the strictly syllabic declamation. The forms are lucid and symmetrical: a reprise of the opening music for the second couplet occurs in a few cases, while in the three *cantiques à danser* from *David triomphant* all three sections are repeated, the last being a refrain; the remaining pieces are through-composed.

The melodies are conventional, resembling the Calvinist metrical psalms in their limited range and simple diatonic intervals. The harmony also reflects the modal tradition; most pieces are in Dorian or transposed Dorian modes and there are four pieces in the transposed Ionian, although the free use of chords on every diatonic degree, like the generally free alternation of major and minor chords, contrasts with later tonal vocabulary. As with the similar *Vingtsix Cantiques ... par Louis des Masures*[20] published in Lyons by Jean de Tournes in 1564, the composer is not named. The style is generally akin to that of the four-voice metrical psalms and *chansons spirituelles* published at Geneva and Lyons around the mid sixteenth century by composers like Loys Bourgeois, Didier Lupi, Philibert Jambe de Fer and Claude Goudimel.[21] None of the Genevan psalm melodies are used in the dramas, but the relationship to older models sacred and secular may be surmised from the broad similarity of the ninth piece, 'Dieu tout puissant', to contemporary courtly pavanes and to the popular chanson *Doulce mémoire*, first published in a four-voice version by Pierre Sandrin in 1538.[22] (See Example 3.) The lighter rhythm of the contemporary branle is illustrated in another *cantique* danced by the *Trouppe* in *David triomphant* which sets the fifth and sixth lines of the *huitain* strophe for solo Tenor, reintroducing the other voices for the final couplet (Example 4).

---

[20] Pidoux, *Le Psautier Huguenot*, II, pp. 146–8. See also L. Guillo, *Les éditions musicales de la Renaissance Lyonnaise* (Paris, 1991), pp. 320–2.

[21] The most likely composer was Claude Goudimel, who lived in Metz from 1557 to 1565 and must have known Des Masures there, since the pair acted together as godparents to a child born on 14 October 1565 (Metz, Archives Municipales, GC 236). The case for Goudimel's authorship is discussed in M. Honegger, 'Les chansons spirituelles de Didier Lupi' (dissertation, University of Paris, 1970), II, p. 149, and all eleven pieces are included in Goudimel, *Oeuvres complètes*, XIV (New York and Basle, 1983), pp. 103–9.

[22] Cf. F. Dobbins, '"Doulce mémoire": a Study of the Parody Chanson', *Proceedings of the Royal Musical Association*, 96 (1969), pp. 85–101.

Example 3a. 'Cantique à danser de la trouppe', from Louis des Masures, *David fugitif* (Geneva, 1566), p. 192 (composer unknown; possibly Claude Goudimel)

Example 3b. 'Doulce memoire', chanson by Pierre Sandrin first published in *Le parangon des chansons* (Lyons: J. Moderne, n.d. [RISM 1538[15]]), fol. 19

Des Masures's *Bergerie spirituelle* (Geneva, 1566)[23] hardly reflects the recent Italian vogue for Arcadian drama, but rather relates to the old French *moralité* tradition adapted to Protestant purposes. The plot involves the rediscovery by Religion of her mother, Truth, awakening after a long sleep and conversing with Error, brother of Ignorance; the work ends with the intervention of Divine Providence. The music comprises three *cantiques* for

---

[23] The *Eclogue spirituelle*, which follows the *Bergerie* in François Perrin's Genevan edition of 1566, includes no music, although it is followed by graces and the monthly consecration with verse by Des Masures set in a similar manner for four voices.

Example 4. 'Cantique à danser de la trouppe', from Louis des Masures, *David triomphant* (Geneva, 1566), p. 144 (composer unknown; possibly Claude Goudimel)

four voices, including the chorus 'Reveillez-vous, reveillez', to which Truth replies alone from behind the curtain.[24] This piece is nothing more than a contrafactum of the *Cantique à danser* from *David triomphant* (see Example 4 above). Similarly, the music for 'Sus bergiers, à ceste fois' comes from the first chorus in *David triomphant* and that for 'O Pere éternel qui les cieux habites' from the final *cantique* in *David combattant*.[25]

While a significant proportion of Des Masures's plays is sung, the new Protestant fashion for associating biblical drama with music reaches its apotheosis with an anonymous play entitled *La musique de David, ou est demonstrée la rejection des Juifs et la reception des Gentils*, published by Jean Saugrin in Lyons in 1566.[26] This

---

[24] Cf. Brown, *Music in the French Secular Theater*, p. 96.
[25] Cf. Goudimel, *Oeuvres complètes*, xiv, pp. 105–7.
[26] The sole surviving copy in the Herzog Albert Bibliothek in Wolfenbüttel (434 Theol. (7)) remained unknown to bibliographers until signalled by Guillo, *Les éditions musicales*, no. 78. The music is reviewed in Dobbins, *Music in Renaissance Lyons*, pp. 268–9.

short single-act drama is presented as a dialogue in verse (mostly decasyllabic) between Abraham (representing Faith), Moses (Law), David (the Psalmist), Jesus Christ (the Prophet), a Jew and a Gentile, expressing the musical and doctrinal harmony between the biblical characters, the rejection of Christ by the Jew and his joyful acceptance by the Gentile. Abraham's opening speech of fourteen decasyllabic lines affirming his faith in God's justice (with echoes of Bèze's play) is followed by three short hexametric strophes, the first on the favourite Protestant theme of Justification by Faith sung with an elaborate melisma (Example 5). Moses enters singing Marot's translation of God's Commandments to the melody of the Genevan Psalter (Example 6).[27] He then sings in dialogue with Abraham in interlocking decasyllabic *épigrammes* of nine, ten and eight lines, before joining him in a duet, singing the *haute-contre* above Abraham's *basse contre* (Example 7). David appears next, praising this harmony before singing his own solo (Example 8). After further dialogue the three agree to sing one of David's psalms, using the first couplet of Marot's translation of *Non nobis domine*, which Claude Goudimel had set for four voices and published two years earlier.[28] Jesus enters next, introducing himself in a high (Superius) voice (Example 9).

In the ensuing dialogue musical terms abound: Jesus offers to teach the others how to sing 'without discord . . . in perfect accord'; David is delighted that their choir is now complete;

Example 5. From *La musique de David* (Lyons: J. Saugrin, 1566), fol. A2^v (author and composer unknown)

[27] Pidoux, *Le Psautier Huguenot*, i, no. 201d.
[28] Goudimel, *Oeuvres complètes*, ix (New York and Basle, 1973), Pseaume cxv, pp. 118–19.

Example 6. From *La musique de David*, fol. A2ᵛ

Example 7. From *La musique de David*, fol. A3

Example 8. From *La musique de David*, fol. A4

Example 9. From *La musique de David*, fol. B2

Superius — Jesus-Christ entre en chantant

Je suis le fils du Dieu vi - vant

Ver - be fait chair par cha - ri - té, Pour sau - ver l'hom- me_en

ve - ri - té Le - quel vers moy se - ra croy - ant.

Moses greets the 'Second David, psalmodising singer'; Jesus explains that he has come down 'to accord human discord . . . to speak to the Jews . . . to speak of [his] new law, full of love, justice and mercy' and suggests that they perform a 'motet', with Faith (Abraham) singing the bass, Law (Moses) the alto (*haute-rencontre*), David the tenor and himself the treble (*dessus*), which he can manage without falsetto ('Sans en rien en mon naturel feindre'). Jesus repeats the Commandments sung earlier by Moses, Abraham welcomes the absence of spinet and lute. Then for the benefit of a Jew who has just arrived on the scene the quartet sing a 'motet' ('La loy de grace et de concorde / Est venue au temps de discorde') using the harmonisation that Goudimel had provided for the first couplet of Bèze's translation of Psalm 59 ('Eripe me de inimicis meis').[29] In the long dialogue that ensues the Jew rejects the new young singer, despite the entreaties of Abraham, David and Moses. Jesus next suggests that instead they should address the Gentile with another song, which turns out to be Marot's translation of the *Nunc dimittis* in Goudimel's four-part harmonisation of 1564.[30] The Gentile is delighted and in extended dialogue agrees to be baptised as a Christian and to embrace the Bible. He then sings the Tenor melody of the preceding *Nunc dimittis*, forswears the false accords of his former false gods and exults in accepting the new faith,

[29] *Ibid.*, Pseaume LIX, pp. 50–1.
[30] *Ibid.*, Le Cantique de Simeon, pp. 151–2.

law, grace and justice. David concludes with a four-line epilogue observing that 'Just as in music, four parts are united without discord. The holy scriptures are in perfect accord despite error and his heretic flock.'

The inclusion in this play of parts of Goudimel's recent psalm settings, as well as the style of the verse dialogue, may indicate that the (clearly Protestant) author was again Des Masures. Another biblical drama that has more dubiously been ascribed to Des Masures (by, for example, the catalogues of the British Library and the Bibliothèque Nationale) is *Josias: tragédie de M. Philone, traduite d'italien en français: vray miroir des choses advenues de nostre temps* (Geneva, 1566).[31] This topical and political interpretation of the biblical account of the destruction of the cult of Baal reflects the Huguenots' hopes under the new French king, Charles IX. While no musical notation is included in François Perrin's printed edition, the stage directions and distribution of lyric verse imply a great deal. Although ignoring the Aristotelian unities, the play is divided into five acts and accords an enormous role to the chorus, including one of Maidens and one of Priests of Baal, each of which also has a 'demichore'. A further chorus of Three Young Princes is actively engaged in the dialogue, each presenting a number of solos. While much of the monologue and dialogue of Josias, his mother Idida, his secretary Joa and the prophet Jeremiah is written in blank verse of alexandrines, a variety of metre and rhyme is found in the extended lyrical sections.

Thus in Act II the Young Princes – Daniel, Benjamin and Juda – offer their suggestions for good government, singing alexandrines, only to be rebuffed by Josias's secretary with: 'Stop that singing . . . it would be better to proceed here in simple speech, so that your words may be heard more distinctly.' But after continuing their alternating *terza rima* strophes in spoken alexandrines, they revert to song for their conclusion. In Act III the Princes' exchanges have alternating rhyme in a variety of short metre; but these are no longer marked 'en chantant'. Act IV is divided by two *pauses*, the second followed by the Priests' alternating chorus and semichorus. Act V brings back the 'Chore

---

[31] London, British Library 11408 aaa.38.

des damoiselles' alternating with their semichorus in a lament on the death of Josias. At this point a topical marginal note in the edition observes: 'Thus all singers, male and female, until the present day, resume their lamentations for Josias.'

Another biblical drama with topical political overtones ascribed to 'Philone', *Adonias: tragedie, vray miroir ou tableau et patron de l'estat des choses presentes* (Lausanne, 1586), also accords a major role to the chorus, but includes no musical notation.[32]

The Protestants' recognition of the power of music and drama as reflected in these plays was tempered by a concern that theatrical performance might occasion irreverence or even immorality among the spectators. This concern was expressed in the Preface to Henri de Barran's *Tragique comedie françoise de l'homme justifié par foy* (s.l., 1554), which concluded that his play's instructional advantage outweighed the danger of profaning the Scriptures. However, in 1572 the Synod of Nîmes proscribed biblical theatre, a proscription confirmed by the Synod of Figéac in 1579. The ban does not seem to have been universally effective, for during the 1580s, as well as Philone's *Josias*, two biblical plays by Pierre Heyns were performed at a girls' school in Antwerp in 1580 and 1582. The first of these, *Jokebed: miroir des vrayes meres*, described as a 'tragi-comedie de l'enfance de Moyse' (Amsterdam, 1597),[33] presents the favourite Protestant subject of human salvation through faith in God. Unusually, it is written entirely in prose except for a single *cantique* in short rhymed verse sung by Jochebed. Heyns's second play, *Le miroir des vefves*, a *tragédie sacrée* telling the story of Judith and Holofernes (Amsterdam, 1597),[34] also illustrates the advantages of homely virtues and faith, again using allegorical figures: two of these (Allegorie and Docilité) conclude Act v after the singing of a 'Cantique de Judith sur le chant du Pseaume 9': 'Non point a nous, ô bon Seigneur / Mais à ton Nom seul soit l'honneur.'

The chorus had also previously played a significant and active part in the Latin biblical tragedies of George Buchanan, written for the Collège de Guyenne in Bordeaux between 1541 and 1544.

[32] Paris, Bibliothèque Nationale Rés. Yf 10bis.
[33] London, British Library 11736 a.23.
[34] London, British Library 11737 aaa.4.

In the first of these, *Baptistes sive calumnia* (London, 1577), choruses occupy 227 of its 1360 lines, and in the last, *Jephtes sive votum* (Paris, 1544), 346 out of 1450. The French translation of *Jepthé* by Claude de Vesel (published in Paris in 1566), like the anonymous author of *La musique de David*, suggests that his choruses be sung to melodies from the Huguenot Psalter (nos. 3, 4, 5, 31, 47 and 81).

André de Rivaudeau's *tragedie saincte Aman* (Poitiers, 1566)[35] follows Protestant models in propagandising a biblical incident (from Esther vii), in describing the chorus of Esther's handmaidens as 'la Troupe' and in giving it a large active singing role in each of the five acts (439 of a total 2093 lines). No music is printed in Nicolas Logeroy's edition, but each commenting intervention designated 'Chant' uses matching strophes of short metre with alternating masculine and feminine rhyme, contrasting with the monologues' ten- or twelve-syllable lines in consecutive rhyme. In Acts ii and iii however the *Troupe* sings in dialogue with Esther and Simeon in the prevailing consecutively rhymed alexandrines; these passages are not designated 'Chant' and may thus have been spoken. But the choruses at the end of the first two acts have regular strophes in short lines with alternating rhyme, and some of these strophes were accorded to a single soloist.[36] Such singing may reflect the influence of Bèze and Des Masures, just as the subject and its classical treatment recall Claude Roillet's *Aman* (Paris, 1556).

CLASSICAL TRAGEDY AND CHORUS; GARNIER AND COSTELEY

The role of music in the classical drama of the humanists is usually less explicit, although choruses played an important structural part in the new Latin and French translations, adaptations and imitations of Euripides, Sophocles and Seneca by Lazare de Baïf, Buchanan, Hervet, La Fontaine, Muret, Dorat, Bochetel,

---

[35] Ed. K. Cameron (Geneva and Paris, 1969).
[36] According to a contemporary report by Rivaudeau's brother-in-law, Michel Tiraqueau, at the first performance in Poitiers on 24 July 1561 the choruses in *Aman* were sung by young men and women to simple tunes like those found in local Poitevin dialect in later collections like the *Gente Poitevinerie*; cf. Lebègue, *La tragédie religieuse*, p. 518.

Sebillet and La Péruse. Most of these tragedies were given by students at the Collège de Boncourt, the Collège de Coqueret, the Collège de Beauvais and the Collège de Clermont in Paris or at the Collège de Guyenne in Bordeaux during the second third of the sixteenth century. But it remains uncertain whether the choruses were spoken, recited or sung. The same uncertainty applies to performances for the court in châteaux or hôtels (there were no permanent royal or ducal theatres in France) or for the citizens of Paris by the professional and amateur troupes (the Confrères de la Passion, the Basochiens and the Enfants sans Souci) in the theatres at the Hôtel de Bourgogne and Hôtel de Reims.

The case for choruses in French tragedies of the sixteenth century being spoken rather than sung was argued in Helen Purkis's article published in 1960.[37] The article sought to refute the claim of Raymond Lebègue[38] that the choruses were sung in court performances of classical tragedies by Jodelle and Filleul. Lebègue based his claim on the *Brief discours pour l'intelligence de ce théâtre* (Paris, 1561) prefacing Jacques Grévin's French adaptation of the Latin tragedy *Julius Caesar*, written eight years earlier by Grévin's teacher, Marc-Antoine de Muret:

In this Tragedy it may perhaps be thought strange that, without the authority of any ancient author, I have made the troop of Caesar's old guard interlocutory and not some Singers or others, as has been the custom. . . . In this I have considered the fact that I am not speaking to the Greeks or Romans but to the French who do not much enjoy those badly prepared singers, as I have often observed in other places where plays have been performed. Moreover since Tragedy is nothing but a representation of truth . . . it seems to me that in those times of trouble for the [Roman] Republic . . . simple people hardly had occasion to sing.[39]

Whether or not Grévin was referring to performances of the new French classical dramas of Jodelle and Filleul, the Latin college plays of Buchanan and Muret or the biblical dramas of Bèze and the Protestants is not clear. Following the statement of

---

[37] Purkis, 'Choeurs chantés ou parlés' (see note 2).
[38] Lebègue, 'Les représentations dramatiques' (see note 2).
[39] For the original French text see J. Grévin, *Théâtre complet*, ed. L. Pinvert (Paris, 1922), pp. 5–10.

Jacques Peletier's *Art poëtique* (1555) that the chorus should 'speak sententiously', along with similar suggestions by other theorists – notably Scaliger (1561), Jean de la Taille (1572), Laudun d'Aiguliers (1595) and Vauquelin de la Fresnaye (1605) – Purkis concluded that the instructive words of moralising choruses would not have been entrusted to singers. She summarily dismissed as mere lyrical convention the clear selection of short or varied metre with regular cross-rhyme for the choruses which contrasted with the invariable alexandrines in consecutive rhyme for the monologues and dialogues; and she asserted that 'a metrical form susceptible to musical setting does not necessarily indicate a musical form'. She could not envisage passages where the chorus sings in dialogue with the main characters (as in the third act of Jodelle's *Cléopatre* or the fourth act of J.-A. de Baïf's *Antigone*) as alternating speech and song, and believed that had this been the case authors would surely have commented on the fact. To support her case she referred to Orsatto Giustiniani's Italian translation of Sophocles' *Oedipus rex* performed for the opening of the Teatro Olimpico in Vincenza in 1585; here Andrea Gabrieli's musical settings, published in Venice in 1591, included only those *chori* which have lyrical structure in strophes and antistrophes, omitting the passages where the chorus was involved as a participant or was not alone on stage.[40]

However her conclusion that we must therefore 'renounce the ideas of sung choruses in classical French tragedy of the Renaissance' is overstated. To suggest that short metre was chosen purely as a mnemonic aid to recitation is simplistic; surely Jodelle's division and designation of the choruses at the end of each act of *Cléopatre* (1552) as 'Strophe', 'Antistrophe' and (in Act IV) 'Epode' reveals at least a lyrical intention. But more important than this, Purkis, like Lebègue and other historians of French Renaissance theatre, believing that no music for any sixteenth-century tragedy or comedy has survived, overlooked some vital evidence provided by contemporary settings of choruses by Robert Garnier, the most prolific and famous French dramatist of the time.

---

[40] L. Schrade, *La représentation d'Edipo tiranno au Teatro Olimpico* (Paris, 1960).

Between 1567 and 1569 Garnier was working in Paris as an advocate to the Parliament. In 1568 Robert Estienne published his first play, *Porcie*, subtitled *Tragédie françoise représentant la cruelle et sanglante saison des guerres civiles de Rome: propre et convenable pour y voir dépeincte la calamité de ce temps*. Ronsard, like Baïf, Belleau, Dorat and Estienne, provided prefatory verse, greeting the young playwright who transforms the French theatrical scene 'from wood to gold' and who despite his 'late arrival on Mount Helicon, leads the way in this glorious art'. Baïf predicted that Garnier's 'grave chanson' would endure for a millennium, while Dorat and Estienne described his work as the 'adornment of French theatre, surpassing even the tragedies of Aeschylus, Sophocles and Euripides'. As the play's subtitle clearly indicates, the author seeks to reflect on the troubles of contemporary France by analogy with the discord and violence of the civil wars of the Roman republic, culminating in the suicide of Brutus, his wife Porcia and her nurse. This analogy is made more explicit in the texts of three choruses from *Porcie* set in four parts and published in 1570 by Adrian Le Roy and Robert Ballard in the *Musique* of Guillaume Costeley, organist in ordinary and valet to King Charles IX. This monumental collection of motets and chansons, including one notable experiment in reviving ancient chromaticism,[41] has prefatory verses by Costeley and his friends Gohory, Belleau and Baïf. Referring no doubt to the new Académie de Poésie et de Musique, Baïf's two sonnets mention his new venture in reuniting music, poetry and philosophy through a revival of the 'ancient numbers' being 'gracefully introduced' by Costeley's songs.[42]

Costeley published the choruses from *Porcie* in random order among the 'Meslange de chansons en façon d'airs'.[43] The first, beginning with the line 'Il n'est trespas plus glorieux', sets the tenth five-line strophe of the 'Choeur des soudars' from the end

[41] K. J. Levy, 'Costeley's Chromatic Chanson', *Annales Musicologiques*, 3 (1955), pp. 213–63.

[42] The prefatory verses, as well as two engraved portraits of the thirty-nine-year-old composer, are reprinted along with some of the music in G. Costeley, *Musique*, ed. H. Expert, Les Maîtres Musiciens de la Renaissance Française 3, 18 and 19 (Paris, 1896–1903).

[43] Fols. 50, 51 and 57. For a modern edition of these pieces presented in alphabetical order of textual incipit see G. Costeley, *Selected Chansons*, ed. J. A. Bernstein, The Sixteenth-Century Chanson 8 (New York, 1989), nos. 6, 13 and 14.

of Act III, appending strophes 11–15. A comparison with the published text of the play[44] suggests that Costeley was interested in the strophes most relevant to contemporary France. Thus he omits the first nine strophes and the final strophe with their specific references to the 'parricide' and campaigns of Caesar, concentrating instead on the rallying cry for the combattants to cease their civil wars and to unite against a common external enemy. The key is provided in Costeley's last strophe which changes the first two lines of Garnier's penultimate strophe from: 'Il me desplaist que le Romains / S'entremassacrent de leurs mains' to: 'Ah Françoys soyons plus humains / Ne nous tuons plus de noz mains'.

The second piece, *Combien roullent ilz d'accidens*, sets three of the six eight-line strophes from the chorus at the end of Act I. Again Costeley omits some strophes (the third, fourth and fifth) and modifies others, this time adding a new final strophe.[45] The slight textual changes in Garnier's first line ('O combien roulent d'accidens'), as in the eleventh ('Ainsi qu'un navire agité' for 'Comme un gallion agité'), are less significant than those in the sixth strophe: 'Nostre Rome qui s'eslevoit / Sur toutes les citez du monde . . .', which Costeley presents as his third strophe: 'Nostre France qui s'eslevoit / Sur tous les royaumes du monde . . .'. The transposition from ancient Rome to contemporary France is made more explicit in Costeley's new final strophe, expressing hope for a revival of fortune, addressed to King Charles IX:

> Helas qui la relevera
> De sa ruine et decadence?
> De vous, o Sire, ce sera
> Le bon conseil et la vaillance
> On voit desja l'experience
> Quand au seul bruit de votre nom
> Devant vous s'enfuit l'arrogance,
> Le feu, le glaive et le canon.

Costeley's third setting, *Heureux qui d'un soc laboureur*, comes from the chorus that follows Porcia's lament at the beginning of

[44]   R. Garnier, *Les tragedies* (Paris, 1585), fols. 23–4; *Oeuvres complètes*, ed. L. Pinvert, 12 vols. (Paris, 1923), I, pp. 65–7; also *Porcie*, ed. R. Lebègue (Paris, 1973), pp. 114–16.
[45]   *Ibid.*, fols. 3ᵛ–4; ed. Pinvert, I, pp. 23–4; ed. Lebègue, pp. 63–5.

Act II.[46] Here the composer retains eighteen of Garnier's thirty four-line stanzas, omitting strophes 4, 6–14, 17 and 28, changing the order of strophes 26 and 27 and modifying a few textual details to suit contemporary royal taste. Thus Costeley changes Garnier's strophe 27 from: 'Enlace d'un noeud Gordien / Nostre peuple Romulien . . .' to 'Enlace d'un noeud soubz tes loix / Tous nos vaillantz Princes Gaulloys . . .', and whereas Garnier's penultimate strophe begins: 'Nous lors, sous l'arbre Palladin, / Voûrons au Dieu Capitolin', Costeley's has: 'Du lys alors dessoubz la fleur / Vourons à Dieu pour le bonheur'. Garnier's reference in his final strophe to 'nos peres vieux' becomes one to 'notre grand roy'. Thus it seems that in all three choruses the play's text is lightly modified to suit performance at the court of Charles IX, even if no such contemporary production is recorded.

The music for these choruses has all the characteristics of later *musique mesurée*, despite the concession to rhyme, observing classical metrical schemes in strictly alternating long and short syllables, including frequent changes of metre.[47] The musical setting is entirely homophonic with occasional ornamental subdivision, using almost exclusively root position chords, with simple melody and supporting parts of limited range.

Garnier's later plays offer similar and even greater opportunities for the chorus, although no further surviving musical settings have yet been found. The same is the case for other humanist tragedies written in France during the religious wars. Thus we have no music for Baïf's translation of Sophocles' *Antigone* (Paris, 1573), or for Jean de la Taille's six *tragédies*, all of which close each act with a classical chorus of appropriate lyrical construction.[48] Few published tragedies explicitly indicate that such choruses were sung. Thus *L'histoire tragique de la Pucelle de Dom-Remy*, a dramatisation of the life of Joan of Arc by the Jesuit Fronton-du-Duc performed for Charles III, Duke of Lorraine, at

[46] *Ibid.*, fols. 5ᵛ–7ᵛ; ed. Pinvert, I, pp. 27–30; ed. Lebègue, pp. 68–73.
[47] Lebègue, *ed. cit.*, pp. 248–9, indicates that Garnier's first-act chorus borrows from Seneca's *Hippolytus* (lines 1123–43) and the second-act chorus from Horace's second epode.
[48] For description and analysis of La Taille's dramas see Lebègue, *La tragédie religieuse*, pp. 397–439. For a modern edition of two of La Taille's tragedies see Jean de la Taille, *Saul le furieux, La famine ou les Gabeonites*, ed. E. Forsyth (Paris, 1960).

the College of Pont-à-Mousson in 1580 and published in a revision by the duke's secretary Jean Barnet at Nancy in 1581,[49] ends each of the five acts with a chorus divided into 'Strophe', 'Antistrophe' and 'Epode', the latter clearly marked 'chantée en musique'. The biblical tragedy *Sichem ravisseur* (Paris, 1589) by François Perrin, a canon of Autun, includes a chorus of Hebrews and one of Sichimites, as well as a *Trope* and *Demy trope* of the Children of Jacob. In Acts II and IV the choruses and troupes alternate alexandrines in dialogue with the principal characters; but they also sing strophic pieces with shorter lines, some of which are described as 'ode', 'odelette' or 'chanson'.

Biblical drama in classical form continued after the accession of Henri IV and the end of the religious wars. Among the most musically interesting was Antoine de la Pujade's *Jacob*, subtitled *histoire sacrée en forme de tragicomédie* (Bordeaux, 1604), which included meticulous stage directions, choruses providing a figurative interpretation of the biblical narrative, a *bergerie* with singing shepherds and an allegorical 'Musique' who plays the lute and sings. However the only play of this period to include notated music was *La Ceciliade* (Paris, 1606), a *mystère* presenting episodes from the life of the 'patrone des Musiciens' with sententious moralising in the humanist manner by Nicolas Soret, 'Maistre de Grammaire des enfans de Choeur de l'Eglise de Paris'. Bound with the play are several choruses set to music by Soret's colleague Abraham Blondet, canon and choirmaster at Notre Dame.[50]

A few tragedies lacking final catastrophe were published as 'tragicomédies'.[51] The earliest of these, entitled *Tragique comedie françoise de l'homme justifié par foy* (s.l., 1554)[52] by the pastor Henri de Barran, represents the new theatre of Calvinist propaganda, continuing the tradition of the morality plays with its allegorical characters but adopting the new classical division into five acts. The new Protestant theatre is also represented by the

---

[49] Fronton-du-Duc, *La Pucelle de Dom-Rémy aultrement d'Orléans, nouvellement departie par actes et representée par personnages* (Nancy: J. Janson, 1581), Paris, Bibliothèque Nationale Rés. Ye 468; ed. D. de Lanson (Pont-à-Mousson, 1859).

[50] A. Blondet, *Choeurs de l'histoire tragique Saincte Cecile* (Paris: P. Ballard, 1606), Bibliothèque Nationale Rés. Yf 3882.

[51] See H. C. Lancaster, *The French Tragi-Comedy (1552–1628)* (New York, 1966).

[52] Paris, Bibliothèque Nationale Rés. Yf 4064.

Tragi-comedie: L'argument pris du troisieme chapitre de Daniel: avec le Cantique des trois enfans chanté en la fornaise (s.l., 1561) written by Antoine de la Croix, with a dedication to the Queen of Navarre. This biblical drama, relating the fate of the three brothers who refuse to worship Nebuchadnezzar as a god, has no formal division into acts but includes dialogue in alexandrines and a chorus of Babylonians who sing in shorter metre at the beginning and end, as well as the three youths who perform the canticle that provides the play's centrepiece. Scévole de Sainte Marthe's *Tragicomedie de Job*,[53] performed in Poitiers in 1572, also includes a single *cantique* written in two strophes of ten seven-syllable lines contrasting with the dialogue's alexandrines. Pierre Heyns's *Jokebed: ... tragi-comedie de l'enfance de Moyse* (Amsterdam, 1597) again includes a single *cantique* with short rhymed verse contrasting with the prose text that prevails throughout the rest of the play.

Outside the Protestant tradition is an anonymous piece entitled *Tragicomedie la Gaule*[54] praising King Charles IX as the saviour of France. The dialogue, in alexandrines, is divided into five acts with choruses in shorter metre at the end of the first three, the second being followed by 'pause et musique'.

THE NEW COMEDY; *INTERMEDI* AND LUTE SONG; RONSARD AND LA GROTTE

No notated music survives for the new French comedies of this period. The elaborate musical *intermedi* that Piero Mannucci composed for a performance of Bibbiena's *Calandria* at Lyons in 1548[55] had limited consequence in France. The prologue to Jodelle's *Eugène* (Paris, 1552) even rejects the classical tradition of entr'acte music in comedy:

> Meme le son qui les actes separe
> Comme, je croy, vous eust semblé barbare
> Si l'on eust eu la curiosité
> De remouller du tout l'antiquité.[56]

[53] *Les oeuvres de Scévole de Sainte Marthe* (Paris, 1579), i, fols. 144–145ᵛ.
[54] Copied between 1560 and 1567 in Paris, Bibliothèque Nationale, MS fr. 838.
[55] For a description of the vocal and instrumental music see Dobbins, *Music in Renaissance Lyons*, pp. 112–17.
[56] E. Jodelle, *Oeuvres complètes*, ed. E. Balmas, 2 vols. (Paris, 1968), ii, p. 12.

However, in 1565 Ronsard published two of the *entremets* (*intermedi*) that he wrote for the 'comedie' *La belle Genevievre*, an adaptation of Ariosto's *Ginevra* presented for the queen mother, Catherine de Medici, in the ballroom at Fontainebleau in February 1564.[57] The first of these entr'actes, 'Pour le trophée d'amour', was set to music for four voices by Henri de Valois's organist and valet, Nicolas de la Grotte, and published in 1569.[58] This homophonic setting with its many repeated notes and changes of metre is akin to those composed a few years later by his colleague Costeley for the choruses of Garnier's *Porcie*, anticipating the *musique mesurée* of Baïf's Académie. An arrangement for solo voice and lute by Adrien Le Roy[59] accentuated the declamatory nature of this setting. The published edition of Baïf's *Le brave* (Paris, 1567) includes five 'chants recitez entre les actes' addressed to Charles IX and other members of the royal family by Ronsard, Baïf, Desportes, Filleul and Ronsard, but it is not clear whether these were ever sung.[60]

There is no evidence for musical requirements in the neo-classical comedies of Belleau, La Taille, Turnèbe, Larivey or Perrin. Following the Greek models of Aristophanes and the Roman models of Plautus and Terence, Jacques Grévin saw his comedies as 'imitation de vie, mirouer des coustumes et image de vérité'. But the prologue to his *Les esbahis* (Paris, 1562) rejects the 'trompettes et tabourins' used in traditional French 'tragedies farcies et farces moralisées', even though in Acts II and V he introduces two serenades sung in Italian to lute accompaniment by the braggart Panthaleone. Another neo-classical comedy, *La comédie nephelocogugle ou La nuee des cocuz* (Paris, 1579), by Pierre Le Loyer, includes a chorus of birds which, like some of the other twenty-two characters, performs 'strophes' and 'odes'. In

---

[57] P. de Ronsard, *Oeuvres complètes*, ed. P. Laumonier., XIII (Paris, 1948), pp. 218–21.

[58] *Chansons de P. de Ronsard, Ph. Desportes et autres mises en musique par N. de la Grotte, vallet de chambre & organiste ordinaire de Monsieur, frere du Roy*, fol. 18. Ed. H. Expert, *La fleur des musiciens de P. de Ronsard* (Paris, 1923; repr. New York, 1965), pp. 62–4. La Grotte omits Ronsard's sixth strophe but appends a new final strophe.

[59] Published in the *Livre d'airs de cour miz sur le luth par Adrian le Roy* (Paris, 1571), fol. 16; ed. A. Mairy, L. de la Laurencie and G. Thibault, *Chansons au luth et airs de cour français du XVIe siècle* (Paris, 1934), pp. 167–9.

[60] J.-A. de Baïf, *Euvres en rime*, ed. C. Marty-Laveaux (repr. Geneva, 1961), III, pp. 183–373.

his preface Le Loyer explains how in the plays of Aristophanes, 'the comic chorus . . . of twenty-four men . . . danced strophes . . . turning to the right, antistrophes . . . turning to the left . . . and epodes . . . without moving'. While he admits to following such models in this play, he does not divide it into acts, although he does include *pauses* which may have involved further music.

Alongside these new classical or Italianate comedies, the medieval tradition of farces and *sotties* including contemporary popular or art song continues, reaching an apotheosis in the *Comédie de la fidelité nuptiale d'une honeste matrone envers son mari*, one of three plays written 'pour l'utilité de la jeunesse & usage des escoles françoises' by Gérard de Vivre of Ghent, a schoolmaster in Cologne.[61] Composed in prose, according to the preface – in 'stile bas' with 'personnages de basse, populaire et moyenne condition' – the play adopts the new classical division into five acts and uses Italianate names for many of the characters. However, the music performed by the seducer Chares in Act III and by his servant Ascanio in Act IV is decidedly French, consisting as it does of lute song arrangements of polyphonic chansons recently published by Pierre Phalèse and Jean Bellère in Louvain and Antwerp. In the first scene of Act II Chares tunes his lute and serenades the virtuous wife Palesta with *Toutes les nuictz que sans vous je me couche*. This is presumably Thomas Crecquillon's four-voice setting of this old *rondeau* fragment first published by Susato in Antwerp in 1549 and reprinted in the many editions of Phalèse's seventh book of chansons between 1560 and 1644. A version for solo lute was included in Phalèse's *Theatrum musicum* in 1571, and a five-voice setting of the same text by Lassus was published in 1563. Although Palesta fails to respond to his appeal, Chares persists with another chanson on his lute. This one, *Susanne un jour*, had appeared in a five-voice setting by Lassus published by Phalèse in 1570 and in a solo lute arrangement in the same *Theatrum musicum* volume of 1571. Despite receiving a dousing from the maidservant Pandelisca, Chares

[61] First published by H. Hendricx in Antwerp in 1577 (British Library 11737 a.38), it was reprinted there in 1580, 1595 and 1602. It was also reprinted in Paris in 1578 and in Rotterdam in 1589.

next plays a 'fantasie' on his lute before continuing with three more chansons, all of which were included in the *Theatrum musicum*: *Bon jour mon coeur* no doubt refers to Lassus's four-voice setting of Ronsard's poem published by Phalèse in 1570, *Douce memoire* to Pierre Sandrin's old setting of King François I's *épigramme* of 1538, reprinted in Phalèse's seventh book, and *Mon coeur se recommende à vous* to Lassus's five-voice setting of Clément Marot's chanson of 1538, which had appeared in Phalèse's third book of 1570.

In Act iii Ascanio emulates his master by tuning his lute and voice and, despite the teasing of a hidden rival, sings Marot's complaint *D'amour me va tout au rebours* which Lassus had set as a five-voice canon in Phalèse's fifth chanson book of 1571. Next he sings Marot's *En entrant en un jardin*, which Claudin de Sermisy had set for four voices before 1531. To this 'another responds in harmony through the window', which encourages Ascanio to sing a 'chansonnette en G'; this turns out to be Marot's drinking song *Changeons propos c'est trop chanté d'amours*, which had long been known in an anonymous four-voice setting published in Pierre Attaingnant's first songbook of 1528. Ascanio ends his serenade with *Qui veut entrer en grace*, another old song by Marot which had been set anonymously for four voices in one of Attaingnant's songbooks of 1529. Thus it seems that while Chares chooses his songs from a modern repertory (all recently published in one lutebook), Ascanio relies on a selection of verses by Marot, all set by older and mostly anonymous composers.

After 1600 there is evidence of musical participation in comedy with the published text of Nicolas de Montreux's *Joseph le chaste* (Paris, 1601), which contains solo song, chorus and instrumental music. However, the first 'comedy' to include notated music was an anonymous *Comoedia D. Guilielmus Dux Aquitaniae*, performed at the Jesuit College in Brussels for William of Orange and Eleanor of Bourbon in February 1614. The text preserved in a manuscript in the Bodleian Library at Oxford,[62] written partly in Latin and partly in French, is based on episodes from the life of Duke William IX of Aquitaine. In Act i scene 2 allegorical characters (Virtue, Nobility, Glory, Honour, Power) alternate

---

[62] Oxford Bodleian Library, MS Add. A 33.

hexasyllabic quatrain strophes lamenting William's decision to support the antipope Pierre Leonin against Pope Innocent II. On folios 19^v–21 the first and third strophes sung by Virtue are notated for solo voice (C1 clef), French lute tablature and viol (F3 clef). In scene 6 Virtue and her companions sing a chorus notated in four parts (fols. 32^v–37), rejoicing at William's changed decision to submit to the Pope. Notated music appears again at the end of Act II, where a chorus of eleven angels perform an *entrée de ballet* to console William after his excommunication and subsequent absolution (fols. 66–9). The third and final act ends with a four-part chorus of triumphant angels who carry William's soul to Heaven (fols. 83^v–87). The musical style of both the solo and four-part pieces is similar to that used in the contemporary *airs* of Gabriel Bataille and Pierre Guédron.

VOICES AND INSTRUMENTS IN THE *PASTORALE*

Although music was used only occasionally in the new French comedies, it plays a most significant part in the new pastoral plays which became fashionable during the second half of the sixteenth century, generally following recent Italian models in recreating Virgil's *Eclogues*. In bowers, grottos and fountains, nymphs, satyrs and shepherds danced and sang the praises of the nobility. As in contemporary pageant, masque and ballet, the participation of both nobility and courtiers may in some cases suggest feigned performance and musical mime. Thus in the *Pastorale* that Jacques Grévin wrote for the double wedding of the French princesses Marguerite and Elizabeth to Duke Phili-bert of Savoy and King Philip II of Spain in 1559, the three shepherds Colin, Tenot and Jacquet, played by the poets Denisot, Jodelle and Grévin, accompany themselves on various rustic instruments (*musette*, *flageol* and *chalemie*) as they perform their nuptial *chansonnettes* for Margot (Marguerite), Philbert (Philibert) and Philippot (Philip II).[63]

Similarly, in the *Bergerie* which Ronsard wrote for Mary Queen of Scots for another projected (but probably ill-fated) performance

---

[63] Grévin, *Théâtre complet*, pp. 223–34.

at Fontainebleau in 1564[64] the cast included 'Le premier Joueur de lyre', 'who speaks the Prologue' in alexandrines, as well as a chorus of twelve shepherds divided into two groups seated on either side of a cavern singing alternating strophes, and a chorus of nymphs who dance and sing another 'chanson' (lines 69–86). A second lyre player declaims more alexandrines shortly before the end (lines 966–96), and the shepherds' chorus concludes the piece with four quatrains of seven-syllable lines. However none of these verses, nor the 'chansons' written for the noble Arcadians (Henri Duke of Orleans, François Duke of Anjou, Henri King of Navarre, Henri de Guise or Princess Marguerite), are found among the many settings of Ronsard that were published around the time.

François de Belleforest's *La Pyrenée et pastorale amoureuse* (Paris, 1571)[65] also scatters songs liberally throughout the dialogue: the shepherd Amato, for instance, sings a seventeen-strophe 'Villanesque', accompanying himself on the 'Mandourre' (p. 15), and later performs an *air* to the lute (p. 27) as well as a chanson (p. 28).

The surviving pastoral plays which include notated music lie outside the new Arcadian vogue favoured at the court. Thus Louis des Masures's *Bergerie spirituelle* (Geneva, 1566) belongs to the old *moralité* tradition and introduces contrafacta of *cantiques* already found in his sacred tragedies (see above, p. 96). Different again was the *Pastorelle sur la victoire obtenue contre les Allemands reytres, lasquenets souyses et françoys rebelles à Dieu et au Roy Treschrestien l'an 1587* written by Loys Papon, a canon of Notre Dame de Montbrison, where it was performed in 1587 for the Duke of Maine, the Archbishop and Governor of Lyons and other local dignitaries. The author's autograph manuscript[66] includes the verse dialogue, a 'Discours' describing the performance, illumi-

---

[64] Ronsard, *Oeuvres complètes*, XIII (Paris, 1948), pp. 75–131.
[65] London, British Library 1073 b4.
[66] London, British Library Harleian 4325 – an elegant little MS of 58 vellum folios (116 × 88 mm) beautifully written and ornamented in gold, bound in embroidered boards. The title page includes a painted device of storm clouds and lightning with the word 'Guise' suspended to a chaplet. Cf. N. Yemeniz, ed., *Oeuvres de Loys Papon* (Lyons, 1857–60); M. J. Keeler, *Étude sur la poésie et sur le vocabulaire de Loys Papon* (Washington, 1930); M. A. Barblan, *Notice sur une pastourelle de Louis Papon* (St Étienne, 1856).

nated drawings of the principal characters and a painting of a scene with singers and instrumentalists, as well as the music for two vocal pieces notated in four parts.

From the *Discours* we learn that the windows were covered while illumination was provided by ninety wax candles arranged in rows as footlights. The stage was concealed by curtains drawn by professional machinists (not actors) to the sound of a band playing on a raised platform on the right-hand side: 'hauboys et autre musique, logée en l'un des costés sur un echafaut, à la main droicte pour ne donner ou recevoir empeschement' (fol. 55ᵛ).[67] This music was not included in the manuscript and may have involved improvised or standard pieces played by the *menétriers* for civic processions, for we are told that 'les Acteurs entroint sur le theatre, marchantz à la Grave cadence de cet harmonie' (fol. 55ᵛ). The eleven actors included eight young musicians (probably choirboys) dressed as shepherds and shepherdesses, while the remaining three, representing Mercury, Ceres and Fame (who pretended to play two trumpets), were adolescents: 'Les Acteurs estoint huict beaus jeunes Enfans, musiciens, vestus en bergers et bergeres . . . et trois adolescents, dond l'un . . . representoit vivement un Mercure . . . l'autre . . . une Ceres . . . et l'autre . . . la Renomée, feignant de soner de ses clerons par intervalles, si proprement que l'on eust jugé que le son en remplissoit la salle' (Figure 3). The *Discours* describes a pyramid, 18 feet high and 4 feet wide at the base, erected and illuminated at the end of Act IV by the shepherds who skilfully danced around it for a quarter of an hour, celebrating the victory of Duke Henri de Guise at Aulneau. This scene is depicted by a painting now inserted into the manuscript's back covers but previously bound in before the *Discours* (Figure 4). The accompanying music, a short *air à danser* for four voices in the strophic *voix de ville* manner, is also provided in its correct position within the play (fols. 44ᵛ–45). The text, comprising five stanzas of four heptasyllabic lines, is set strophically with the first stanza underlaid and the remaining stanzas appended in the usual manner. The piece could hardly be simpler – strictly symmetrical in structure, homophonic in texture and tonal in harmony

---

[67] The foliation given here is recently added.

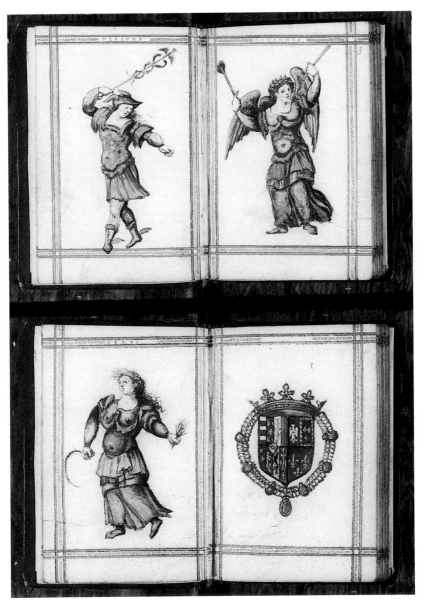

Figure 3   Mercury, Fame and Ceres. Drawings from Loys Papon, *Pastorelle* (London, British Library MS Harleian 4325, fol. 3). (Reproduced by permission of London, British Library)

Figure 4 Loys Papon, *Pastorelle*, Act IV, final scene, performed in the Salle de Diane, Montbrison Cathedral (London, British Library MS Harleian 4325; painting inserted at end of MS, dated 1588)

(Example 10). It would have offered no memorising problems to the young choristers who played the shepherds, but the low range of the Bass is curious and may suggest the aid of one of the adolescents, a non-acting adult or instrumental support; it may be significant that in the illustration Fame is miming while the band is playing, although the only instruments visible, natural trumpets rather than the 'haubois' (shawms) mentioned in the description, could not manage any of the parts of this music.

The other notated music occurs at the beginning of Act III, where Mercury, Fame and four shepherds (Coridon, Themis, Paris and Cloris) enter with palms in their hands and sing a hymn to victory, 'comm'il est noté cy appres' (fols. 24^v–25), while the remaining characters (Ceres and the other shepherds Sylves, Sylvie, Alexis and Amarillis) listen in awe to the harmony on the other side of the stage (Example 11). The four parts here are more restricted in range (none exceeds a sixth) and better situated for young voices (SSAT). The facile triadic harmony and homophonic texture would again offer no performance problems, while even the change from duple to triple metre for the final line would have been familiar through dance-couples,

Example 10. 'Air à danser', from Loys Papon, *Pastorelle*, Act IV scene 2 (British Library MS Harleian 4325, fols. 44^v–45; composer unknown)

119

Example 11. From Loys Papon, *Pastorelle*, Act III scene 1 (British Library MS Harleian 4325, fols. 24ᵛ–25)

chansons, *voix de ville* and *noëls*. The ensuing dialogue between four of the shepherds is similarly arranged in quatrains of alexandrines with consecutive rhyme, each followed by the 'Victoire' refrain assigned to Fame, who is supposed to be playing her trumpet (*trompe*) as well as singing.

This grand but undramatic piece in the classical five-act format, involving mostly a verse description of battle with praise for the victors, lasted nearly five hours; it clearly required all the visual and aural *divertissement* that could be offered. Accordingly five *intermedi* were performed by eight actors from an Italian *commedia dell'arte* troupe entertaining the distinguished audience with comic dialogue, acrobatic antics, songs and dances as the *Discours* explains:

affin de les delecter d'une varieté l'on introduict, par cinq fois, huict acteurs d'une Comédie Italienne, de trois Pantalons servys d'un seul Zani et toutz trois amoureux d'une mesme signore: un Gratian qui la vouloit obtenir par arguments de Pedant, un Rodrigue par armes, un des Pantalons par noblesse de sa race, l'autre par l'ostentation de ses moyens, l'autre par l'appareil de ses festins, enfin Zani qui se fist servir et honorer de toutz cinq, comme Seigneur et prince, les fist chanter, checun d'eux a part, une chansson pour faire preuve qui avoit plus belle voix, les fist dancer les sonnettes pour faire voir qui serait plus dispos et leur fist courre une bague sur des chevaux moulés pour cognoistre le plus adroict et digne d'avoir la faveur de la damoyzelle [fol. 56ᵛ]⁶⁸

Five *intermedi* with 'music variously composed of all kinds of voices and instruments with new words and tunes especially written for this subject' also accompanied the pastorale *L'Arimène ou berger desesperé* written by Nicolas de Montreux for the Duke of Mercoeur and performed at his chateau in Nantes in 1596.⁶⁹ The final interlude presents 'Orpheus in the Underworld with his lute in his hand . . . charming the spirits with his song'. At the end of this interlude verses in honour of the duke were performed by Monsieur d'Arenes 'chantant sur sa lyre'. This music has not survived. Nor has that of the chansons sung by

[68] 'To provide variety on five occasions there were eight actors of an Italian troupe, with three Pantalones served by a single Zanni, all three being in love with the same *signora*; [also] a Graziano who sought to procure her with his pedant's arguments, a Rodrigo by [feats of] arms, one of the Pantalones by the nobility of his race, another by the ostentation of his means, the third by his air of pomp; finally Zanni, who managed to be served and honoured by all five as Lord and Prince, made each of them sing in turn a solo song to prove who had the finest voice, made them dance to show who was the best at it, and made them joust on plaster-cast horses to see who was the most skilful and worthy to have the lady's favour'. This unusually detailed account seems to have eluded A. Baschet, *Les comédiens italiens à la cour de France* (Paris, 1882), which traces the successes of the Gelosi, Confidenti and Raccolti troupes in France during the last three decades of the sixteenth century.
[69] The text was published in Paris in 1597 under the author's usual pseudonym: Ollenix du Mont-Sacré (British Library 11737 a.5). The lavish staging is described in the preface to this edition and is commented by T. E. Lawrenson, 'La mise en scène dans *L'Arimène*', *Bibliothèque d'Humanisme et Renaissance*, 18 (1956), pp. 286–90, and by Purkis, 'Les intermèdes', pp. 301–4.

the shepherds Alexis and Coridan in *La chaste bergere*, written by La Roque de Clairmont for Queen Marguerite and published at Rouen in 1599.[70]

These various dramatic sources serve to illustrate the fact that music played an important part in much French drama of the late sixteenth century. As well as the continued tradition of including popular songs in *mystères*, *moralités* and *farces* we find a new vogue for simple choruses, adapted or composed in the manner of the contemporary *noëls* and chansons (for Aneau), metrical psalms and canticles (for Coignet, Bienvenu and Des Masures), *musique mesurée* (for Garnier and Ronsard) or *voix de ville* and *airs* (for Papon). The inclusion of notated vocal music is important and invaluable, even if it is incomplete, for it provides concrete examples of the kind of lyrical adornment that choirboys or non-professional musicians could provide. The manuscript of Loys Papon is particularly detailed and evocative; although it fails to record the instrumental entr'actes or the music of the Italian comedians, it provides information which may shed light on performances of similar plays closer to the court. The anonymity of some of the music may be deserved; but this holds even for courtly works like the famous *Balet comique de la royne* (1581) whose music, if more elaborate, is hardly more distinguished.[71]

Goldsmiths' College
University of London

---

[70]   British Library C.38 a.35. Another edition was printed by C. de Montreuil in Paris in 1609 (British Library 242 f.37).

[71]   Later reports identified [Lambert de] Beaulieu and Jacques Salmon as the composers. See C. and L. MacClintock, *Le Balet comique de la Royne* (Rome, 1981).

Early Music History (1994) Volume 13

RICHARD FREEDMAN

CLAUDE LE JEUNE, ADRIAN WILLAERT AND THE ART OF MUSICAL TRANSLATION

In calling for a new history of French music and musical life of the second half of the sixteenth century, Howard Mayer Brown's paper has presented scholars with a number of formidable challenges. It admonishes us to re-examine nearly every facet of what remains largely an enigma of music history. Simultaneously exacting and encyclopedic, it considers in turn each of four themes: the relation of words and music; the means and character of print culture; musical styles and genres; and (perhaps most important of all) the social context of the chanson itself – what Brown called 'the anthropology of the French chanson'. His essay concerns the problems and perspectives of Renaissance musicology: how we hear and how we explain the music of the past in relation to those who first made and heard it. It thus requires us to reconsider our assumptions about the nature and workings of historical change, the status of canonical styles and those who promoted them, and the very place of music in culture.

The focus of my response to this expansive challenge for renewed study of music in late sixteenth-century France is *Amour, quand fus-tu né?*, a musical dialogue cast in the form of a sonnet that appeared at the conclusion of Claude Le Jeune's *Le printemps* of 1603. The work is in many ways an embodiment of the varied sorts of perspectives and processes adduced in Brown's paper. It reveals, for instance, Le Jeune's careful musical reading of a French dialogue by Philippe Desportes, a text whose complex cross-cutting of themes, syntax and poetic form doubtless posed a number of pressing problems for the French composer. But my interest in this particular dialogue extends well beyond the confines of the work itself. The piece occupies, for instance, a curious position in the printed record of Le Jeune's compositional career, appearing at the very end of a posthumous publication otherwise devoted chiefly to his well-known experiments with ancient musical prosody, the *musique mesurée à l'antique*, as cultivated some three decades earlier at Jean-Antoine de Baïf's celebrated Académie de Poésie et de Musique. The delay in publication of this repertory (and the several other stylistic threads drawn together in this print) cries out for explanation in light of the clear classicising tendency among French printers of the late sixteenth century. As their several retrospective anthologies amply demonstrate, firms like Le Roy and Ballard seemed especially concerned to confer lasting authority on current musical production as the heir to a long tradition of musical expression allied with both the immediate French past and the distant heritage of antique culture.

Le Jeune's adaptation of Willaert's dialogue *Quando nascesti, Amor?* also speaks to the manifest pluralism of French musical culture during the third quarter of the sixteenth century. In this work, as in several other of his secular compositions, we may detect the deep impression made by the Italian madrigal and its allied genres upon composers of Le Jeune's generation, who plainly found in these repertories much that was worthy of musical emulation. The cultivation of Italian musical models, moreover, is but one facet of an extensive interest in and debate about Italian language, poetry and manners in and around the French court during the third quarter of the sixteenth century. Thriving alongside the *air* and *musique mesurée*, long regarded as the sole authentic expressions of French culture of the late sixteenth century, the varied threads represented by Le Jeune's reworking of Willaert's composition suggest a model of musical history that resists the presumption of monolithic national styles so long promoted by nineteenth-century historiography. What is more, that reworking can also serve as an emblem of still more fundamental concerns that seem to have been at the heart of music and musical representation in Renaissance France. In this era, as the manifesto of Baïf's Académie amply demonstrates, aesthetic forms served not just to entertain, but as the direct means to social and even moral reform. The story of Le Jeune's dialogue, in short, is the complex story of French music itself, a tale of changing artistic responses to the changing audiences and attitudes that shaped their production. In this respect *Amour, quand fus-tu né?* speaks directly to Howard Mayer Brown's synoptic challenge to the study of French Renaissance music.

WILLAERT'S READING OF SASSO

The prospect of setting Sasso's dialogue no doubt presented Willaert with some important compositional challenges. For the musical reader the central dilemma of this text is how to balance the formal demands of rhyme with the at times competing requirements of the dialogue. Indeed, Sasso seems to have constructed his poem with an ear towards the strong sense of anticipation created by precisely this effect: here answers come to rest convincingly at the ends of poetic lines, while the questions that prompt them generally do not (only two of the eight questions posed here take up an entire line of verse). Willaert, a composer well known for his awareness of the syntactic subtleties of his chosen texts, evidently respected the ways in which Sasso the poet artfully manipulated the conventions of lyrical form so as to support the discursive language it frames. Throughout the poem, Willaert scrupulously follows Sasso's lead in creating musical divisions that track the syntactic articulations of the dialogue, carefully delineating question and response even when the rhetorical divisions fail to coincide with the end-rhymes of the sonnet itself.[1]

As in the three other seven-voice dialogues (all settings of sonnets by Petrarch) that conclude the *Musica nova*, Willaert preserves a general musical division between two choirs of four voices (they often share the Bassus or Septa voce) that is doubtless intended to reflect the two participants in the dialogue. The cadential gestures that underscore these antiphonal choirs likewise serve to give voice to the complementary rhetoric of question

---

[1] Further on Willaert's habits as a musical reader, see H. M. Brown, 'Words and Music: Willaert, the Chanson, and the Madrigal about 1540', *Florence and Venice: Comparisons and Relations*, 2 vols. (Florence, 1979–80), II, pp. 217–66; the same article appeared in French translation as 'Paroles et musique: Willaert, la chanson et le madrigal vers 1540', *La chanson à la Renaissance*, ed. J.-M. Vaccaro (Tours, 1981), pp. 209–42. More recently on madrigal texts and their musical readers, see M. Feldman, 'The Composer as Exegete: Interpretations of Petrarchan Syntax in the Venetian Madrigal', *Studi Musicali*, 18 (1989), pp. 203–38.

Panfilo Sasso, *Quando nascesti amor?*[2]

> 'Quando nascesti amor?' 'Quando la terra
> Si riveste di verde e bel colore.'
> 'Allhor di che nascesti?' 'D'un ardore
> Ch'otio e lascivia in se rachiude, e serra.'
> 5   'Chi ti constrinse a farne tanta guerra?'
> 'Calda speranza, e gelido timore.'
> 'In cui fai la tua stanza?' 'In gentil core
> Che sotto il mio valor tosto s'atterra.'
>
> 'Chi fu la tu nutrice?' 'Giovenezza.'
> 10 'E le serve che furno a lei d'intorno?'
> 'Vanità, gelosia, pompa e bellezza.'
>   'Di che te pasci?' 'D'un parlar adorno.'
> 'Offendeti la morte o la vecchiezza?'
> 'Non, ch'io rinasco mille volte il giorno.'

and answer in the poem, with the low tessitura and medial cadential positions of the former contrasting with the expansive vocal ranges and secure cadences used for the latter (as for example in the probing gesture to A in bar 13 and its convincing reply to F in bar 21). Only for the final line of verse, in fact, does Willaert use all seven voices simultaneously, doubtless in an effort to underscore the pointed significance of the concluding epigram, 'Non, ch'io rinasco mille volte il giorno', which convincingly reverses all previous discussion of death and age even as it returns (bars 81–107) to the theme of birth first raised at the outset of the poem. Just as the respondent appropriates the initial concern with origins to make a clear point about destinations, so too does Willaert's musical setting eventually appropriate the low tessitura and even some of the thematic material from the opening of the setting for this final and most expansive musical

---

[2]   The text given here follows that printed in Willaert's seven-voice setting from the *Musica nova* of 1559. See A. Willaert, *Opera omnia*, ed. W. Gerstenberg, 13 vols., Corpus Mensurabilis Musicae 3 (Rome, 1965), xiii, pp. 103–7. This reading differs slightly in wording, but not rhyme scheme or overall syntax, from the one transcribed from the *Opere del preclarissimo poeta Miser Pamphilo Sasso* (Venice, 1519) by Jacques Lavaud in *Un poète de cour au temps des derniers Valois: Philippe Desportes (1546–1606)* (Paris, 1936), p. 181.

Philippe Desportes, *Amour, quand fus-tu né?*[3]

> 'Amour, quand fus-tu né?' 'Ce fut lors que la terre
> S'émaille de couleurs et les bois de verdeur.'
> 'De qui fus-tu conçeu?' 'D'une puissante ardeur
> 'Qu'oisivité lascive en soy-mesmes enserre.'
> 5   'Qui te donne pouvoir de nous faire la guerre?'
> 'Une chaud' esperance et une froide peur.'
> 'Où te retires-tu?' 'Dedans un' jeune coeur
> Que de cent mille traits cruellement j'enferre.'
>
> 'De qui fus-tu nourry?' 'D'une douce beauté,
> 10   Qui eut pour la servir jeunesse et vanité.'
> 'De quoy te repais-tu?' 'D'une belle lumiere.'
>   'Crains-tu point le pouvoir des ans et de la mort?'
> 'Non, car si quelque-fois je meurs par leur effort,
> Aussi-tost je retourne en ma forme premiere.'

gesture (compare the Bassus and Quinta parts of bars 86ff with those of bars 1ff).

The melodic and contrapuntal construction of Willaert's setting also succeeds in capturing many of the nuances of Sasso's dialogue, reflecting both the local meaning of the words at hand and some of the ways in which they might have been emphasised in speech. In line 11 of the poem, for instance, allusions to 'pompa e bellezza' prompt a rapid succession of melodic ornaments and text repetitions that suggests ostentation itself. In its treatment of the final line of the poem, moreover, Willaert musically inscribes both the meaning of the text and its emphatic enunciation: the convincing interjection 'Non' thus interrupts the final cadence of the preceding line and is separated from the line it

---

[3] The reading here follows the one used by Le Jeune in his *Le printemps* of 1603 rather than the slightly different text given in the *Amours de Diane* of 1573. See Le Jeune, *Le printemps*, 3 vols., ed. H. Expert, Les Maîtres Musiciens de la Renaissance Française 12–14 (Paris, 1900–01; repr. New York, 1963), III, pp. 112–33, and P. Desportes, *Les amours de Diane*, ed. V. E. Graham, 2 vols. (Geneva, 1959), I, p. 73. The Italian model for Desportes's sonnet was first publicly identified by H. Vaganay, 'Un modèle de Desportes non signalé encore', *Revue d'Histoire Littéraire de la France*, 10 (1903), pp. 277–8. See J. Vianey, *Le Pétrarquisme en France au XVIe siècle* (Montpellier, 1909), pp. 227–35, on Desportes's early borrowings from Italian sources. Victor Graham and others have since uncovered direct Italian models for a number of Desportes's lyrics.

begins by a rest (bars 81–2), while the seemingly countless staggered entries that soon unfold in all seven voices (bars 83–105) are an apt representation of the multiple rebirth suggested by the concluding words of the poem.

DESPORTES'S READING OF SASSO

At first glance, Philippe Desportes's *Amour, quand fus-tu né?* seems but an over-literal translation of Sasso's sonnet. The octave of the French text, for instance, preserves not only the rhyme scheme of the original poem but much of the vocabulary of its model. Indeed, at times Desportes's poem is little more than the Italian words recast as their French cognates: 'D'un ardore / Ch'otio e lascivia in se rachiude, e serra' thus yields 'D'une puissante ardeur / Qu'oisivité lascive en soy-mesmes enserre'. Perhaps not surprisingly, the first half of the French version also preserves the complex relationship between syntax and form that Willaert's musical setting was careful to observe, wherein questions generally end in mid verse, and their responses enjamb two successive lines, coming to a convincing halt only with the ensuing end rhyme. But if the opening eight verses of Desportes's translation seem slavish in their close adherence to the design, meaning and even sound of Sasso's model, the concluding six verses are remarkable for the ways in which they suddenly depart from Sasso's script. Here the French poet consciously avoids the cognate vocabulary that dominates the first half of the poem, and likewise rejects the original alternating rhyme scheme (*cdc dcd*) in favour of the less regular *ccd eed*. Perhaps more importantly, in the second half of his sonnet Desportes radically alters the disposition of question and answer penned by Sasso: what was originally a terse reply in line 9 ('Giovenezza') becomes instead a longwinded response that absorbs the sense of Sasso's verses 9, 10 and 11 in a single pair of lines ('D'une douce beauté, / Qui eut pour la servir jeunesse et vanité'). The effect of this compression is that each of the ensuing lines of the Italian original regresses by one position in the French translation, such that Desportes now extends Sasso's concluding epigram ('Non, ch'io rinasco mille volte il giorno') across a pair of verses ('Non, car si quelque-fois je meurs par leur effort, / Aussi-tost je retourne en ma forme premiere').

128

The French text, in short, is far more than a literal translation of its Italian model: rather, it is a subtle reworking that first adheres closely to and then radically departs from the form and language of that poem. By these means Desportes negotiates a seemingly impossible terrain between literalism and free paraphrase that is to a great extent also at the heart of Le Jeune's setting of the same text, a work that likewise embodies unlikely compromise between the French poem it sets and the musical model upon which it is directly based.

LE JEUNE'S READING OF DESPORTES AND WILLAERT

Like Desportes's translation, Claude Le Jeune's composition begins as little more than a musical transliteration of Adrian Willaert's setting of the Sasso poem. Indeed, so careful was Le Jeune to preserve the melodic, contrapuntal and formal profile of the earlier master's work that Kenneth Levy considered the dialogue hardly an independent composition at all, but instead 'principally a job of editing which naturalized the Willaert for French consumption'.[4] At least as far as the first half of the piece is concerned, Levy's disclaimer seems fair enough: Le Jeune follows precisely the antiphonal scheme adopted by Willaert, opening with largely the same melodic ideas and coming to rest upon the same cadential tones as had the earlier master. Despite Levy's scepticism, however, there are some clear signs that Le Jeune was doing more than simply editing Willaert's piece for use with a French contrafactum. Early on in the composition, for instance, Le Jeune interpolates a brief but aurally striking passage of direct chromaticism (f', then $f\sharp'$ at the word 'puissant' in bar 16), and later adds a piquant $c\sharp'$ to a cadence on A (bar 75).[5]

---

[4]   K. Levy, 'The Chansons of Claude Le Jeune' (Ph.D. dissertation, Princeton University, 1955), p. 221.

[5]   The printed Ebs at 'douce beauté' in bar 57 simply realise alterations demanded by the polyphonic context, and would in any event have been added by Willaert's readers as early as 1559. The direct chromaticism of bar 16, of course, returns in Le Jeune's other experiments with the antique genera. See his *Quell' eau, quel air* from the *Livre des meslanges* of 1585, transcribed in modern edition in Le Jeune, *Mélanges*, ed. H. Expert, Les Maîtres Musiciens de la Renaissance Française 16 (Paris, 1903; repr. New York, 1965), pp. 4–10.

Such local touches notwithstanding, Le Jeune's most arresting manipulation of his model comes in the second half of the piece, which by no coincidence is also where Desportes departed quite strikingly from the literal imitation of Sasso's poetic model. The French poet, it will be recalled, enjambed the reply that begins in the middle of line 9 with the ensuing line of text ('D'une douce beauté, / Qui eut pour la servir jeunesse et vanité'), in contrast to the terse reply and then the new query that marked off lines 9 and 10 from one another in the Italian original. Le Jeune at first seems to have ignored utterly the syntactic and rhetorical changes wrought by Desportes, preferring instead to continue with precisely the antiphonal pattern adopted by Willaert. Thus what should logically have been given to a single musical persona is instead divided between choirs that had previously been used exclusively for different speakers in the dialogue. Worse still, Le Jeune next repeats the text of line 10, which is after all a fragmentary and dependent relative clause ('Qui eut pour la servir jeunesse et vanité'), with yet another of Willaert's antiphonal responses, this time the one that originally accompanied line 11 of Sasso's poem. Preserving Willaert's thematic design, cadential plan, and registral shifts, Le Jeune here does explicit disservice to the first tercet of the poem as offered by Desportes (see Example 1).

Le Jeune's apparent preference for close musical imitation over careful poetic reading, however, is itself part of a remarkably subtle transformation of both musical model and literary text that unfolds in the remaining measures of the work. Indeed, the apparent misreading of Desportes's poem seems now to have been part of a deliberate effort by Le Jeune to realign Willaert's original musical material with its corresponding passages in the French poem. Thus the music for Sasso's verse 12 (Willaert, bars 71–6) is joined to Desportes's verse 11 (Le Jeune, bars 73–9), and the musical question originally posed in verse 13 (Willaert, bars 76–83) likewise appears for the corresponding French query in verse 12 (Le Jeune, bars 78–84). This, in turn, brings Le Jeune to the core of the challenge presented by Desportes's rewriting of Sasso: the epigrammatic couplet that expands considerably the gesture of reversal ('Non') and mani-

Example 1. Claude Le Jeune, *Amour, quand fus-tu né?*, bars 56–73. Edition after Le Jeune, *Le printemps*, 3 vols., ed. H. Expert, Les Maîtres Musiciens de la Renaissance Française 12–14 (Paris, 1900–01), III, pp. 112–33. Readings confirmed against the original source.

56

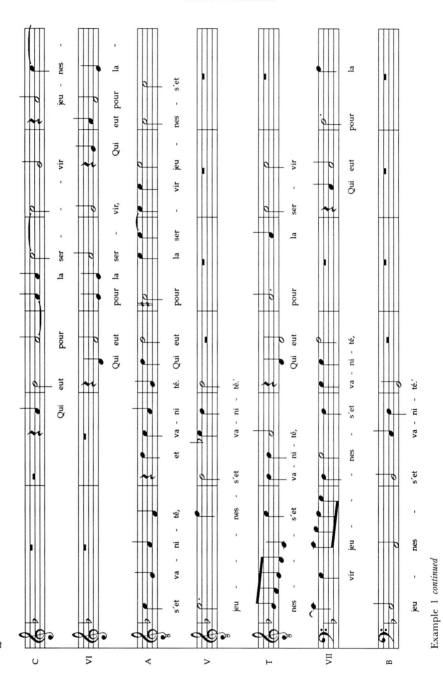

Example 1 continued

Example 1 *continued*

133

fold rebirth ('ch'io rinasco mille volte') that Sasso invoked in a single line of verse (see Example 2).

Like Willaert, Le Jeune seizes upon the interjection 'non' as a means to interrupt (and in some respects to thwart) the warning of mortality offered implicitly in the preceding question. But, though realising that he still has much text ahead of him, he does not continue with Willaert's next melodic idea. Instead he composes what at first glance seems entirely new music for the remainder of line 13, counterpoint which itself leads smoothly into the music for the final verse of Desportes's poem (see Example 3). It is here that Le Jeune at last turns to the signal motive of Willaert's concluding passage, a falling third used to create an imitative stretto that captures well the notion of perpetual rebirth suggested in Sasso's last words. For Le Jeune, too, the short, imitative motives succeed in conveying the pledge of immediate renewal that Desportes cast as the last line of his couplet (see Le Jeune's Superius in bars 94ff, 'Aussi-tost je retourne', in Example 3). But on close hearing this melodic motto may also be detected at work in the music for the penultimate verse (see Le Jeune's Septa pars in bars 86–7, at 'si quelque-fois je meurs'). In this respect Le Jeune's setting responds directly to the ways in which Desportes expanded Sasso's poem, not just the ways in which he narrowly imitated it. Balancing the at times competing needs of the French text and the Italian musical dialogue, Le Jeune here demonstrates both a subtle command of the complex relationship between words and music and his recognition of the lasting authority of worthy models. As a result, *Amour, quand fus-tu né?* strikes a delicate balance between imitation and innovation as they manifest themselves in the rapprochement of French and Italian musical traditions.

LE JEUNE'S DIALOGUE' IN ITS MUSICAL AND CULTURAL CONTEXTS

Amours, quand fus-tu né?, as already noted, was issued at the very end of Claude Le Jeune's *Le printemps*, the posthumous collection (consisting largely of his celebrated *musique mesurée* settings) brought out by the composer's sister, Cecile, in 1603.[6] That the

---

[6] The entire print, together with its dedications and prefatory poems, was issued in modern edition by Henry Expert (see note 3 above).

Example 2. Adrian Willaert, *Quando nascesti, Amor?*, bars 79–84. Edition after Willaert, *Opera omnia*, ed. W. Gerstenberg, 13 vols., Corpus Mensurabilis Musicae 3 (Rome, 1965), XIII, pp. 103–7.

Example 3. Claude Le Jeune, *Amour, quand fus-tu né?*, bars 81–114. Edition after Le Jeune, *Le printemps*, 3 vols., ed. H. Expert, Les Maîtres Musiciens de la Renaissance Française 12–14 (Paris, 1900–01), III, pp. 112–33. Readings confirmed against the original source.

136

Example 3 *continued*

137

Example 3 *continued*

Example 3 *continued*

139

Example 3 *continued*

from Le Jeune's pen and additional poetic stanzas drawn from *La sepmaine*, a creation cycle by the Calvinist writer Guillaume Salluste du Bartas first issued in 1578.[9] In the second of these works the new stanzas (each with its own new music) do more than merely elaborate the mimetic counterpoint of Janequin's narrative chanson: they also reinterpret the preceding stanzas of descriptive writing, offering not the nightingale but the classical Philomel as the musical voice of crowning perfection, whose song is quite literally likened to Le Jeune's own previous 'completion' of Janequin's vocal quartet through the addition of a fifth voice.

The next two *vers rimés* from *Le printemps* touch upon still other aspects of Le Jeune's interests as a composer. *Ma mignonne je me plain*, for instance, is a long, multi-part chanson (for two to eight voices) that borrows its tenor melody from a four-voice setting of this text by the French composer Nicolas.[10] Of course such musical reworking of borrowed melodies had long been accepted

---

[9]   Le Jeune's additional poetic stanzas for *Le chant de l'alouette* and *Le chant du rossignol* were drawn from the same section of Du Bartas's long poem. See Du Bartas, *La sepmaine*, ed. Y. Bellenger, 2 vols. (Paris, 1981), II, pp. 229–30 (Premier semaine, Ve jour, vv. 615–18, for *Le chant de l'alouette* and vv. 619–34 for *Le chant du rossignol*). Levy ('The Chansons of Claude Le Jeune', pp. 140–1) seems to have been unaware that the additional poetic stanzas for *Le chant du rossignol* came from the same source as those for *Le chant de l'alouette*. A modern edition of Janequin's *Or sus vous dormes trop* (*Le chant de l'alouette*) appears in C. Janequin, *Chansons polyphoniques*, ed. A. T. Merritt and F. Lesure, 6 vols. (Monaco, 1965–71), I, pp. 106–14. First issued in 1528, this chanson was reprinted as late as 1559, when it appeared in a book issued by the firm of Le Roy and Ballard. For a modern edition of Le Jeune's version of this composition, see Le Jeune, *Le printemps*, I, pp. 92–115. A modern edition of Janequin's *En escoutant le chant mélodieulx* (*Le chant du rossignol*) appears in Janequin, *Chansons polyphoniques*, II, pp. 197–202. First issued in 1544, this chanson was reprinted as late as 1559, when it appeared in a book issued by the firm of Le Roy and Ballard. A setting of the same text by Pierre Certon also appeared in 1559; for a modern edition see P. Certon, *Complete Chansons Published by Le Roy and Ballard*, ed. J. A. Bernstein, The Sixteenth-Century Chanson 6 (New York, 1990), pp. 51–5. For a modern edition of Le Jeune's version of this chanson, see Le Jeune, *Le printemps*, I, pp. 50–68.

[10]   A modern edition of Le Jeune's *Ma mignonne je me plain* appears in Le Jeune, *Le printemps*, II, pp. 1–63. Le Jeune had previously borrowed the tune for his four-voice setting in 1575. For a modern edition of this arrangement, see C. Le Jeune, *Complete Unpublished Chansons*, ed. J. A. Bernstein, The Sixteenth-Century Chanson 16 (New York, 1989), pp. 24–7. For a modern edition of Nicolas's setting of *Ma mignonne je me plain* (from Le Roy and Ballard's *Second livre de chansons* of 1564) see Nicolas, *Complete Chansons Published by Le Roy and Ballard*, ed. Hyunjung Choi, The Sixteenth-Century Chanson 20 (New York, 1991), pp. 126–8. Pierre Certon evidently also used the tenor of Nicolas's chanson in his own setting of this text issued in *Les meslanges de Maistre Pierre Certon* (Paris: Du Chemin, 1570).

as common currency in the economy of the sixteenth-century chanson. *Du trist' hyver* presents still another facet of Le Jeune's compositional arsenal, in this case a profound assimilation of formal types and musical procedures explored principally in the mid sixteenth-century Italian madrigal. Rife with lyric variety and with the affective gestures of an extended diatonic compass (notably the sweep to C♯, G♯ and D♯ at the words 'bless' à mort'), Le Jeune's setting of this anonymous sestina suggests the perfect seasonal alternative to the descriptive patter song of the Janequin chansons and the cogent Nicolas melody reworked elsewhere in the volume.[11] *Amour, quand fus-tu né?*, in short, was not merely appended to *Le printemps* as a musical afterthought bearing little direct relation to the rest of the collection. Rather, it seems to be one of several pieces – each patently quite different from the *vers mesurés* settings they surround – carefully distributed throughout the volume. Taken together, these *vers rimés* settings constitute a broad narrative of stylistic renovation metaphorically embodied in the seasonal cycle suggested in the texts and musically developed in the adaptation of mid sixteenth-century melodies and techniques. Le Jeune's (and Desportes's) adaptation of the Willaert dialogue thus forms a logical conclusion to this narrative of compositional borrowings and stylistic alternatives: it reworks music by an older master in ways designed to highlight the process of renewal itself. Viewed in this light, the concluding epigram so artfully expanded by Desportes and Le Jeune ('Non, car si quelque-fois je meurs par leur effort, / Aussi-tost je retourne en ma forme premiere') answers not only the immediate questions posed in the dialogue itself, but those posed by the broader 'dialogue' among rival styles and historical models in sixteenth-century France. No wonder Le Jeune's posthumous editor saw fit to issue this piece at the end of a print so thoroughly devoted

---

[11] Levy ('The Chansons of Claude Le Jeune', pp. 223–6) connects *Du trist' hyver* with other Italianate pieces by Le Jeune, and in turn with the broad – but in his view exclusively musical – vogue for Italian fashion that appears among the works of Caietain, Maletty and Boni. Further on the musical aspects of that movement, see F. Dobbins, 'Les madrigalistes français et la Pléiade', *La chanson à la Renaissance*, ed. Vaccaro, pp. 157–71. A modern edition of *Du trist' hyver* appears in Le Jeune, *Le printemps*, III, pp. 47–86.

to the adaptation of ancient Greek prosody to modern musical practice.

There is good reason to locate the source of Le Jeune's interest in the Willaert–Sasso dialogue in a courtly milieu steeped in a range of musical, literary and even philosophical concerns every bit as varied as *Le printemps* itself. This posthumous volume, as many writers have noted, testifies to the musical means that Le Jeune (like Jacques Mauduit and Thibault de Courville) employed in the service of Jean-Antoine de Baïf's *vers mesurés* during the years around 1570.[12] But the volume also affords ample testimony that French musical practice of the late sixteenth century (even that centred on the ruling élite) should not be so neatly circumscribed as a monolithic repertory. Of signal importance in this received musicological view of a largely uniform French practice is the extent to which the many 'Italianate' chansons among the works of Le Jeune and his contemporaries have been characterised as foreign imports into a strictly French courtly idiom. Clearly this simplistic view of a purely French style needs to be refined, especially in light of the overwhelming evidence of the thorough integration of French and Italian musical traditions among the works of Le Jeune and several of his contemporaries.[13] Willaert's *Musica nova*, of course, must have been well enough known in France for Le Jeune to have connected Desportes's translation with Willaert's setting.[14] Lighter Italian genres, too, had circulated there at the latest by the 1580s: as Isabelle His has recently demonstrated, many of the works in

---

[12] Several of D. P. Walker's important studies of Le Jeune's settings of *vers mesurés* have recently been reprinted in a single volume, *Music, Spirit and Language in the Renaissance*, ed. P. Gouk (London, 1985).

[13] Levy's accommodation to this national model of musical history led him to classify Le Jeune's 'Italianate' chansons as a separate type of work from the remainder of his output, positing an undocumented Italian journey during the composer's early career. See Levy, 'The Chansons of Claude Le Jeune', pp. 191–241.

[14] According to Mary Lewis (personal correspondence of 19 November 1993) a copy of the *Musica nova* now in the collection of the Paris Conservatoire (Rés. 1202) seems to bear the marks of early French ownership. The title page of the cantus book, she reports, bears a signature in a northern hand, 'Barbara [?] de Bonhomme.' The binding papers and the binding itself appear to be of French provenance. My thanks to Dr Lewis for kindly sharing with me the results of her extensive research with the Gardane sources.

Le Jeune's successful *Meslanges* of 1585 are polyphonic elaborations (with French texts) of villanellas from Italian prints of the 1560s and 70s.[15] Finally, Le Jeune's *Dodecacorde* of 1598 adopts the system of modal ordering favoured by the Italian theorist Zarlino over that promoted by Glarean.[16]

Le Jeune's adaptation of Willaert's dialogue, moreover, ought also to be seen as symbolic of the need to consider musical style as more than a series of essentially internal and autonomous formal developments. Baïf's experiments in his Académie, after all, were undertaken as much for their moral and social efficacy as for their narrowly aesthetic virtues.[17] So, too, should Le Jeune's interest in Italian musical ideas be understood in light of the widespread cultivation of Italian letters and manners at the French royal court during the third quarter of the sixteenth century. Jean-Antoine de Baïf, long projected as the literary arbiter of taste behind the quintessentially French neo-classical experiments in his Académie, borrowed extensively from Italian models, as his own translation of the Sasso dialogue *Quando nascesti, Amor?* confirms.[18] Philippe Desportes, of course, played a central role in this advocacy of Italian culture, drawing a surprising proportion of his models and ideas from Italian poetic sources of the mid sixteenth century. It seems no coincidence that several

---

[15] See I. His, 'Les modèles italiens de Claude Le Jeune', *Revue de Musicologie*, 77 (1991), pp. 25–58.

[16] On Le Jeune's *Dodecacorde contenant douze pseaumes de David, mis en musique selon les douze modes* . . . (La Rochelle, 1598) and its use of Zarlino's disposition of the modal types, see C. Le Jeune, *Dodécacorde, comprising Twelve Psalms of David Set to Music according to the Twelve Modes*, 3 vols., ed. A. H. Heider, Recent Researches in the Music of the Renaissance 74–6 (Madison, WI, 1988), I, pp. xiii–xvi. Bonniffet (*Un ballet démasqué*, p. 403) cites a French translation, 'probablement de la main même de C. Le Jeune', that joins Le Jeune's ideas on musical theory with those of Zarlino (Paris, Bibliothèque Nationale, n.a.fr. 4679). Scholars have evidently overlooked this and other sources of Zarlino's theories in French.

[17] On the moral and philosophical platforms of the Baïf circle, see F. A. Yates, *The French Academies of the Sixteenth Century* (London, 1947), pp. 69–76. The famous letters patent of the Académie, issued to Baïf by King Charles IX in 1570, appear on pp. 319–22 of this volume. Concerning the later history of academic discussion of the moral virtues of art, especially as voiced in Desportes's thought, see R. J. Sealy, *The Palace Academy of Henry III* (Geneva, 1981). A mid sixteenth-century Latin music treatise in the hand of a royal mathematician, Christophorus Mondoreus, was apparently once in Desportes's possession. The book, with the poet's name on the title page, is preserved as Oxford, Bodleian Library, MS Bodl. 224.

[18] A modern edition of Baïf's nineteen-line *chansonette mesurée* appears in his *Chansonnettes*, ed. G. C. Bird (Vancouver, BC, 1964), pp. 100–03.

of the sonnets and dialogues that he based closely on Italian
models are also among the poems set to music by Le Jeune,
Nicolas de la Grotte, Guillaume Costeley and Fabrice Marin
Caietain – all composers closely associated with those élite circles
in which the Italian vogue was so strong.[19] Indeed, were it not
for the extensive cultivation of Italian literature, manners and
even music in France during the period under discussion, we
would be hard pressed to account for the equally extensive
literature (in both prose and poetry) devoted to the polemical
criticism of this trend. Henri Estienne's *Deux dialogues du nouveau
langage françois italianizé* of 1578, to mention but one of these
Italophobic texts, is an exhaustive and philologically detailed
consideration of the enormous inroads made by Italian words –
and what, for Estienne, are the plainly anti-Gallic mentalities
they reveal – that had recently become fashionable in France.
Through his interlocutors, Philausone and Celtophile, Estienne
offers a scathing critique of those courtiers who cultivate a form
of French adulterated with borrowed words and speech, seeing
the deliberate adoption of this foreign manner as symptomatic of
a deep-seated cultural malaise behind the deceptively nonchalant
façade of courtly life.[20] Identifying ethical behaviour with the use
(and misuse) of language, Estienne condemns the Italian vogue
at court as a means of bolstering the authority of the French
vernacular and the philological research that establishes its auth-
enticity. Indeed, Estienne himself was at the time engaged in a
long polemical debate among French scholars as to the status
and value of translation itself, defending the craft as one that

---

[19] For a survey of Desportes's poetic currency among chanson composers of the late
sixteenth century, see P. Verchaly, 'Desportes et la musique', *Annales Musicologiques*,
2 (1954), pp. 271–345. Further on the Italian models for Desportes's writings, see
the sources listed in note 3 above.

[20] Estienne attacks so many aspects of courtly behaviour and language that it is difficult
to know where to begin listing them. See H. Estienne, *Deux dialogues du nouveau langage
françois italianizé et autrement disguizé, principalement entre les courtisans de ce temps* (Paris,
1578); the dialogue was issued in a modern edition in 1883. Further on the reception
of Italian manners and language in France during the second half of the sixteenth
century, see J. Balsamo, 'Les traducteurs français d'ouvrages italiens et leurs mécènes
(1574–1589)', *Le livre dans l'Europe de la Renaissance*, ed. P. Aquilon and H.-J. Martin
(Paris, 1988), pp. 122–32, and *Idem, Les rencontres des muses: italianisme et anti-italianisme
dans les lettres françaises de la fin du XVIe siècle*, Bibliothèque Franco Simone 19 (Geneva,
1992).

presumes philology as the central discipline for humanist scholarship.[21]

This rich contextual dialogue about the status of competing artistic visions of Renaissance language and style typifies the latent programme at work in Le Jeune's posthumous *Printemps*, a print that draws together and juxtaposes rival approaches to the chanson as they were informed by masters of the immediate and not so immediate past. This classicising tendency, explicit in the manifestos of both the *Printemps* and Baïf's Académie, seeks to confer special authority on the artistic enterprises of an age crying out for new moral and social order. The study of the musical rapprochement between chanson and madrigal during the third quarter of the sixteenth century, in short, should be placed in the context of the compelling debates that raged at the time about the origins and destination of French culture itself. As Howard Brown's final essay reminds us, this work has only just started.

Haverford College, Pennsylvania

[21] On the long French debate about the status and meaning of Horace's advice on translation, which embroiled not only Henri Estienne but also Estienne Dolet and even Heinrich Glarean, see G. P. Norton, '*Fidus interpres*: a Philological Contribution to the Philosophy of Translation in Renaissance France', *Neo-Latin and the Vernacular in Renaissance France*, ed. G. Castor and T. Cave (Oxford, 1984), pp. 227–51, and *Idem, The Ideology and Language of Translation in Renaissance France and their Humanist Antecedents* (Geneva, 1984), esp. pp. 57–112. The sixteenth-century French discussion of theories of translation and imitation should be viewed against the intellectual background of the years around 1500 as presented by Howard Mayer Brown in 'Emulation, Competition and Homage: Imitation and Theories of Imitation in the Renaissance', *Journal of the American Musicological Society*, 35 (1982), pp. 1–48.

Early Music History (1994) Volume 13

ISABELLE HIS

ITALIANISM AND CLAUDE LE JEUNE*

In section III of his paper '*Ut musica poesis*', Howard Mayer Brown remarked upon Italian musical presence in France in three main areas: music theory, techniques of composition and interpretation, and poetry. The works of Claude Le Jeune (*c*. 1530–1600) seem to me to illustrate his comments in a particularly striking fashion, and although my study of Italian influence on Le Jeune's work is incomplete, I think it is possible to make some preliminary observations.

There is no reliable testimony to prove that Le Jeune travelled to Italy as did so many of his contemporaries. This lack is perhaps due only to the fact that none of his contemporaries thought it necessary to mention an Italian visit which was nothing exceptional; it is only from a single verse in a prefatory sonnet that we know that Séverin Cornet, Le Jeune's exact contemporary and, like him, a native of Valenciennes, travelled to Italy in his youth. For Le Jeune, a curious anecdote related by Mersenne in his *Harmonie universelle* might be considered evidence of a voyage to Italy:

Et l'on tient que Claudin Le Jeune ayant monstré de ses pièces de Musique à 5, 6, & 7 voix aux Maistres de Flandre et d'Italie, qu'ils ne voulurent seulement pas les regarder, & qu'il n'eut point d'audience, qu'après avoir composé à deux parties, ausquelles il reüssit si mal, qu'il avoüa luy-mesme qu'il n'entendoit pas la vraye composition de la Musique.[1]

*This article is a reworking of my 'Aspects italianisants de l'oeuvre de Claude Le Jeune', *Musique vocale de la Renaissance italienne*, ed. J. Viret (Lyons, 1992).

[1] 'And they say that Claude Le Jeune showed his musical works in five, six and seven parts to the masters of Flanders and Italy, who refused even to look at them or give him an audience until he had composed for two voices, which he did so badly that

This story should be treated with caution, however. Since Mersenne is (perhaps too much) interested in demonstrating that it is more difficult to write a duo than a trio, even for an already highly experienced composer, it is not entirely convincing when told about a composer of Le Jeune's strengths, and so supplies no firm biographical evidence. Examination of Le Jeune's music remains the only reliable means of measuring Italian influence upon his style.

Le Jeune was unusual in applying techniques drawn from music theory developed and published in Italy, and he was one of the few musicians to adopt immediately Zarlino's theory of twelve modes as discussed in the 1573 edition of the *Istitutioni harmoniche* – that is, twelve modes beginning with that on C rather than D. His reputation is due in part to a zeal bordering on militancy in this respect; both the *Dodecacorde* (1598) and *Octonaires* (1606) are conceived and organised according to Zarlino's theory, for which they serve as a practical demonstration.[2] In his famous preface to the *Dodecacorde* Le Jeune could have removed, by mentioning Zarlino, any ambiguity arising out of a title that evokes Glarean, but he does not; on the contrary, he displays remarkable prudence in stating that to comment on 'la dissention des Anciens, & leurs diversitez d'opinions sur tels noms, requiert un plus curieux esprit que moy, qui ay mieux aimé estre leur disciple, que leur juge' ('the dissent among the ancients, and their differing opinions on the names [of the modes], demands a more inquiring spirit than mine, who have preferred to be their disciple rather than their judge'). Nevertheless, he does continue by supplying the number of the mode of each piece, which allows the volumes to be employed for didactic purposes.[3] It is not surprising, then, to find the names 'Zarlin'

he himself admitted that he did not understand the true composition of music.' Facsimile ed. F. Lesure (Paris, 1965), II, p. 202.

[2] Le Jeune's collection of *Melanges* (1585) features a completely original organisation, apparently intermediate between the theories of Glarean and Zarlino. See I. His, 'Le *Livre de melanges* de Claude Le Jeune (Anvers: Plantin, 1585) au coeur du débat modal de la seconde moitié du XVIe siècle', *Claude Le Jeune et son temps*, ed. P. Bonniffet (Berne, forthcoming).

[3] Brossard (*Catalogue*, 1724, in Paris, Bibliothèque Nationale, Rés. Vm^8 21) comments on the *Octonaires*: 'les Maîtres du Mans, de Rouen &c qui envoyent des paroles pour composer des Motets pour les prix qu'on y distribue le jour de Sainte Cecille tous les Ans marquent toujours le mode sur lequel il faut qu'ils soient composez, et ne manquent point de renvoyer auxd. Octonaires *de Claudin le Jeune* pour y voir et examiner comment chaque mode y est traité et noté' ('the masters from Le Mans,

and 'Claudin' united under the rubric of 'moderns' in Antoine Parran's *Traité de la musique* of 1639; in the preface to the *Dodeca-corde* Le Jeune even speaks of his own project, to write a treatise on the modes ('ceste matière mériteroit un traitté à part, que je prendray courage de faire'). This engagement with Zarlino's writings is entirely exceptional; to my knowledge, no other musician, even in Italy, became such an advocate of the new theory. Was it because Le Jeune was a Huguenot and therefore free of ecclesiastical tradition that he showed such initiative, or did he promote the new theory in his capacity of academician? Lassus and Palestrina, his two great contemporaries, remained faithful to eight-mode theory despite their Italian careers.

The other Italian theorist whose writings made a demonstrable impact in France was Nicola Vicentino. As Brown noted, Guillaume Costeley and Anthoine de Bertrand were among his readers, and so was Le Jeune, several of whose pieces employ the chromatic genera as described by Vicentino in his *L'antica musica ridotta alla moderna prattica*. The famous air *Quel est devenu ce bel oeil*, labelled 'cromatique', and the chanson spirituelle *Povre coeur entourné*[4] both refer to antiquity through the use of the chromatic tetrachord, producing a characteristic 'demonstration chromaticism'.[5] The use of the tetrachord is less pronounced and less motivic in the chanson than in the *air*, but in both cases only those intervals belonging to the genera are included. Elsewhere Le Jeune employs the tetrachord in a more localised fashion; in a posthumously published *chanson spirituelle*, *Hélas mon Dieu*, he reserves it for the invocation of God that begins and ends the chanson. Unlike Bertrand, Le Jeune was apparently uninterested in the

---

Rouen and elsewhere who send words for setting as motets [to compete] for the prizes awarded on St Cecilia's Day each year always indicate the mode in which they should be composed and never fail to refer to the said *Octonaires* of Claude Le Jeune to find out and study how each mode is dealt with and noted'). The manuscript Paris, Bibliothèque Nationale, n.a.f. 4679 shows that the *Dodecacorde* was studied as a treatise.

[4]   The *air* is edited by D. P. Walker and F. Lesure in Le Jeune, *Airs of 1608*, 4 vols., AIM Miscellanea 1–4 (Rome, 1951–9); the chanson, with its variants, is edited in I. His, 'Les *Mélanges* de Claude Le Jeune (Anvers: Plantin, 1585): transcription et étude critique' (Ph.D. dissertation, University of Tours, 1990). It is also included in The Sixteenth-Century Chanson 16, ed. J. A. Bernstein (New York, 1989).

[5]   See J. Chailley, 'Esprit et technique du chromatisme de la Renaissance', *Musique et poésie au XVIe siècle*, ed. J. Jacquot (Paris, 1954), pp. 225–39.

enharmonic genera.[6] Although Le Jeune does not speak of the genera in any of his prefaces, his music testifies to his interest in the questions discussed by Vicentino.

On the more general level of compositional technique, Le Jeune's works are not lacking in references to Italy. First of all there are of course his 43 canzonettas, 37 of which were published in 1586 by Le Roy and Ballard, making Le Jeune the most important 'italianising' composer in terms of quantity in the firm's catalogue (see Brown's Appendix 7). Virtually all of them are reworkings and elaborations for four, five and six voices of a simple three-voice repertory, *villanelle alla napolitana* or villotte, published in Italy.[7] Le Jeune's models seem to derive from two sources: anonymous volumes published between 1555 and 1562, which furnish the basic material for the four-voice canzonettas, and later volumes, printed between 1567 and 1585, whose authors (Giacomo Celano, M. A. Mazzone, Giacomo Moro, G. D. da Nola, G. A. Veggio, G. B. Moscaglia) are identified, and who supply models for Le Jeune's five- and six-voice canzonettas. The differing number of voice parts signals a difference in construction as well as in the source of the model. With few exceptions, the pieces for four voices keep the simple form of their models (/:A:/B/:C:/) and cite fairly complete segments of the canto of the model in alternation in the superius and tenor voices, in a manner similar to that employed by Franco-Flemish composers for the *chanson rustique*. In his canzonettas for five and six voices, Le Jeune treats his models more freely: repeats are not literal, citations from the model are more fragmented and diffuse, and the reworking is more highly elaborated, particularly in the context of text expression. Le Jeune frequently transforms his models in order to illustrate certain words: he changes the placement of repeat signs to keep together phrases belonging to the same semantic unit; he adds accidentals on key words such as 'distrugge', 'lagrima' or 'pianti' and supplies an appropriate contrapuntal treatment for others such as 'fiamma' or 'fuggi'; and he sometimes transforms the metre according to the meaning

---

[6]   On Bertrand's use of the genera, see J.-M. Vaccaro, 'Les préfaces d'Anthoine de Bertrand', *Revue de Musicologie*, 74 (1988), pp. 221–36.

[7]   See I. His, 'Les modèles italiens de Claude Le Jeune', *Revue de Musicologie*, 77 (1991), pp. 25–58.

of the verses. All these procedures are borrowed from the madrigal and paradoxically reintroduced into a simple repertory characterised by lack of concern for text. The response of this learned musician to the requirements of these dialect poems is at times fairly sophisticated. For example, the sense of the final verse of the four-voice canzonetta *Oime crudel*, 'Mi farai rinegar la patienza' ('You will make me lose patience'), dictates that the final repeat should be varied rather than literal. Similarly, the final verse of *Sta costante*, which concerns an irresistible attraction ('che tu me tiri com'a calamita' – 'for you attract me like a magnet'), justifies an unusual final cadence on a degree not used earlier in the piece. These canzonettas, some described as 'madrigales' in the contents list of the *Second livre des meslanges* of 1612, thus replicate the formulaic structure of the villanesca while adopting the performing forces and compositional techniques of the madrigal, which incidentally render their strophic form uncomfortable and out of place.[8] Of course, in working in this genre Le Jeune was part of a general trend, illustrated in the 1550s by the four-voice works of Adrian Willaert and his pupils as well as by Lassus, and in the 1570s by the five- and six-voice pieces of Giovanni Ferretti, a composer from Liège whose Italian transformation was so complete that his original name in French is unknown.[9] In taking up Brown's question ('a certain number of French composers who, so far as we know, never went to Italy – Jean de Castro, Pierre Clereau, Claude Le Jeune and Guillaume Tessier – also set Italian poems, a phenomenon that demands an explanation'), I would like to underline that Le Jeune wrote a large number of Italian pieces compared to other composers. Furthermore his Italian output consists entirely of canzonettas on borrowed models, with madrigals notably excluded. To contribute to this repertory, which required some knowledge of Italian musical as well as poetic sources, would have been more difficult in France, given the diversity of those sources (at least thirteen collections, some of which furnished

---

[8] The supplementary strophes of text, printed below the music in the first edition of the *Mélanges* of 1585, disappear from the Parisian editions of 1586–7 and 1606 and are not included in the *Second livre de meslanges* of 1612; it is in the latter volumes that the Italian pieces are designated as madrigals.
[9] See C. Assenza, *Giovan Ferretti tra canzonetta e madrigale* (Florence, 1989).

153

four or five models each) and their publication dates. (Some of the canzonettas from the *Melanges* of 1585, which was ready for publication in January 1582, are based on models not published until 1582 and in some cases not until 1585.)

Le Jeune wrote no Italian madrigals; it could be claimed, however, that he composed in the genre (though on French texts) in his chansons, some of which are monuments to Italianism. *Du trist'hyver la rigoureuze glace* features a number of characteristic elements: the sestina form, generating a cyclic chanson in seven sections; the five-voice texture; the through-composed and contrasting writing, which highlights the numerous images of the poem (birds, skies, the sea) or other evocative words ('seul' or 'privé', for example, where Le Jeune plays on the suppression of voices). A number of other chansons display similar Italian influence,[10] but only in *Un jour estant seulet* does it extend to this degree. Based on Marot's French translation of a canzone by Petrarch, *Un jour estant seulet* is also a cyclic chanson. Petrarch's *Standomi un giorno* inspired several madrigalists, including Orlande de Lassus.[11] Like Castro's madrigal, Le Jeune's chanson refers to Lassus's setting, although Le Jeune was working with Marot's translation of the text.[12] The links between the two pieces are announced from the beginning, as Le Jeune cites the opening motive of Lassus's madrigal, first in inversion and then literally (see Example 1). What is most striking is how Le Jeune borrows from Lassus as if from a reservoir of madrigalisms, within the limits permitted by the French text, which corresponds to varying degrees with the Italian. Example 2 shows two instances of parallelism between corresponding passages in the two versions. The later version does, however, show signs of a desire to improve on Lassus's version; Le Jeune introduces new text painting (on 'mêlés', 'serpenteau' and 'bec', for example), but more important, structures his piece differently. Lassus had treated Petrarch's text in six sections, the final section covering the concluding *commiato*; Le Jeune gives the conclusion greater emphasis by increasing the

[10] Examples include *Rossignol mon mignon*, *D'où vient l'amour* and *J'ay senti les deux maux*.
[11] Settings exist by Arcadelt (or Gero), Perissone, Lassus, Rampollini, Castro and Del Mel.
[12] Castro's madrigal is edited in J. A. Bernstein, The Sixteenth-Century Chanson 5 (New York, 1989).

Example 1. Opening bars of (a) Orlande de Lassus, *Standomi un giorno* (1557), and (b) Claude Le Jeune, *Un jour estant seulet* (1585)

(a)

(b)

number of voices to six and treating it separately. Can we speak of 'Italianism' here? Certainly, even if Lassus was Italian only by adoption.

The same question could be asked about the relationship between Le Jeune's chanson *Amour, quand fus-tu né?* and Willaert's madrigal *Quando nascesti, Amor?*, published in the celebrated *Musica nova*.[13] The nature of this relationship is in some measure

---

[13]   See R. Freedman, 'Claude Le Jeune, Adrian Willaert and the Art of Musical Translation', pp. 123–48 above.

Example 2. Parallelism in corresponding passages in Lassus, *Standomi un giorno*, and Le Jeune, *Un jour estant seulet*

exceptional, and it is difficult to find a word to characterise it; 'parody' seems too weak, and Kenneth Levy's term 'translation' is perhaps too strong,[14] given the transformation of the model, particularly in the distribution of the voices and the treatment

---

[14] 'The Chansons of Claude Le Jeune' (Ph.D. dissertation, Princeton University, 1955), pp. 221–2.

Example 2 *continued*

of poetic lines. Be that as it may, Le Jeune's setting was probably intended as a gesture of homage and admiration to a composer whom one could imagine among the 'Maistres de Flandre et d'Italie' – those masters who, according to Mersenne, judged Le Jeune so harshly, since he borrows Willaert's music, reworking it to accommodate a French translation of the text. Furthermore, Le Jeune's choice of this particular madrigal is significant, since it represents one of the important novelties of Willaert's collection, the *dialogo*. Indeed, despite its posthumous publication, *Amour, quand fus-tu né?* could signal an effort by Le Jeune to adopt one of the latest Italian innovations and import it to France; interestingly, the rest of Le Jeune's work features several other pieces for seven and eight voices attesting his interest in the new styles of dialogue and double-choir composition.

Mais qui es-tu dy moy is the only dialogue other than *Amour, quand fus-tu né?* to be written for seven voices; the voices are clearly divided into two unequal choirs representing Man (four low voices) and Religion (three high voices). In other words, Le Jeune writes for a true double choir, unlike Willaert, who created with seven voices the illusion of an eight-voice double choir by using the bass of the low-voiced choir to support the high-voiced one. The music of *Mais qui es-tu dy moy* is thus clear and didactic, reflecting a text that elucidates the allegorical figure of the Reformed church,[15] perhaps in order to facilitate performance by Protestant aristocrats.[16] This dialogue, published only five years after Willaert's *Musica nova* (admittedly a very late publication[17]), was one of the first to be printed by Le Roy and Ballard, before those of the *Livre de chansons nouvelles a cinc parties, avec deux dialogues à huict d'Orlande de Lassus* (1571). Another dialogue, this time between a man and his heart, *Arreste un peu mon coeur*, is an eight-voice setting of a sonnet by Desportes. Here Le Jeune treats only the first quatrain as a double choir, setting the rest of the poem for varying combinations of voices to vary the responses of the interlocutors, in a technique frequently employed by Willaert and his emulators.[18] Le Jeune's version is much more up to date than Costeley's five-voice setting (1570), in which the three middle voices sing continuously, joined sometimes with the superius and sometimes with the bass.

Amour et Mars and *May fait les bois*, both for eight voices, are

---

[15] This figure, which can be seen on title pages by the printer Haultin of La Rochelle, shows a winged woman, poorly dressed but radiant, holding an open book, treading on a skeleton, and leaning on a cross from which a horse's bit is suspended.

[16] The *Dix pseaumes* (1564) are dedicated to 'Messieurs de la Noe et de Teligni' and the preface explains that Le Jeune was in their service.

[17] See H. Meier, 'Zur Chronologie der *Musica nova* Adrian Willaerts', *Analecta Musicologica*, 8 (1973), pp. 71–96.

[18] See A. Carver, *Cori spezzati: the Development of Sacred Polychoral Music to the Time of Schütz*, 2 vols. (Cambridge, 1988), i, pp. 12–14.

not true dialogues but settings of texts constructed around anti-thesis ('l'un' and 'l'autre' in *Amour et Mars*, 'may' and 'moy' in *May fait les bois*). The first of these features varying combinations of voices in representing Ronsard's verses;[19] the second employs two unchanging choirs. Le Jeune also left a motet, *Adiuro vos filiae Ierusalem*, in which the eight voices underline first the dialogue, then the long enumeration from the text drawn from the Song of Songs;[20] here, other than the conventional tutti to end the sections, only a few special passages employ one or two voices drawn from the opposite choir. This Latin work, the five chansons for seven and eight voices, two *dialogues en forme d'air* published in 1608,[21] and a psalm setting in *musique mesurée* for eight voices in double choir,[22] could all have been performed with some sort of staging, even if minimal. One can imagine such performances of these pieces, with the possible exception of *Mais qui es-tu dy moy*, in the context of meetings of the Académie de Poésie et de Musique founded by Jean-Antoine de Baïf and Thibault de Courville in 1570, for they all display evidence of Le Jeune's experiments with prosody.

An exceptional work which merits discussion as an Italian-inspired variant of the dialogue principle is *Quae celebrat thermas*, a ten-voice Latin echo piece published at the end of the *Melanges* of 1585. There is only one known concordance for the text, a variant version preserved in the Altus part of an earlier anonymous manuscript in the Vatican library.[23] Le Jeune's echo piece can be compared to two similar works by Lassus, *O la o che buon echo* (1581) for eight voices and *Valle profonde* (1584) for ten voices, but in Lassus's works the second choir systematically repeats the entire text and music sung by the first choir. Le Jeune employs a more sophisticated procedure, using his second choir to echo only the rhyme, a partial repetition leading to plays on words which give savour to this type of piece (see Example 3). The text, inspired by Ovid's *Metamorphoses*,[24] represents the impossible

---

[19] A four-voice setting of the text by Guillaume Boni was published in 1576.
[20] *Song of Solomon* v.8–17, vi.1, ii.16–17.
[21] *Ninfe qui m'as asservi* and *Si onc feu d'amour*, ed. in Walker and Lesure, *Airs*, nos. 47 and 55.
[22] The measured psalm is *Loué-tous ce Dieu qui est dous*; see Carver, pp. 40–1.
[23] See A. Silbiger, 'An Unknown Partbook of Early Sixteenth-Century Polyphony', *Studi Musicali*, 6 (1977), pp. 43–67. [24] *Metamorphoses*, book 3, verses 379–401.

Example 3. From Claude Le Jeune, *Quae celebrat thermas* (1585)

dialogue between Narcissus and the nymph Echo, who can express her love only by repeating the ends of Narcissus's phrases. The musical treatment of the echo here is closely associated with Ovid's fable explaining the acoustic phenomenon of the echo. Lassus's *O la o che buon echo* is, by comparison, much more simple and playful; the singers joke with the echo and order it to be silent. In the almost entirely homophonic *Quae celebrat thermas*, the second choir begins by responding with silences, then with partial repetitions, and finally with echoes of complete phrases; the interjections are built into a dramatic progression. Since this Latin song in some ways closely resembles *musique mesurée*, and the partial repetitions are often rhythmically altered to reflect the prosody of the new word created by the echo,[25] I am reminded of Baïf's Académie, whose Italian connections should perhaps be re-examined. We know that in 1584 the Ferrarese court, famous for its private concerts, received a certain Courville (probably one of the two sons of Thibault), who was recommended by 'Monsieur Bayf'.[26] Italian academies were certainly much admired in France, *a fortiori* by the son of Lazare de Baïf, French ambassador to Venice in the early part of the century and linked at least with the Accademia dei Filleleni.[27] The principle of measured poetry itself, of which Jean-Antoine de Baïf was the main proponent in France, had antecedents in Italy.[28]

What were Le Jeune's models for his echo piece? I mentioned above an earlier concordance preserved in the Vatican library, but it seems more likely that to understand this piece we should turn to Lassus or even to other Italian composers. *O la o che buon echo* was published in Paris in 1581 in Lassus's *Libro di villanelle, moresche, et altre canzoni,* but the piece is written for only eight voices and the text does not feature a true poetic echo. There are two isolated cases of echo songs in the French repertory: Janequin's setting of Joachim du Bellay's *Dialogue d'un amoureux et d'Écho,*[29] for which only the Bass part survives, and

---

[25] See I. His, 'Claude Le Jeune et le rythme prosodique: le tournant des années 1570', *Revue de Musicologie,* 79 (1993), pp. 201–26.

[26] See A. Newcomb, *The Madrigal at Ferrara, 1579–1597,* 2 vols. (Princeton, 1980), I, pp. 203–4. Newcomb notes the Italian influence on Thibault de Courville, very evident in his *air Si je languis* (1614).

[27] See F. A. Yates, *The French Academies of the Sixteenth Century* (London, 1947), p. 6.

[28] *Ibid.,* p. 7. See also F. Liuzzi, *I musicisti in Francia* (Rome 1946), pp. 97–9.

[29] Piteuse Echo, qui erres en ces bois,
Repons au son de ma dolente voix
D'ou ay-je peu ce grand mal concevoir,
Qui m'oste ainsi de raison le devoir? De voir.
Qui est l'autheur de ces maulx avenues? Venus.
Comment en sont tous mes sens devenus? Nuds.
Qu'estois-je avant qu'entrer en ce passaige? Saige.
Et maintenant que sens-je en mon couraige? Raige.
Qu'est-ce qu'aimer, & s'en plaindre souvent? Vent.
Que suis-je donq', lors que mon coeur en fend? Enfant.
Qui est la fin de prison si obscure? Cure.
Dy moy, quelle est celle pour qui j'endure? Dure.
Sent-elle point la douleur qui me poingt? Point.
O que cela me vient bien mal à point!
Me fault il donq' (ô debile entreprise)
Lascher ma proie avant que l'avoir prise?
Si vault-il mieux avoir coeur moins hautain,
Qu'ainsi languir soubs espoir incertain.

a chanson for four voices by Gentian, in which the echo effect is produced by the same four singers, who can sing the repetitions more softly.[30] On the other hand, Italian music prints feature more developed echo pieces for six, eight and ten voices from 1561 onwards,[31] and one of the most prolific composers of echo songs was the Ferrarese Lodovico Agostini, who published five such pieces in two volumes with significant titles: *L'echo, et enigmi musicali a sei voci* (Venice: Gardano, 1581) and *Il nuovo echo a cinque voci* (Ferrara: Baldini, 1583). The preface to the latter volume evokes these pieces 'ne' quali sono arteficiosamente imitate le risposte, ch'Echo suol fare naturalmente alla voce altrui' ('in which are made by means of artifice the responses which Echo would make naturally to the voice of others'). Agostini's echo technique differs, however, from Le Jeune's; in his six-voice collection, the *sesto* part alone sings the echo, and in the five-voice book only the *quinto* responds.

Another of Le Jeune's works, this time on a French text, also employs echo technique. *O voix ô de nos voix* is a chanson in two

(Piteous Echo, who wander in these woods, / Answer the sound of my plaintive voice. / Whence can I have conceived this great pain / That takes away from me the exercise of reason? From seeing. / Who is the author of these pains befallen? Venus. / How have my senses become from them? Laid bare. / What was I before I took this path? Wise. / And now what do I feel in my valour? Madness. / What is it to love, and to complain of it often? Wind. / What am I then, when my heart breaks from it? A child. / What is the end of this dark prison? Care. / Tell me, what is she for whom I suffer? Harsh. / Does she not feel the pain that wounds me? Not at all. / O how bad this is for me to hear! / Must I then (o feeble enterprise) / Release my prey before I have caught it? / Thus is it better to have a heart less proud / Than to languish so with uncertain hopes.) This text was published in 1549.

[30] Gentian's chanson appears in Attaingnant's *Trente quatriesme livre* (1549), and sets the following text:
Quel est le coeur qui ce vaincueur a prins? Cueur aprins.
Quelle est la peine quelle endure? Dure.
Qu'auront les tiens qui tant apres ont cours? Prompt secours.
Par ton secours seront ilz resiouys? Ouys.
Mais qu'auront ilz parfaicte iouyssance? Iouyssance . . .
(What is the heart that this victor has seized? Tamed [?] heart. / What is the pain that endures? Harsh. / What will yours have, that have pursued so much? Swift help. / By your help will they be glad? Yes. / But will they have perfect pleasure? Pleasure . . .).

[31] Examples include Bertoldo's *Son io son altri* (6 vv., 1561); Marenzio's *O tu che fra le selve* (8 vv., 1580); Anerio's *Iam da sommo* (8 vv., 1585); Mosto's *Ecco, s'in questi boschi* (10 vv., 1578); and Oristagno's *Quanto più al mio gran duol* (10 vv., 1588). See T. Kroyer, 'Dialog und Echo in der alten Chormusik', *Jahrbuch der Musikbibliothek Peters* (1909), pp. 13–33. See also E. Vogel, A. Einstein, F. Lesure and C. Sartori, *Bibliografia della musica italiana profana pubblicata dal 1500 al 1700*, 3 vols. (Pomezia, 1977), index.

sections, the first for six voices (setting the first quatrain, in 'normal' verses) and the second for eight (setting the rest of the sonnet, written in echo verse).[32] The change in performing forces is evidently dictated by the need for a double choir to highlight the echo effect, and the two-section structure is also indicated by the text. The subject of this poem is similar to that of *Quae celebrat thermas*; apparently Le Jeune used echo technique only for texts relating to the myth of Echo. As for the division of the sonnet into two sections, it may be noted in passing that here too an Italian influence on Le Jeune is discernible. He adopts the practice employed by Willaert in all the sonnet settings of the *Musica nova* with the exception of the seven-voice dialogues, dividing the sonnet into two sections, one setting the quatrains and a second setting the tercets. Le Jeune followed this pattern of division systematically in all but four of his fifteen sonnet settings,[33] the four exceptions being sonnets with such special literary features as dialogue, anaphore or echo, which in each case give rise to different formal solutions: continuity, double

---

[32] O voix ô de nos voix le pourtrait sans visage,
L'image sans peinture, et sans langue la voix,
Qui nous donne toujours és lieux obscurs et coys
De la fin de nos mots un plaisant tesmoignage.
    Que cachent les amans en leur courage? Rage.
Qui fait qu'ils sont ainsi, & chauds & froids? Effroys.
Mais n'esperent-ils pas quelque-fois? Quelquefois.
Et qui est-ce à la fin qui les soulage? L'age.
    C'est donc bien une chose amère qu'aymer? Mer.
Mais qui fait cet amour trop amer? Trop pâmer.
Où est donc de ce Dieu l'aesle folle? Elle vole.
    D'où est-il descendu, est-ce des cieux? Des yeux.
On peut donc sans danger, de toy estre amoureux,
Puis qu'on ne void en toy qu'une aveugle parole.
(O voice, o of our voices the portrait without a face, / The image without painting, and voice without tongue, / Who in dark and quiet places always gives us / A pleasant testimony to the ends of our words? / What do lovers hide in their valour? Madness. / What makes them so, both hot and cold? Fright. / But do they not hope, sometimes? Sometimes. / And what is it that in the end brings them relief? Age. / Then it is thus a bitter thing to be in love? Sea. / But what makes this love so bitter? Too much swooning. / Where is then the wild wing of this god? It flies. / From where is it come, from the heavens? From the eyes. / Then one may be in love with you without danger, / For we see nothing in you but blind words.)
This song was published in 1612.

[33] *Rossignol mon mignon* (1572), *O pas en vain perdus* (1572), *Quell'eau quel air* (1585), *L'aspre fureur* (1585), *Je ne me plain* (1585), *Si ma dame eust jadis* (1585), *Amour & Mars* (1585), *Arreste un peu mon coeur* (1585), *Voicy du gay printemps* (1603), *Amour, quand fus-tu né?* (1603), *Certes mon oeil* (1612), *Quand sur nostre horizon* (1612), and *O voix ô de nos voix* (1612).

choir or asymmetric division.[34] The consistency of his normal division of the sonnet is unusual, however, as it was not a general convention.[35]

I have already addressed indirectly the question of poetic Italianism in discussing *Amour, quand fus-tu né?*, a translation by Philippe Desportes of Panfilo Sasso's *Quando nascesti amor?*, and *Un jour estant seulet*, Marot's translation of Petrarch's *Standomi un giorno*. These two cases are unusual in that they involve musical as well as literary relationships between the Italian versions and their translations. Kenneth Levy has remarked that two other texts set by Le Jeune refer to Italian models: *O pas en vain perdus, ô espérances vaines*, in which Baïf was inspired by Petrarch's *O passi sparsi, o pensier vaghi e pronti*, particularly the first quatrain; and *Arreste un peu mon coeur* by Philippe Desportes, which is related to Della Casa's *Stolto mio core, ove si lieto vai*.[36] Moreover, Le Jeune's two cyclic chansons, *Un jour estant seulet* and *Du trist'hyver la rigoureuze glace*, settings of a canzone and a sestina respectively, have to my knowledge few equivalents in the contemporary French repertory. Levy notes that Le Jeune's is the only known canzone setting in French, and that only Caietain, an Italian working in France, set to music another sestina in French (*A la doulce ombre*, an anonymous translation of *A la dolce ombra* by Petrarch).[37] Even more interesting, to my mind, are some of Le Jeune's *airs mesurés*, which set French translations (by Baïf?) of Italian poems probably transmitted by the little collections of villanesche and villotte of the type Le Jeune used as sources for his canzonettas. To begin with, the most famous of these, *Une puce j'ay dedans l'oreille* is probably derived from *No pulice m'entrato nell'orecchia*, published by Baldassare Donato in his *Primo libro di canzon villanesche alla napolitana a quatro voci* (Venice: Gardano, 1550):[38]

---

[34] *Amour, quand-fus-tu né?*, *Amour et Mars*, *Arreste un peu mon coeur*, and *O voix ô de nos voix*.

[35] See J.-P. Ouvrard, 'Le sonnet ronsardien en musique: du *Supplément* de 1552 à 1580', and I. Bossuyt, 'Jean de Castro: *Chansons, odes et sonets de Pierre Ronsard* (1576)', both in *Revue de Musicologie*, 74 (1988), pp. 149–64, on pp. 159–61, and pp. 173–87, on p. 177.

[36] Levy, 'The Chansons of Claude Le Jeune', pp. 302 and 231.

[37] *Ibid.*, p. 215.

[38] Reproduced in facsimile by F. Dobbins in 'Les madrigalistes français et la Pléiade', *La chanson à la Renaissance*, ed. J.-M. Vaccaro (Tours, 1981), p. 170.

No pulice m'entrato nell'orecchia	Une puce j'ay dedans l'oreille helas!
Che nott'e giorno mi fa pazziare	Qui de nuit et de jour me fretill'et me mord
Non saccio che mi fare	Et me fait devenir fou
Corr'in qua, corr'in la	Nul remède n'y puis doner
Piglia questa, piglia quella	Je cours de ça je cours de la
Dammi soccorso tu,	Oste la moy
faccia mia bella.	Retire-la moy je t'en pri
	O toute belle secour moy
E tanto da saltare s'apparecchia	Quand mes yeux je pense livrer au someil
Per nullo modo nol posso pigliare	Elle vient me piquer, me demange, et me point,
Non saccio . . .	Et me garde de dormir
	Nul remède . . .
Et quando tu ti pensi haverlo in mano	D'une vieille charmeresse aydé me suis,
Piu d'uno miglio salta da lontano	Qui guérit tou-le monde et de tout guerissant,
Non saccio . . .	Ne m'a sceu me guerir moy
	Nul remède . . .
Quando si mett'in cusitura vecchia	Bien je sçay que seule peux guerir ce mal
Ma non fa altro se non pizzicare	Je te prie de me voir de bon oeil, et vouloir
Non saccio . . .	M'amolir ta cruauté
	Nul remède . . .
Cosi interviene a chi in donna se fida	J'ay souvent dedans l'oreille farfouillé,
D'esser content ogn'uno si sconfida	Ni je n'ay par amour, ni par art su trouver
Non saccio . . .	La maniere de l'oster,
	Nul remède . . .

This fairly free translation, popular with musicians no doubt primarily because of the erotic allusions evoked by the phrase 'to have a flea in one's ear',[39] is not the only one of its type. I have identified two other texts, both from the same anonymous volume titled *Il quinto libro delle villotte alla napolitana* (Venice:

[39] See C. Duneton, *La puce à l'oreille* (Paris, 1978). The expression meant 'to suffer from the itches of love'.

Gardano, 1566), which are similarly related to texts set by Le
Jeune as *airs mesurés*:

All'arma all'arm o fidi miei pensieri	Arm'arm'arm'arm'arm'arm' ô mes loyaux pensers
Corrette tutt'in guardia del mio core	Acourez acourez a la guarde de mon coeur.
Che s'avicina 'l mio nemic'amore	Voicy Amour mon ennemy qui s'approchant me court sus
Armative di ghiaccio e di disdegno	Barre la porte leve le pont, sur la muraille bon guet
Alzate il ponte e state alla diffesa	Tant que dicy tourne son host, honte & domaige trouvant
Accio che 'l traditor perda l'impresa	Arm'arm . . .
Ma si per capo de inimici viene	Si la cruelle qui ne pardonne & jamais ne perdit
Quelle che sempre vinci e mai pardona	Chef se présente des ennemis randre a la fin se faudra
Pregate Iddio che ve la mandi bona	Qu'on prie Dieu plus qu'a rigueur soit a mercy.
	Arm'arm' . . .
Pur combatete ogn'hor fin alla morte	Faiste effort & retenez la place tant que pourrez,
E se vi buttera le mure a terra	Mais si du fort elle boulle- verse & parapet & rampart
Rendetivi gridando a bona guerra.	Tous luy crians a bonne guerre sortez.
	Arm'arm' . . .[40]

The translation here is much more faithful; it involves all the
strophes, even if Baïf did use the first couplet of the Italian text
as a refrain, which lengthens Le Jeune's setting considerably in
comparison with the music of the Italian original. This *air* opens
La guerre de Claude Le Jeune, a long narrative cycle which was
probably performed at the 'Magnificences' celebrating the

---

[40] The version published in the *Airs* of 1608 results from a later revision; it features
rhyming verses, which Baïf did not use. The revisions are probably the work of
Agrippa d'Aubigné and/or Odet de la Noue (see the preface to the Walker and
Lesure edition of the *Airs*). I have given here Baïf's version as set by Thibault de
Courville (published in *Airs mis en musique par Fabrice Marin Caietain* [Paris: Le Roy
and Ballard, 1578]) since it is probably closer to the text set by Le Jeune before the
revisions were effected.

wedding of the Duc de Joyeuse in 1581.[41] The theme of the 'battle of love' is fairly common in such occasional works, but it is interesting to note that this one begins with an *air* based on the text of an anonymous three-voice villotta.

A final example, perhaps the most diverting of all, is the *air Trinke trink trink pon pokras*, which is as far as I know the only case of a French 'tudesque' (see Table 1 for text). The Italian *tedesca*, rooted in the *mascherata* and the *canto carnascialesco*, takes its themes from the reputed German love for the bottle.[42] The text of the anonymous 'todesca' of the 1566 collection is given in Table 2. The rapport between *Trinke trink trink pon pokras* and the Italian text of 1566 is clear; the first two strophes are obviously related, if my necessarily somewhat hypothetical (and incomplete) translation of the former is accepted. As in the two preceding *airs*, Le Jeune does not use the music of his Italian model; he improves on it by using the special characteristics of *musique mesurée* to underline the bacchic nature of his 'tudesque': the asymmetric alternation of long and short note values creates an effect that represents perfectly the unsteady walk of a drunkard. These three examples drawn from Le Jeune's numerous *airs* are only a small sample of the relationships that I believe remain to be found between this repertory and that of the little volumes published in Italy, which were apparently well known in France.[43]

In conclusion I will mention yet another link between Le Jeune and Italy, through a sonnet by La Boëtie, *J'ay senti les deux maux*; Le Jeune was the only composer, other than the madrigalist Marc'Antonio Ingegneri, to set it as a chanson. The poem was published by Baïf in 1573, but in a version slightly different from that used by the two composers. Le Jeune's chanson, printed in the *Melanges* of 1585, was probably written much earlier, whereas Ingegneri's setting, his only French chanson, was published in 1580. The music of the two settings is unrelated except in the division of the sonnet into two parts

---

[41] See F. A. Yates, 'Poésie et musique dans les "Magnificences" au mariage du duc de Joyeuse', *Musique et poésie au XVIe siècle*, ed. Jacquot, pp. 241–64.

[42] Some of the best-known examples of the genre are Lassus's *Matona mia cara* (1581), the 'imitatione del tedesco' (*Mi star pone compagne io*) in Orazio Vecchi's *Veglie di Siena* (1604), and the 'Thedesco' in Adriano Banchieri's *Barca di Venetia per Padova* (1623), which repeats 'Brindes io io io sgott mi trinc con el flascon'.

[43] For example, the *air* text which begins 'A l'aid à l'aid'helas je suis blessé / A l'eau à l'eau dedans dehors je suis tout en feu' resembles 'Aqua madonna al foco' or 'Aqua aiuto al foco'; a more systematic study of such relationships is needed.

Table 1 Anon., *Trinke trink trink pon pokras*

Original text set by Le Jeune	Modern French	English translation
Trinke trink trink pon pokras	Je bois, bois, bois du bon hypocras	I drink, drink, drink some good hypocras
Moy ne trinker haûtre fin	Je ne bois pas d'autre vin	I don't drink any other wine
L'haûtre nut gout par mon foy	L'autre pas bon par ma fôi	Others are no good, by my faith
Il m'a gorché l'estomal	Il m'engorge l'estomac	They give me stomach-ache
Moy si trinker haûtre fin	Moi si je bois d'autre vin	Me if I drink another wine
Tout melanklik fâché moy	Moi tout mélancolique et fâché	Me all sad and angry
m'ôte tout mon pon kouleur	Il m'ôte toute ma bonne couleur	It takes away my good colour
Ch'aûne suich komm peurre fraesch	Jaune suis comme beurre frais	Yellow I am like fresh butter
Faire moy brint fin pokras	Le vin d'hypocras me fait [?]	Good hypocras makes me [?]
Piau fénir teint continent	Puis devenir incontinent	Then become all of a sudden
Moy choyous, chanter parlér,	Moi joyeux, chanter, parler,	Me happy, singing, dancing
Point me gouchér, schlofe point	Point me coucher, point dormir	Don't go to bed, don't go to sleep
Fair'amour tréproprement,	Faire l'amour très proprement,	Make love very properly
Prendre, fouéter, kot léfér:	Prendre, fouetter, lever la cotte,	Take, whip, lift up the shift,
Moy si nut maitresse fut	Si ma maitresse n'y est pas,	If my mistress isn't there
Fut le chambrier aussi pon.	Le chambrier est aussi bon.	The servant will do just as well.
Kant chouér treffort me suich	Quand je suis tombé très fort	When I've fallen very hard
Las, reposser, bien me dorm:	Las, je me repose, je dors bien	Tired out I rest, I sleep well
Sonche plaissant soer de nuich	Songe plaissant soir de nuit(?)	Pleasant dreams evening and night(?)
Mons de champons, stans de fin.	Monts de jambon, étangs de vin.	Mountains of ham, pools of wine.
Fut il en partis hurous	Que soit heureux en parti	Happy is he
Ki brémir truf fin pokras.	Celui qui premier trouve du vin d'hypocras.	Who first found the wine of hypocras.

168

Table 2

Anon. todesca from *Il quinto libro delle villote alla napolitana* (1566)	French translation	English translation
Trinc e got e malvasia Mi non trincher altro vin Ch'altro vin star pisinin Si mi fa doler mia pansa Fa venir il mio voltin Di color di melaranza Volentier mi sta far danza Piste trinc e romania.	Je bois un verre de malvoisie Je ne bois pas d'autre vin Car un autre vin est de l'eau de flaque Et il me donne mal au ventre Il fait devenir mon visage Couleur d'orange douce Je me mets volontiers à danser A cause de cette orgie de vin romain.	I drink a glass of malvoisie I don't drink any other wine Other wines are pond water And give me stomach ache It turns my face The colour of sweet oranges I willingly get up and dance Because of this orgy of Roman wine.
Trinc e got io io io Trinc e got e malvasia Mi non trincher altro vin	Je bois un verre, moi moi moi Je bois un verre de malvoisie Je ne bois pas d'autre vin.	I drink a glass, I I I I drink a glass of malvoisie I don't drink any other wine.
Mi levar da mezza notte Quand'el di de San Martin Vo spinar tutte le botte Mi vol biber da matin Vin e car il mio cusin Si mi fa balar per via.	Je me lève à minuit Quand c'est le jour de la Saint Martin Et je tire du vin de tous les tonneaux Je veux boire dès le matin Le vin est mon cher cousin Il me fait danser dans la rue.	I get up at midnight On St Martin's Day And I pull wine from all the barrels I want to start drinking in the morning Wine is my dear cousin It makes me dance in the street.
Trinc e got e malvasia Mi non trincher altro vin.[44]	Je bois un verre de malvoisie Je ne bois pas d'autre vin.	I drink a glass of malvoisie I don't drink any other wine.

[44] According to Jean Guichard, to whom I am grateful for the French translation, the dialect forms here are more characteristically Venetian. There are no German words; only the word 'trinc' recalls the German 'trink'.

and in the time signature, but it is possible that Le Jeune, or his chanson, served as an intermediary in transmitting the unpublished version of the sonnet to Italy.

Le Jeune was highly engaged with the theoretical writings of Zarlino and Vicentino, and was interested equally in Italian musical forms (villanesca or villotta, *dialogo*, *eco*, madrigal cycles) and texts (*tedesca*, canzona, sestina). This strand joins the two other major influences on his work: the Franco-Flemish contrapuntal tradition (cantus firmus, canons and other technical features) and of course *musique mesurée à l'antique*. His debt to Italy is found not only in his settings of Italian texts (i.e. in the canzonettas): he also employs translations, parodies which conceal their relationships from the non-specialist. That is why it is likely that further study of his works will reveal still more links with the country that may have welcomed him as it did so many other musicians.[45]

University of Rennes

---

[45] A manuscript mass attributed to Le Jeune survives in the chapter archives of Turin, a city whose position on the border between France and Italy is important.

Early Music History (1994) Volume 13

MARGARET M. McGOWAN

THE ARTS CONJOINED: A CONTEXT FOR THE STUDY OF MUSIC

The conditions of artistic production in late sixteenth-century France required musicians and poets, composers and painters, choreographers and performers to work together. They shared the same objectives and they worked from the same aesthetic principles.[1] Their common experience suggests that, as historians and analysts, we can enlighten the study of one art form – music or the dance, for example – by placing it within the context of others, assessing their interaction and their shared purpose.[2] If this assumption is accepted we must consider issues of production, that is those practical matters concerning technique and the varied conditions of performance; we must examine the audience's expectations of those events which drew together the arts into a single spectacle or in a sequence of festivals and which relied for their inspiration on intellectual currents nourished through renewed acquaintance with ancient sources;[3] and we need to assess the nature of the works themselves, their impact on the status of the artist (broadly defined), and on the social and political benefit for the patrons. There is inevitably much overlap across these three areas of production, expectation and outcomes, yet, in the discussion which follows, attempts will be made to keep them separate.

---

[1]   For a discussion of interart analogies, see my book *Ideal Forms in the Age of Ronsard* (Berkeley and Los Angeles, 1985), chapter 2, pp. 51–88.

[2]   In '*Ut musica poesis*' the late Howard Mayer Brown stressed the intellectual order posited by poets and musicians; the present paper tries to extend that work to include social, humanist and artistic trends which brought all arts closely together at this time.

[3]   F. A. Yates, *The French Academies of the Sixteenth Century* (London, 1947), and J. Jacquot (editor of *Les fêtes de la Renaissance*, Paris, 1956, 1960, 1975) have demonstrated how Renaissance artists used ancient sources in their search for the therapeutic 'effects' they thought could be produced through different forms being appropriately conjoined.

Some reflections on the French 'prince of poets' published at the end of the sixteenth century serve to set the scene. In his life of Ronsard, however prejudiced his views and however unfaithful his massaging of the biographical material, Claude Binet was accurate in his highlighting of the poet's taste for other forms of art since Ronsard himself confirmed in his poems their appeal to him. Of his love of painting, sculpture and music, Binet has this to say:

La peinture et la sculpture, comme aussi la Musique, luy estoient à singulier plaisir; et principalement aimer à chanter et à ouyr chanter ses vers, appelant la Musique soeur puisnée de la Poésie, et les Poètes et Musiciens, enfans sacrez des Muses que sans la Musique la Poësie estoit sans grace, comme la Musique sans la melodie des vers, inanimée et sans vie.[4]

(Painting and sculpture, as well as music, gave him particular pleasure. He especially enjoyed singing his own verses and hearing them sung, naming Music as the younger sister of Poetry, calling both poets and composers the sacred children of the Muses, and maintaining that Poetry without Music was graceless, and that Music without the harmonies of verse was inanimate and lifeless.)

The biographer has stressed the ease with which a writer can pass from comment on one art to another, and especially the interdependence of poetry and music, conceived of by Ronsard as inseparable and self-enhancing both in his writings and in their effects. This breadth of interest, essential for a poet who sought to emulate Greek and Latin masters, was also necessary to satisfy the increasing ambitions of princely patrons.

CONDITIONS OF FESTIVAL PRODUCTION

The most striking (and perhaps the most obvious) feature of artistic production in the second half of the sixteenth century in France is its diversity. An enormous range of entertainments was given, from elaborate and magnificent set pieces wrought with skill and prepared with infinite care, to much more modest performances conceived in haste and performed impromptu. This

---

[4] C. Binet, *La vie de Pierre de Ronsard*, version C, ed. P. Laumonier (Paris, 1909), p. 45 note 12.

range can best be illustrated by reference to Abel Jouan's account
of Charles IX's journey with his mother through France in the
years 1564–6.[5] The royal departure from Fontainebleau was
marked by a musical and martial festival which combined songs
of greeting (with verses composed by Ronsard), a banquet whose
courses were interrupted by concerts performed on a variety of
instruments, and a tourney between Greeks and Trojans whose
quarrel was announced in a series of sung monologues. The
occasion was appropriately splendid; the size of the musical
ensembles was large and variable according to need; costumes
matched the character of the singers or players; décor enhanced
the magnificence; and the most prominent artists were used.[6]
The climax of the royal tour, reached at Bayonne in 1565, took
the form of a complex series of entertainments involving musical
performances beside a lake; musical preludes sung at a banquet
in preparation for the tournament; musical accompaniments to
the triumphal cars which brought in those who were to fight the
next day; and a banquet whose courses were introduced by
dancing nymphs whose songs entertained the company and who
rounded off the evening's festivities with a ballet.[7] The events
had been long in preparation and impressed the Spanish visitors.

In addition to these extended fêtes, Charles IX had ample
opportunities during his journey to appreciate more humble offer-
ings in which music played a central role, and where the emphasis
was often regional: at Montpellier, on Christmas Day 1564,
citizens came 'en un grand convoy, qui estoit devant son logis,
[pour offrir] une dance que l'on appelle la Treille, et dansoient
au son des Trompettes, tenans en leurs mains des cerceaux tous
floriz, et des Danseurs tous masquez et revestuz' ('in a great
procession to his lodging [to perform] a dance called *la Treille*;
they danced to the sound of trumpets, holding floral hoops in
their hands; the dancers were well dressed and masked').[8]

---

[5] For a modern edition of Abel Jouan's *Recueil et discours du voyage du roy Charles IX*,
    see *The Royal Tour of France*, ed. W. McAllister Johnson and V. E. Graham with
    many additional documents gleaned from provincial as well as Paris archives (Toronto,
    1979).
[6] McAllister Johnson and Graham, pp. 75–6, and Appendix I, pp. 147 ff., for the
    Fontainebleau fêtes.
[7] *Ibid.*, Appendix XXI, pp. 328 ff., for a description of the events at Bayonne.
[8] *Ibid.*, pp. 101–2.

The simplicity of this local homage to the king was in marked contrast to the intricate set pieces which had been arranged in June 1564 by the municipality of Lyons where, for example, at the porte Bourgneuf, from the top of a theatre structure, Apollo harangued the king, and then the nine Muses from within a rock

commencerent à fredonner de fort bonne grace leurs instrumens musicaux divers: et à ceste melodie s'adjoingnit une autre harmonie de Musiciens, posez en la concavité dud. theatre superieur, lesquelz desgorgeans voix melodieuses, chanterent en Musique excellente le cantique suivant: 'Chante du siecle d'or les Divines douceurs'.[9]

(began to pluck their diverse musical instruments with good grace; to this melody were joined other harmonies from musicians hidden in the well of the theatre above, from which came the sound of melodious voices singing in excellent harmony the following canticle: 'Sing the divine pleasures of the golden age')

A multi-layered structure, voices and instruments interweaving, and the diversity of instruments give some indications of the artistic ambitions of the second city of France,[10] but also remind us of the richness of source material, scattered over the regions of France in the archives, that still awaits analysis. It is important to remember that, although the accident of document survival has concentrated attention on Paris and on productions for the court, festivals (both secular and religious) were enjoyed with enthusiasm elsewhere in France,[11] and especially at times when the court came to visit and when attempts to respond to its taste reproduced well-known figures – Apollo and the Muses – who were to appear at regular intervals in other places (*Le ballet des Polonais*, 1573, for instance).

The taste of individual patrons also affected the nature of production. For Catherine de' Medici, who loved luxury in all its forms and who recognised the valuable contribution festivals could make in controlling and disciplining members of the court,[12]

---

[9] *Ibid.*, pp. 187 ff., for a description of the king's entertainment at Lyons in the summer of 1564.

[10] A clear idea of the nature of music-making in Lyons can be gained from Frank Dobbins's detailed account in *Music in Renaissance Lyons* (Oxford, 1992).

[11] I am not convinced that we can, in our present state of knowledge, assume that Paris was the centre and that artistic production elsewhere should be seen as the periphery, as Howard Mayer Brown implies on pp. 25 and 29 of '*Ut musica poesis*'.

[12] In her letter to Charles IX (September 1563), Catherine recalls the advice given to her by her father-in-law, François I; he had argued that it was politic to engage

dancing was her favourite art. She is said to have choreographed those dances performed by her ladies at Bayonne in 1565; certainly, dancing was at the centre of most fêtes performed at the Valois court when her authority was in the ascendant. In his memoirs (although these are often unreliable) Brantôme, who knew members of successive generations at court, recalled of Catherine: 'Elle inventoit tousjours quelque nouvelle danse ou quelques beaux ballets, quand il faisoit mauvais temps'.[13]

According to Pierre Paschal, the taste of Henri II was equally broad, even when we make allowance for the historian's will to flatter and bathe in reflected glory:

Tout ainsi qu'il [Henri II] aimoit la cognoissance de toutes choses humaines, aussi se delectoit-il singulierement de l'Architecture. Il feit bastir en plusieurs endroits, au temps de son règne ... Il faisoit faveur aux gens de lettres, tant de son naturel, qu'incité par l'exemple du feu Roy François son pere: et faisoit principalement cas des beaux esprits qui peuvent rendre immortels les faicts des grans et illustres personnages. Il entendoit la langue latine, et sçavoit des lettres suffisamment. Il parloit Italien et Espagnol bien proprement. Il estoit amateur de la Musique.[14]

(Just as he [Henri II] favoured knowledge of all things human, so he delighted particularly in architecture. During his reign, he had buildings erected in many places ... Through his own taste, but also inspired by the example of his father Francis I, he was a good patron of men of letters showing especial favour to those able to grant immortality to the deeds of great and illustrious persons. He understood Latin; had a fair knowledge of letters; spoke Italian and Spanish well. He was a fair performer in music.)

This vision of the king as ideal monarch or as universal man was not an uncommon one in sixteenth-century writing; it recurred especially when attacks on the tyranny of princes became more frequent and when a fiercer defence was required; but it is unusual for the panoply of talents cited to be extended to music.

In the case of Charles IX, his love of poetry and music is well known through his poetic exchanges with Ronsard, through the attention he gave to every musical event he encountered from his journeys around France, and from his letters patent for the

nobles in entertainments in order to ensure relative harmony at court: *Lettres de Catherine de' Medici*, 5 vols., ed. M. Le Cte Hector de la Ferrière (Paris, 1885), ii, p. 92.
[13] Brantôme, seigneur de Bordeille, *Oeuvres complètes*, 8 vols. (Paris, 1823), v, p. 36.
[14] P. de Paschal, *Journal de l'année 1562* (ed. Paris, 1950), p. 12.

Académie de Poésie et de Musique, 1570.[15] Jouan reported, for example, that Charles IX had been installed in the main street in Narbonne on 3 January 1565 to hear a concert which had been prepared by the 'enfants de la ville'. These performed sweet music and sang joyous verses ('Si l'allegresse et les jeux . . .'). The king's pleasure was evident: 'Le Roy qui aimoit la musique les écouta fort humainement'.[16] It seems that his pleasure derived (in part at least) from his own knowledge of music, poetry and the dance for, as Archange Tuccaro confidently claimed at the beginning of *L'art de sauter* (1599), 'Il [Charles IX] estimoit être chose tres honorable de sçavoir toutes sortes de bals et de danses esquels par dessus tout la mesure et cadence est necessaire'.[17]

Henri III seems to have had more limited preferences and to have focused his interest on philosophical debate, if the evidence of the discussions at the Académie du Palais is a serious guide,[18] and if Belleau's assessment of him is accurate. In the poet's dedication of *Les amours* to Henri III, he asserted: 'Vous estes le Prince de ce monde qui prend plus de plaisir à discourir des secrets de la Philosophie, et choses naturelles, et qui plus honore ceux qui font exercice en le mestier' – an unusual tribute for a poet who doubtless sought his patronage.[19]

Such diversity of taste in patrons contributed to the wide range of fêtes which can be found in the second half of the sixteenth century. Their nature was also affected by the different locations in which festivals took place: a main street in a provincial town; a temporary platform hastily arranged; the splendid space of bishops' palaces or of town halls; or the rocking boards of a river barge. Even at the court itself, ostensibly one place (and often wrongly thought of as a coherent entity), even there, heterogeneity was the principal characteristic. For the Fontainebleau fêtes of 1564, the entertainments were dispersed, scattered around different apartments and palaces: first in the logis of the Duc

[15] Letters patent published in full by Yates in *French Academies*, pp. 319–20.
[16] See McAllister Johnson and Graham, Appendix v, pp. 187 ff., for a description of the king's visit to Narbonne.
[17] A. Tuccaro, *L'art de sauter* (Langres, 1599), sig. a ijv.
[18] For a discussion of the activities of the Académie du Palais, see Yates, *French Academies*, pp. 27 ff.
[19] R. Belleau, *Oeuvres poétiques* [1569], ed. C. Marty-Laveaux, 2 vols. (Paris, 1877–8; repr. Geneva, 1965), II, dedication to *Les amours et nouveaux eschanges*.

d'Orléans; then at the residence of the Cardinal de Bourbon; and finally, in the Vacherie of the queen mother. Although there might have been little to differentiate the physical settings arranged in the palaces of the Duc d'Orléans and of the Cardinal de Bourbon, Catherine's dairy was something else entirely. Built to match the assumed simplicity of pastoral life, it imitated the habits of shepherds, and the rustic entertainments arranged were intended to match their cadre.

It is mistaken to think of the court as a single focus for festival. In 1572, for example, the wedding of Henri de Navarre and Marguerite de Valois was celebrated with entertainments in the Louvre and then in the city of Paris, first at the Hôtel de Bourbon and later at the Hôtel d'Anjou. Responsibility for celebrating important political events (whether marriages or births, baptisms or visits of foreign princes) was collective and dispersed and, in consequence, the conditions of production could vary greatly.

Actual settings for festival inevitably had an impact on the nature of the music-making. If we consider two entertainments, both given in Paris in 1558, some idea of the nature of the differences can be gauged. At the banquet following the wedding of Mary Queen of Scots to the dauphin, the royal party returned to the Louvre for ballets and masques. For one of the ballets, the twelve performers (all royal princes) made their entrance into the hall on horseback, their mounts being artificially made; each appearance was accompanied by a troop of 'pelerins . . . chantans melodieusement avec instrumens en toute perfection la musique, hymnes et cantiques, à la louange des mariez et du mariage'.[20] Although the music has not survived, it is clear from the official account that the music-making was ambitious, for these singers and players who accompanied the entries were different from those who played for the dancing.

The music which Etienne Jodelle planned for the city's entertainment for Henri II was more integrated with the marine theme he had chosen. Acknowledging the central role of music at the beginning, 'sçachant que la beauté d'une mascarade est la musique', he planned to have Orpheus come on stage singing

[20] *Discours du grand et magnifique triumphe faict au mariage de . . . François . . . et . . . Marie d'Estrevart, roine d'Escosse* (Paris, 1558), sig. C.iv.

177

the praises of the king – 'Si jamais rochers et bois . . .'; the power of his music was (as in the myth) to attract 'deux rochers plains de musique'. From within these rocky structures was to come the song of Satyrs and of Nymphs very deliberately conceived in a sweet and simple style using 'vers intercalaires' to achieve this direct effect.[21] The practical problem was, however, that the rocky structures were too large to get into the hall!

An even more ambitious role for music can be seen in the pastoral play *L'Arimène* performed in 1596 at the Duc de Mercoeur's country home in Nantes. Here an elaborate theatre setting had been constructed in which a system of periaktoi turned at bidden intervals to change the scenery *à vue d'oeil* for the interludes which were performed between the acts. These interludes bore no relation to the play, being modelled on ancient practice as their author Nicolas de Montreux indicates in his dedication to the duke, addressing him thus: 'l'imitation des antiques vous a parue belle et legitime'.[22] The interludes combined theatrical display with musical entertainment. The first showed Jupiter at war with the giants; Helen of Troy's story provided the second; Andromeda's escape was the subject of the third; Jupiter and Argus were represented in the fourth; and, for the climax, Orpheus and Eurydice and the power of music. Music was present throughout the performance, skilfully concealed behind the periaktoi: 'Derriere les Pantagonnes estoit la musique, composée diversement de toutes sortes de voix, et d'instrumens, dont les paroles et les airs estoyent neufs, et faicts pour ce seul subject'.[23] The nature of the music's newness must remain obscure; but, within the play, there were conventional love songs, echo effects, songs praising the power of the lyre or indulging lovers' complaints. It was, however, in the final interlude that the role of music was dominant. Orpheus is summoned:

> Sus donc, Orphee, or sus prestre de Thrace
> Descen en bas, et va fleschir l'audace
> Par bon doux chant des infernaux esprits.[24]

[21] See McAllister Johnson and Graham's edition of *Le recueil des inscriptions, 1558* (Toronto, 1972), pp. 103–5, for Jodelle's account of this spectacular disaster.

[22] *L'Arimène* by Ollenix du Mont-Sacré [pseudonym for Nicolas de Montreux], Paris, 1597, sig. A.iiv.

[23] *Ibid.*, sig. A.iiij.

[24] *Ibid.*, fol. 122.

Quickly the infernal spirits succumb to Orpheus' magic, his song having the same effect as enchantment, and even Cerberus is put to sleep by his musical power. *L'Arimène* gave much emphasis to music, offering a blend of intimacy in the lovers' exchanges within the pastoral and of more overwhelming musical power in the interludes, ending on tones of praise when Monsieur d'Avenes, who played Orpheus, 'couronna l'oeuvre, chantant sur la lyre des vers fort agreables en l'honneur du Prince'.[25]

Even in this detailed account of the performance of *L'Arimène*, there is little precise evidence of the character of the singing or playing, and although the verses survive, the music does not. Yet some music does exist for Loys Papon's *Pastorelle* which he composed in 1587 to celebrate the recent French victory over German mercenaries and which was performed in the Salle de Diane, at Montbrison; it was decorated with tapestries and portraits for the occasion.[26] The first two acts are devoid of music, which war had banished from the land; it bursts out in triumph at the end of Act III scene 1 where the triple victory roll:

> Victoire io victoire aux fidelles Françoys,
> Victoire io victoire au grand Roy des Gauloys,
> Victoire io victoire aux loys de nostre Eglise;[27]

is repeated several times until the shepherds recognise the source of these harmonies as belonging to Fame. The cries of triumph are sung to an unadorned melody which is integrated into the overall simplicity. Music and dancing also appropriately contributed to the climax of the play where, in Act V, a pyramid symbolising the victory of right causes has been constructed *à vue d'oeil*, fires of triumph have been set alight beneath it, and the rustic performers dance 'autour, l'espace d'un quart d'heure, avec telle dexterité qu'il estoit impossible de faire mieux'.[28]

[25] *Ibid.*, fol. 123ᵛ.

[26] I wish to thank Dr Frank Dobbins for drawing my attention to this work of which a manuscript presentation copy survives in the British Library (Harleian 4325); rather crude watercolour drawings show the costumes for Mercury, Ceres, Fame and two shepherd couples and the general disposition of the scene and hall. There have been two modern printings: the first by N. Yemeniz (Lyons, 1857), the second by C. Longeon (1982).

[27] *Pastorelle*, fols. 24ᵛ–25. A fervent catholic and priest, Papon seeks not only to praise French glories (particularly those of the Guise) and to extol peace returned but also to promote the cause of the church.

[28] Papon appended to the end of his presentation copy an account of the performance from which this extract is taken, fol. 56ᵛ.

From Papon's own observations we know that the musicians were accommodated in a small gallery erected for the purpose, out of the way of entrances and exits. Describing the stage, Papon remarks:

le tout se couvrait par fois soubz deux Rideaus qui se tirants par les deux bouts bouchoint toute cette magnificence:[29] pour n'estre couverts que lorsqu'au son des hautboys, et autre Musique, logee en l'un des costes sur un eschafaut, a la main droicte pour ne donner ou recepvoir empeschement, les Acteurs entroint sur le theatre, marchantz a la grave cadence, de cet harmonie: et des qu'il[s] rentroint, la scene finie, le Rideau estoit reserré par les hommes Expres à cet office.[30]

(The whole was covered from time to time beneath two curtains which were pulled from two ends to cover up all this magnificence; only covered when – to the sound of oboes and other music, lodged on each side of the stage, on the right hand side in order to prevent any obstruction – the actors entered on stage, walking in slow rhythm which matched the music. When, once the scene had ended, they withdrew, the curtain was drawn back again by men specifically appointed to this task.)

In addition to the music needed for the *Pastorelle* itself, music and dancing played a role in the interludes taken from the *commedia dell'arte* which were imported by Papon 'affin de les [the spectators] delecter d'une varieté'. The interludes were linked by a common theme. Three aspirants sought the hand of a beautiful signora, and each had to prove his worth in singing, dancing and tilting: first, by 'une chansson pour faire preuve qui avoit plus belle voix'; then by dancing a moresque 'les fist dancer les sonnettes';[31] and finally, by 'courre une bague, sur des chevaux moulés, pour cognoistre le plus adroict'.[32] These competitive trials, for which no further detail is available, were designed to lend variety and to respond to the spectators' ability to distinguish good and indifferent performances.

---

[29] Despite these grandiloquent tones, the scenery appears relatively rudimentary, tapestries providing the walls on which a series of portraits were affixed.

[30] *Pastorelle*, fol. 55ᵛ. Papon seems to use the word *scene* to mean *act*.

[31] T. Arbeau, *Orchésographie* (Paris, 1589; trans. M. S. Evans, New York, 1948, p. 177), explains how this *moresco* was performed with bells attached to the dancers' legs.

[32] *Pastorelle*, fol. 56ᵛ. These interludes taken from the repertory of the *commedia dell'arte* are further proof of the enduring Italian influence in France at this time, and that it went well beyond the court.

The varied settings of these four events – two in 1558 and the plays of 1587 and 1597 – give some notion of what was intended. It is also possible to glean other indications of value relative to music from the many extant descriptions of festivals. Jouan's account of the February 1564 fêtes at Fontainebleau, for which Ronsard composed all the verses, describes the scene at the home of the Duc d'Orléans; after the trumpets had ceased their noise, three Sirens greeted the king outdoors, accompanying themselves on the lute; their final stanzas of praise were taken up by three ensembles and repeated on the *basse contre*. Additionally, hidden within a fountain was a band of violinists who performed a concert which lasted as long as it took the king to walk from the gardens and into the banqueting hall. There, more music awaited him, for a gallery had been constructed at one end to accommodate the music: 'la salle estoit bien accoustrée et au bout d'icelle avoit dressé un petit lieu eslevé en forme de gallerie pour mettre la musique'.[33] Each course was brought in with music: a concert of trumpets and sackbuts; or four voices accompanied by 'une Espinette, un dessus de viole, un dessus de flute, un Bourdon'. The dinner ended with goddesses bearing gifts, and singing songs of praise, each one with a different instrument. Then the company moved outdoors again where Greeks and Trojans, ready to do battle, first expressed their differences in song. Jouan does not always trace such variety or remember to give the words of the songs, but the official scribe does so for the fêtes at Bayonne (June 1565), where a herald appears before the king at a banquet to expound in song the quarrels that have broken out between the Britons and the Irish and which will be settled only the next day in jousts. The account stresses, in particular, the clarity of delivery, the appropriateness of the tone which matched the sense of the words, and the fact that each sung speech was followed by a concert with all the musicians playing together:

commença le Deputé de la grand Bretagne à réciter sur sa lyre ce qui s'ensuit, chantant à haute voix, tellement qu'il estoit oüi de tous ceux qui estoyent en la salle, avecques grand plaisir, pour sa voix qui estoit excellente, et pour le ton et chant qui estoit si bien accommodé aux

---

[33] McAllister Johnson and Graham, *The Royal Tour*, Appendix v, pp. 147 ff.

paroles, qu'on entendoit tout ce qu'il recitoit, comme s'il eust parlé, et n'en perdoit on une seule syllabe, tant il prononçoit nettement et distinctement accordant sa voix à sa lyre parfaitement:
'Huict chevaliers de Bretagne la grande . . .'
Ce couplet achevé, se fit un consort de musique de tous les instruments ensemble.[34]

(Then the Deputy from Great Britain began to recite what follows, accompanying himself on his lyre in such a way as to be heard with pleasure by all those in the hall, for his voice was excellent, its tone and singing manner ideally suited to the words; everything he recited was understood just as if he had spoken; not a syllable was lost, for he pronounced the words clearly and distinctly, perfectly harmonising his voice to the sound of his lyre:
'Eight knights from Great Britain . . .'
As soon as he had finished singing his couplet, a consort of music burst forth from all the instruments together.)

This degree of insistence on clarity and on the harmonising of voice and instrument is unusual in these sources, but it serves to underline the perceived relationship between music and poetry, the former (as Ronsard and Pontus de Tyard seem to have advocated) as servant of the latter.[35] Descriptions of festivals given at court assume that the spectator's appreciation is founded on knowledge and on the ability to differentiate different kinds and different levels of skill.

AUDIENCE EXPECTATION

The competence of the courtier in matters of dancing and music should not be underestimated. On the whole, as the accounts of court festivals imply, spectators were expected to be able to judge the niceties of musical composition, to appreciate the intricacies of dance steps, and to admire the variations which professional dancers and musicians introduced in their performance to avoid monotony.[36] The rich and unbroken tradition of works on courtly

[34] *Ibid.*, Appendix xxi, pp. 328 ff.
[35] The passage cited from the Bayonne fêtes confirms the hierarchy discussed by Brown in '*Ut musica poesis*', pp. 4–12, where relevant passages from Pontus de Tyard's *Solitaire second* are analysed, followed by an appraisal of various settings of Ronsard's poems.
[36] Monique Rollin has shown how, for a slightly later period, dance music was printed to allow for variations to be introduced impromptu in performance, 'La musique de ballet dans les tablatures de luth: souvenir et source d'inspiration', *Cahiers de l'IRHMES*, 1 (1992), pp. 53–75.

behaviour (starting with Castiglione whose *Libro del cortegiano* was available in many translations and adaptations, and including *La civil conversazione* of Guazzo or *L'honneste homme ou l'art de plaire à la court* copied from earlier traditions by the bourgeois writer Nicolas Faret) had laid out clear rules and expectations concerning artistic performance for nobles and their ladies.[37] These included knowledge of the various arts, ability to perform most with skill but not ostentatiously, and the recognition and appreciation of those skills in others. Italian influences were strong in the social conditioning which was to make increasing demands on poets and painters, musicians and choreographers. This is apparent from the authors of books on manners, from the artistic demands of Catherine de' Medici and her Italian entourage, from books on dance technique, and from the presence of Italian dancing masters in France throughout the second half of the sixteenth century; such masters as Palvallo and Pompeo Diabono came across the Alps from 1554.[38]

In practice, noble men and women were often performers – singers and/or dancers – alongside professionals in court entertainments. This mixed participation is recorded for the marriage festivities of Henri de Navarre (1572) for example, and for the *Balet comique de la royne* (1581). However, in trying to establish more clearly the expectations of the audience in the second half of the sixteenth century, it is perhaps instructive to consider also less well-known instances of amateur and professional mix such as in Jacques Yver's *Le printemps* (1572) or Claude Gauchet's *Plaisir des champs* (1583).

Le printemps is a long fictional work which deserves closer analysis. Jacques Yver creates an imaginary, idyllic place in Poitou, with a gorgeous castle filled with noble rooms of great magnificence and peopled with lively, cultured souls whose task is to fill the five days they are to stay there with suitable

---

[37] Castiglione's *Book of the Courtier* was first published in French as *Le parfait courtisan* in 1538; Guazzo's *La civil conversazione* was published in Brescia in 1574; and Faret's adaptation of these traditions came out in Paris in 1632.

[38] G. Nakam, *Montaigne en son temps* (Paris, 1982), p. 56, commenting upon Montaigne's references to Italian masters in *De l'institution des enfans*, offers this information: 'La cour prend des leçons de danse, sous la conduite du maître italien Ludovico Palvallo, et s'enthousiasme pour le célèbre milanais Pompeo Diabono arrivé en France en 1554.'

entertainment and pleasure. What is striking about their pastimes is the ease of intercourse between the social classes, with nobles and peasants joining together in music and dance and using musical instruments belonging to both sets: 'Lors apres maintes dances compassees, ores au son du luth, ores du flageolot, ou de la cheurie, dont les villageois de ce pays sçavent tous jouer'.[39] Equally interesting are the constant shifts between songs and dances, the former sung to dance tunes: 'Puis estant lassez de danser en chappellet, commencerent la Gaillarde, chansons *gaillarde* ... apres les Damoiselles commencerent à chanter force Vaudevilles'. After the epithalamia composed to celebrate several rustic marriages, the fifth day ends with more songs – *branles de Poitou* (pp. 388–91).[40]

The ease of transference in this rustic setting has its learned counterpart at court, as has most recently been examined by Pierre Bonniffet in the context of Baïf's *Le printans*.[41] In his analysis, which sets out to demonstrate the links between word and music in Baïf's work, Bonniffet extends that linkage to include the dance, arguing that Baïf's profound knowledge of Greek allowed him to understand both the closeness of dance and verse, 'les *pieds* dans les vers et les *pas* des danseurs', and the natural, innate affinity which existed between song and dance.[42] These affinities Baïf sought to capture in his *vers mesurés* apt to serve the rhythms required by dancing. Bonniffet maintains (with reason) that Baïf's *Chansonettes* were *chansons à danser*, and that in composing them as he did, he was consciously emulating ancient Greek practice:

> Car leurs vers avoyent la mesure,
> Qui d'une plaisante bature
> Frapoit l'oreille des Oïans,
> Et des chores la belle dance,
> En chantant gardoit la cadence
> Au son des Hauboys s'éguyans.[43]

---

[39] *Le printemps*, Paris, 1572, fol. 10ᵛ.

[40] *Ibid.*, fols. 164ᵛ–165.

[41] Pierre Bonniffet, *Un ballet démasqué: l'union de la musique au verbe dans 'Le printans' de Jean-Antoine de Baïf et Claude Le Jeune* (Paris and Geneva, 1988).

[42] *Ibid.*, pp. 153–6.

[43] This is the first strophe of the dedication to the Duc d'Alençon of *Les jeux* (1573); it is cited by Bonniffet on p. 155.

(Because their [the Greeks'] verse was measured / And with a pleasant beat / Struck the ears of the listeners / While the beautiful dances of the chorus / In their song kept time with the beat / As they disported themselves to the sound of oboes.)

Marin Mersenne was later to make even more explicit the natural extending and fusing of dance and poetic rhythms.[44] To return, however, to Yver's work of the same title as that of Baïf; it is evident that, in his fictionalised world, the same pleasures in the same forms are shared by both the rural community and the visitors imbued with evident culture of the court; secondly, that there is mutual understanding and appreciation of the qualities of performance (a point made clearly in the discussions on the value of dancing which brings to an end the third day's activities);[45] and thirdly, that the connections between verse, music and the dance are perceived as close sometimes to the extent that the forms seem interchangeable – an effect which is achieved apparently with great naturalness here but which was sought more consciously and more learnedly in Baïf's *Le printans*.[46]

For a sight of connoisseurship fully displayed, one could turn to Ronsard's evocation of Marguerite de Navarre dancing with her brother Charles IX in *La charite*, or to her solo performance as set out in the sonnet beginning 'Le soir qu'Amour vous fist en la salle descendre'. Both poems assume that the reader, through his or her knowledge of the dance, has the equipment to recreate the scene; and both poems have received much attention.[47] A similar appreciation of virtuosity can be found in Claude Gauchet's poem *La feste du village avec la dance*.[48] At the centre of village life, Gauchet places music and dancing, and he represents both arts as being emblematic of youth, of joy and celebration,

---

[44] *Harmonie universelle* (Paris, 1636), proposition xx, p. 391, 'Les Compositeurs de balets donnent à leurs Branles, et autres pieces qui servent à la recreation: car ils usent des mesmes pieds qu'Anacreon, Pindare, Theocrite, et les autres Poëtes, encore qu'ils ne suivent autre chose que leur genie et qu'ils n'en ayent point oüy parler: c'est pourquoy l'on peut appeler chaque espece de vers, Branle, Courante, etc. suivant le mouvement du vers.'

[45] *Le printemps*, fol. 165ᵛ.

[46] Bonniffet rounds off his argument about Baïf's collection of poems thus: 'on peut voir dans *le Printans* le premier monument de la musique de danse au XVIe siècle', *Un ballet démasqué*, p. 156.

[47] *Ideal Forms*, pp. 221–6.

[48] *Le plaisir des champs* (Paris, 1583), pp. 57 ff.; Gauchet, almoner of the king, dedicated his work to the Duc de Joyeuse two years after the *Balet comique de la royne* (1581).

and both as being natural and spontaneous expressions of feeling. Such spontaneity does not, of course, preclude virtuosity; the skills and appreciation of them are caught in Gauchet's account of Michaut and Marion's love game/dance where the man's gaucheness and limitations are ironically contrasted with the maiden's imitative power and endurance:

> Michault prend Marion, la tire de la dance,
> Et apres avoir faict une humble reverence
> Il la baise à la bouche, et cliquetant les dois
> Montre qu'à bien dancer il ne craint villageois;
> Or' il a les deux mains au costé, puis se tourne,
> Et devant Marion presente sa personne,
> Puis resaultant en l'air gambade lourdement;
> Hault troussant le talon d'un sot contournement.
>   La fille s'en hardit, et son homme regarde
> Et à tout ce qu'il faict de pres elle prend garde:
> S'il faict un sault en l'air, Marion saute aussi:
> S'il dance de costé, elle faict tout ainsi;
> Tant qu'à les voir dancer à tout le monde resemble
> Qu'ils ayent recordé leur tricotis ensemble.
>   Or Michault ayant faict, suant et halletant,
> Son devoir de dancer le bouquet, bien content,
> Le Livre entre les mains de Marion, puis passe
> Et seule la laissant se remet à sa place:
> Marion tourne au tour, et si bien se conduit
> Qu'au vueil des assistans prend Sandrin qu'elle suit,
> Qui luy preste la main comme par moquerie,
> Puis dançant de plus beau saulte comme une pie . . .[49]

(Michault claims Marion and draws her into the dance / And after performing a humble reverence / He kisses her on the mouth, and snapping his fingers / Shows that no villager could rival him in dancing well / With his hands on his hips he turns, / And, before Marion, presents his person, / Then jumping again into the air he tumbles rather heavily / Shaking his heel high foolishly yet nimbly. / The girl gains confidence, and watching her man closely / She takes in everything he does: / If he jumps high in the air, Marion does too, / If he dances sideways, so does she exactly the same; / Such that those who saw them dance / Thought they had rehearsed their measures together. / Then Michault having finished dancing *le bouquet* / Well pleased with himself, breathless and sweating hard, / Delivers the flowers into Marion's hands, retires / And leaving her

---

[49]   *Ibid.*, p. 68.

alone, he goes back to his place. / Marion moves around the company, and holds herself so well / That to the delight of those there, she chooses Sandrin and follows him / He offers his hand as if in mockery, / Then dancing even better, leaps like a bird [magpie].)

The spirit of rivalry and the sense of an audience enjoying that competitiveness are the dominant themes, and they show how similar were the attitudes – at least those depicted in poems – of the lower and higher classes towards music and dancing. The frequent blurring of the lines between the two social levels are further illustrated by the *Recueil de ballets* of the violinist Michel Henry where he records those occasions at which he played in the Louvre and then proceeded to perform the same work in the town; in 1597, for example, 'sortis du Louvre, les amis de M. Henry diffusaient largement en ville les danses qui venaient de réjouir les grands'.[50]

In the circumstances of sharing a common experience it is not surprising that whatever the artistic activity – music, poetry, painting or dancing – the same terms were used to evaluate their nature, their status and their objectives. 'Grace', 'harmony', 'order'/'skill', 'speed', 'ease'/'sweetness', 'virtuosity', 'smoothness' recurred each time a writer attempted to convey the effects produced in performance.[51] The knowledgeable audience had no difficulty (apparently) in responding differentially to such terms which, in making judgments, placed music alongside other art forms and on the same plane. In Hugues Salel's poem *Chant poétique présenté au roy le premier jour de l'an 1549*, the homage takes the form of a ballet, composed by Apollo, danced and sung by all the gods to please Jupiter: 'Et quant à quant balèrent et chantèrent'. Jupiter discriminated; he admired the songs performed by the Muses,

> Chacune adonc ses forces esprouva
> De bien chanter . . .

but he particularly extolled the dangerous leaps of the Satyrs:

[50] See F. Lesure, 'Recueil des ballets de Michel Henry' [*c.* 1620], published in *Fêtes de la Renaissance*, ed. Jacquot, I, pp. 205–20.
[51] For a discussion of this common language, and concerning interart analogies more generally, see *Ideal Forms*, pp. 51–63.

Là firent [les Satyrs] saults, virevoustes, gambades,
Tours, et contours, passepieds par compas
Des bransles gais, gaillardes, et cinq pas.[52]

(Then each muse gave proof of her power of singing . . . / The
Satyrs performed leaps, jumps and somersaults, / Their figures and
windings and their measured capers, / Gay branles, galliards and
cinquepaces.)

It was well known and generally accepted in the Renaissance
that makers (painters, composers and poets) claimed also to be
thinkers. Performers (dancers, players, poets) similarly claimed
to know about theory. As Howard Mayer Brown made clear in
his discussion of Pontus de Tyard's contribution to mid-century
debates, poetry, music and dancing were often combined, and
when they worked thus in harmony, they were thought to have
extraordinary powers of elevation. In the *Solitaire premier*,
Pontus de Tyard expressly linked this power of expression with
knowledge and moral enlightenment: 'Davantage les Muses . . .
entrelacées l'une avec l'autre dancent en chantant des Hymnes,
appropriez aux louanges des Dieux, et signifie tel entrelacement,
que la vertu ne peut estre separée ou desjointe des studieux et
sinceres amateurs de sapience et doctrine.'[53] ('Moreover, the
Muses . . . entwined one with the other, danced and sang hymns
designed to praise the gods, and such entwining signified that
virtue cannot be separated nor disjoined from those who actively
and sincerely seek formation and knowledge'). Earlier in the
same text Pontus de Tyard had summarised the effect on the
soul of music, poetry and dance conjoined as 'a tirer l'ame
embourbée hors de la fange terrestre'. Similar claims were made
at the end of the century, notably by the acrobat Archange
Tuccaro who argued that 'le but de la danse . . . c'est la vertu'.[54]

Such powers of elevation claimed for the arts fed into other
objectives set by poets, composers, choreographers and painters.
In the context of the court, they shared the same aims: enhanced
status for themselves and for their patron. In their works, their
object was to celebrate and to praise; and to this end, *chanter*

---

[52] H. Salel, *Oeuvres poétiques*, modern edn (Paris, 1930), p. 301.
[53] *Solitaire premier*, ed. Lapp, p. 42.
[54] Tuccaro, *L'art de sauter*, fol. 28ʳ.

became synonymous with *louer*, and both verbs were used inter-changeably by Pontus de Tyard in the *Solitaire premier*, and by others. It suffices to cite Pasquier's letter to Ronsard (1555), where poetry and celebration are put together in a striking way, to assess how widespread this view had become. Pasquier ends his letter with this resounding affirmation: 'Car quant à la plume du Poëte, elle doit estre vouée à la celebration de ceux qui le méritent'.[55] The authority for such views was ancient and went back at least to Hesiod whose poem began with a gesture of celebration that linked dancing and music in the action of the Muses which Pontus de Tyard reproduced as fact in the *Solitaire premier* (see above) and which Tuccaro recalls in *L'art de sauter*.[56] Thus, all the arts shared a common language in their mutual assessment of quality and in the way they described their aims and achievements. Tuccaro's *L'art de sauter* (1599) can be seen as providing the culmination of half a century's thinking on the value of combining the arts and on the effectiveness of the works produced through such linking.

Behind the assertions of poets and composers, of choreographers and artists, lay the influence of the past. They all referred more or less precisely to classical texts, and often to the same ones: to Plato and Lucian; to Pliny, Hesiod and Homer; but especially to Plato. He is the source most cited by Tuccaro, for instance, who, at the beginning of his book, used Plato to justify the role of the arts in the Republic, and again when he argued the connections between dance and virtue. From Plato, Tuccaro's argument widens out to define the harmonic correspondances that were thought to exist between 'le bal des astres' and 'la musique des sphères', and to claim those similar harmonies which were achieved when music, dance and poetry were combined in spectacle. The argument is long, convoluted and complex but it is worth citing in full:

Ils [les Grecs] afferment mesmes qu'ils ont esté trouvez à l'imitation du mouvement et tour des cieux et des progrez divers, droits et obliques, des retrogradations et diversitez des conionctions et aspects des

---

[55] Cited in P. Champion, *Ronsard et son temps*, I (Paris, 1925), p. 31.
[56] Tuccaro, *L'art de sauter*, fol. 38ᵛ, 'Hesiode au commencement de ses vers voulant louer les Muses, escrit qu'elles sautent et ballent souvent entre-elles de fort bonne grace'.

planettes. Toutes lesquelles choses si on vouloit considerer parfaitement, on pourroit paravanture cognoistre qu'elles sont iustement imitees et representees au bal; d'autant que la diversité des mouvements faicts à l'opposite l'un de l'autre par ceux qui dansent, n'est qu'une generale imitation du mouvement des cieux, et le retour qu'on faict en arriere au bal et à la dance n'est autre chose que vouloir imiter honnestement la retrogradation des planettes. Il y a plus, que les passages qui sont representez tenants un de leurs pieds arrestez et remuantz l'autre c'est comme une similitude des estoilles errantes, quand elles sont suyvant les Astrologues, en leur degré. Et les Voltes dont on use en ballant, ne sont autre chose que les espies qu'on tient estre és cieux, les conjonctions alternatives qu'on faict apres une separation proportionnee du bal et de la dance; et puis ces belles et diverses retraictes, droictes et obliques, qu'on exerce avec tant de grace, sont les mesmes conjonctions et opposites triangulaires et quadrangulaires, voire sexangulaires qui interviennent tous les iours entre les planettes en leurs spheres celestes . . .[57]

(The Greeks even affirm that they sought to imitate the movement of the heavens, their diverse motions, straight and oblique, their retrograde movements and the diverse aspects and conjunctions of the planets. All these things, if they are closely considered, can be seen to be perfectly imitated and represented in dancing; the more so since the movements back and forth performed by those who dance are nothing other than an imitation of heavenly movement, and the steps one takes backwards in dancing or during a ball are nothing more than the wish to imitate accurately the retrograde motions of the planets. And there is more; those steps which are made showing one foot motionless while the other moves are nothing other than a likeness to the wandering stars as they are followed in their detail by astrologers. The leaps that one performs in dancing are nothing other than markers that are thought to be in the heavens, the alternating conjunctions one makes after an appropriate separation in dancing; and then, those beautiful and diverse withdrawings, straight and oblique, that one performed with such grace, are the same three- or four-part, even six-part, conjunctions and oppositions which intervene every day between planets in their celestial spheres.)

In this passage which sees almost systematic proportions and correspondances between the harmonic effects engineered by man – through music or dance –and those created in nature, Tuccaro is both making explicit the ambitious claims which artists had long sought, and reminding us of the broad context –

---

[57]   *Ibid.*, fol. 36.

cosmic even – in which artistic performance (whether music, dancing or poetry) was placed in the second half of the sixteenth century in France.[58]

THE WORKS: PRAISE, PROPAGANDA AND POLITICS

In the late Renaissance, poets and princes had rediscovered affinities from which other artists – composers or painters – also benefited. Their interdependence and self-reinforcing status could be illustrated from any of the composite court festivals of the period. Three examples, mounted in successive years, have been chosen here to demonstrate the political and social consequences of the arts conjoined and to show the place of music in this context where the arts are so interrelated. The examples all occurred during the most active years of the Académie de Poésie et de Musique when we know that poets, composers and choreographers worked together in a common cause, promoting their own image and that of their art, and projecting an upbeat view of their princely patrons, and also at a time when Orlande de Lassus was in Paris[59] (invited by his editor Adrian Le Roy, at whose house he stayed until after August 1573 when he participated in the fêtes for the Polish ambassadors; he was the composer who, for French poets, symbolised the musical power attributed in mythology to Orpheus or to Mercury).[60]

The first occasion concerns the marriage of Charles IX in 1571, which was organised according to a simple processional structure on the familiar theme of celebration.[61] Jamyn, Jodelle

---

[58] Howard Mayer Brown has stressed the cosmic context in which music was placed by musical theorists at this time; see '*Ut musica poesis*', pp. 3–4.

[59] H. Chamard, *Histoire de la Pléiade*, 4 vols. (Paris, 1939), III, p. 357, note 1. Lassus paid his first visit to Paris in 1571 when he dedicated a new book of five-part chansons to Charles IX; see J. Roche, *Lassus* (Oxford, 1982), p. 45, and for a full account of this visit, A. Sandberger, 'R. Lassus' Beziehungen zu Frankreich', *Sammelbände der Internationalen Musik-Gesellschaft*, 8 (1906–7), pp. 355 ff.

[60] Ronsard wrote of Lassus that he 'semble avoir seul desrobé l'harmonie des cieux pour nous à resjouir en la terre' (cited by Champion, *Ronsard et son temps*, IV, p. 135); and Jodelle compared him to Mercury: 'Mercure aussi, qu'on fait fort subtil inventeur, / En musique, peut estre, est la Musique mesme, / Haussant, baissant, partout ce beau vol enchanteur' (cited by Champion, III, pp. 247–8).

[61] The details of this indoor festival are less well known than that other processional celebration, the royal entry into Paris: *L'entrée à Paris de Charles IX*, ed. F. A. Yates (Amsterdam, 1974).

and Ronsard all participated, and their verses were played and sung in a series of alternating *soli* and *ensembles* by musicians hidden in triumphal cars: 'vers intercalaires chantez et sonnez par les musiciens estans dans le creux du char'.[62] As they had been for earlier royal festivities,[63] the gods were present at the ceremony, brought triumphantly into the banqueting hall. Seven gods first sang together, followed by a vocal concert provided by the Muses whose singing culminated in a solo *récitatif* performed by Cléion in honour of the queen mother. One by one triumphal cars came forward: that of the Moon combining the properties of Abundance and Sleep; Mercury drawn by Genius; Venus, accompanied by the three Graces and pulled along by Cupid; then that of the Sun, showing the four seasons, and drawn along by Aurora; finally Mars, all bristling, appeared. Each entry was marked by music-making, and its lavish décor was enthusiastically received by the élite audience which had crowded into the Louvre. In her verses, Cléion had made it clear that what the spectators had seen was a replication of what occurs in the heavens:

> ... tous ces chars, tous ces animaux-ci,
> En or et en argent, et en couleurs aussi,
> Et presque ces mouvemens, en splendeurs, et au reste
> Imitent quasi l'ordre et matiere celeste.
> L'appareil ample et digne, et propre à chacun Dieu
> S'est fait tel que voyez, pour en temps et en lieu
> Qui seroit propre, orner un si haut mariage ...[64]

(... all these cars, all these animals / In gold and silver, and in colour too, / And almost these movements in splendour / Virtually imitate heavenly order and matter. / The noble and ample show, appropriate to each God / Was done as you see, for a time and in a place / Which would be a fitting adornment to such a noble marriage)

Once more the cosmic context is emphasised as the cars, their richness, their movement, order and colour imitated their heav-

---

[62] See E. Jodelle, *Oeuvres complètes*, 2 vols., ed. E. Balmas (Paris, 1968), II, pp. 268–74.
[63] The tradition was well established. For an earlier example of the French court mirrored in Olympus, see Mellin de Saint-Gelais, *Chanson des astres* (otherwise called 'Chanson appelée le Ciel*, sur les dames de la cour de Françoys Ier. Elle se chante sur l'air du Curé de Créteil, 1544', note in the *Recueil de Maurepas*), published by P. Blanchemain, *Oeuvres poétiques*, 3 vols. (Paris, 1873), I, pp. 121 ff.
[64] Jodelle, *Oeuvres*, II, p. 272.

enly counterparts and were thus entirely appropriate to this royal occasion. Social dancing closed the evening's entertainment when spectators and performers mingled together as they had done at the wedding of Mary Queen of Scots in 1558.[65]

The second event, the marriage of Henri de Navarre to Marguerite de Valois in August 1572, inspired a much more complex set of entertainments where the celebratory theme (which started in processional mode) was dramatised, and where dancing, music, décor and combat were fused into a more coherent whole.[66]

On the first evening (19 August) a ballet with musical entertainment was performed at the Hôtel d'Anjou by members of the French court, some of whom were disguised as sea creatures to blend into the marine symbolism which formed the subject of the ballet. Eleven triumphal cars brought the performers into the hall; they depicted rocks covered with shells and sea creatures carrying musicians and surmounted by colonnaded temples in each of which sat a sea god enthroned and dressed in gold cloth and robes of diverse colours. Sometimes a car was shaped in the form of a fish or a sea lion or, for the one carrying Neptune and the King of France, a colossal shell. After the triumphal procession had been completed, all the splendidly attired arrivals got down from their vehicles, and princes and princesses together performed their dancing. Simon Goulart unfortunately provides no information about the nature of the dancing; he does however give some details concerning the music, providing a glimpse of the scale of the performance and of the quality of the singing of Etienne le Roy who was to enchant the French court on many further occasions:

Premierement se presenterent trois grands chariots qui estoient trois grands rochers ou escueils de mer tous argentez: et sur chascun desdits chariots y avoit cinq musiciens iouans de diverses sortes d'instrumens qui rendoyent une grande melodie. Deux desdits chariots marchoyent accouplez ensemble. L'autre marchoit seul à leur queüe: à la cime duquel estoit le chantre tant renommé, Estienne le Roy, qui faisoit retentir toute la salle de sa voix harmonieuse.[67]

---

[65] *Discours du grand et magnifique triomphe*, sigs. B iij–iv.
[66] The most detailed account of the proceedings can be found in S. Goulart, *Mémoires de l'estat de France* (s.l., 1578), 3 vols., I, fols. 262^r–270^v.
[67] *Ibid.*, fol. 236^v.

(First came three vast cars which were three huge rocks or seashells, all silvered; and on each were five musicians playing diverse instruments which produced great harmonies. Two of the cars came in joined together. The third came behind; on its crown sat the celebrated singer Estienne Le Roy, who made the whole hall resound with his harmonious voice.)

The next day's fêtes had been long in their preparation. The Salle de Bourbon in the Louvre was filled with theatrical machinery: looking towards the stage, on the left-hand side was situated hell, its cavernous mouth filled with devils performing tricks and with a rotating wheel which never ceased its noisy movement except when the doors of hell were shut. On the right was paradise, guarded by the king and his two brothers. The two places were separated by a river in which Charon on his boat was visible. Beyond paradise, and away from the spectators at the end of the hall, the Elysian fields could be perceived. They clearly impressed Goulart, for he described them in detail:

A l'un des bouts de la salle, et derriere le Paradis estoyent les champs Elisées, assavoir un jardin embelly de verdure, et de toutes sortes de fleurs: et le ciel empyree, qui estoit une grand' roüe avec les douze signes, sept planettes, et une infinité de petites estoilles faites à jour, rendant une grande lueur et clarté, par le moyen des lampes et flambeaux qui estoyent artificiellement accomodez par derriere. Ceste roüe estoit en continuel mouvement, faisant aussi tourner ce jardin, dans lequel estoyent douze nymphes fort richement accoustrées.

(At one end of the hall, behind paradise, were the Elysian fields, namely a garden beautified with greenery and with all sorts of flowers; and the highest heaven which was a great wheel with the twelve signs of the zodiac, the seven planets, and an infinity of tiny transparent stars which gave out great light and dazzle by means of the many lamps and torches which were artificially fixed behind. This wheel moved continuously, making the garden move also in which were twelve nymphs richly dressed.)

The décor seems to have been particularly ambitious (perhaps anticipating the use of periaktoi as for *L'Arimène*), and what is noteworthy is the very deliberate antithesis which the designers sought to make between the dark wheel in the mouth of hell and the luminous dial that dominated the celestial sky. Dramatic tension was thus implicit in the scenery, and it was made explicit through the armed encounters which formed a significant part of the performance. One by one challengers ('chevaliers errans') come forward to test their skills against those of the king and his brothers, one by one they are repulsed and dragged off to hell by eager devils. When all challenges have ceased, the doors of hell are closed and, on the instant, harmony breaks forth:

A l'instant descendirent du ciel Mercure et Cupido, portez par un coq, chantans et dansans. Le Mercure estoit cest Estienne le Roy, chantre tant renommé lequel descendu en terre se vint presenter aux trois chevaliers, et apres un chant melodieux, leur fit une harangue, la quelle paracheva, il remonta sur son coq tousjours chantant, et fut reporté au ciel.[68]

(On the instant, Mercury and Cupid, carried on the back of a cock, came down from heaven and began singing and dancing. Mercury was that celebrated singer Estienne Le Roy who, as soon as he touched the earth, came to present himself to the three knights. After his melodious song, he harangued them; that completed, he remounted the cock, and as he continued to sing he was transported back to heaven.)

The peace which follows the victory of the French king and his brothers is given overt approval by the heavens through this descent of the messenger of the gods. Further confirmation is brought by the action of the king himself who makes his way, together with his two brothers, into the Elysian fields which welcome them, releasing to their care the twelve heavenly nymphs who had sparkled in that place from the beginning of the performance. These ladies are brought by their three knights to the centre of the hall where 'elles se mirent à danser un bal fort diversifié, et qui dura plus d'une grosse heure'. Characteristically, Goulart does not comment on the pattern of figures they performed, only on the length of time they took. It is not unreasonable to suppose that the movements were like those performed by the twelve nymphs at the end of the *Balet comique de la royne* (1581). In the same fashion as in the later ballet, they have come to bring harmony through their dancing and to consecrate the peace that the king's presence and his actions have brought about.[69] We have come full circle back to the parallels summarised by Tuccaro whereby harmonic correspondences carefully

---

[68] *Ibid.*, fol. 269ʳ.
[69] This ballet is followed by further displays of martial skills among the challengers released from hell, before fireworks end the proceedings.

contrived, through heavenly music and dancing, are echoed on earth.

In many respects, the third event picks up the themes and artistic threads that have already been articulated in the two earlier fêtes. The visit of the Polish ambassadors to Paris in 1573 offered another opportunity to underline the importance of artistic activity in the context of the court, and momentarily to divert attention away from the mounting tensions of civil and religious strife.[70] A mobile rock brought the nymphs into the hall, nymphs the court had seen at Lyons in 1548 and 1564, at Fontainebleau in 1558 and 1564, and in the Louvre two years previously. They sang verses composed by Jean Dorat which unashamedly extolled the provinces of France and its king.[71] The celebration ended with a ballet danced by sixteen ladies representing the six provinces of France; it was intended that they should give physical expression through their movements to those virtues which had already been articulated in song. Their dancing lasted a long time and, according to d'Aubigné, the ballet was performed twice, first with masks, and then without. Choreographed by Beaujoyeulx (who was later to design the *Balet comique de la royne*[72]), the work moved through a series of well-controlled figures which challenged the memory and the skills of the dancers. Eye-witnesses agree about its complexity: Brantôme, for instance, reports that the spectators were amazed that the dancers were able to perform the choreographic difficulties without fault. They danced to the sound of thirty violins:

sonnans quasi un air de guerre fort plaisant, elles vindrent marcher soubs l'air de ces violons, et par une belle cadence, sans en sortir jamais, s'approcher et s'arrester un peu devant Leurs Majestez, et puis après danser leur ballet si bizarrement invanté, et partant de tours, contours et destours, d'entrelasseures et meslanges, affrontemens et

---

[70] For a study of the precise context of these fêtes, see my article 'Une affaire de famille: les fêtes parisiennes en l'honneur d'Henri, duc d'Anjou, roi de Pologne', *Arts du spectacle et histoire des idées*, introduced by J.-M. Vaccaro (Tours, 1984), pp. 9–20.

[71] The verses were composed in Latin and published in *Magnificentissimi spectaculi* (Paris, 1573).

[72] Dorat, *Magnificentissimi spectaculi*, fol. Fiv, 'Sed quis tam varias saltandi expressint artes, / Quas Belloioius mille Choragus habet? / Quod solum potuit, pictis, Baptista tabellis, / Expressit prima, caetera carmen habet'.

arrets, qu'aucune dame ne faillit se trouver à son tour ny à son rang
... et dura ce ballet bizarre pour le moins une heure ...[73]

(to the sound of a somewhat martial air which was very agreeable,
they came in moving to the violins' beat and dancing a beautiful
measure which they sustained as they came towards their Majesties
and stopped in front of them; then began their ballet of such strange
invention: through so many steps winding, curling, encircling, coming
together and parting, stopping and restarting and during which no lady
missed her way nor lost her place, this ballet lasted more than an
hour.)

D'Aubigné confirms that the ballet was complicated and that
the music on which the figures were based was diverse and ever
changing. It appears that the Polish ambassadors were well
satisfied with the efforts which had been made to entertain them:

Les Polonais admirèrent les confusions bien desmeslées, les chiffres bien
formez du ballet, les musiques différentes, et dirent que le bal en France
estoit chose impossible à contrefaire à tous les rois de la terre.[74]

(The Poles admired the intertwinings of the dance so well executed,
the numbers so well formed, the diverse music, and they reported that
dancing in France could not be emulated by any king on earth.)

In his fine overview of the position of music in France in the
second half of the sixteenth century, Howard Mayer Brown
concluded: 'We should never consider French music in isolation
from poetry or dance'.[75] In this paper, an attempt has been made
to situate music in the social and courtly context to which it
belonged and to link it with those other arts which gave music
its variety and its vigour. Musical scores and precise detail on
technique are still lacking, yet the documents which have been
examined suggest that the following three conclusions are valid.
First, that music was indeed the servant of poetry and the dance,
supporting the meaning of words and echoing the rhythms of
the dance. Secondly, through their association with other artists
in festivals at court, musicians acquired enhanced status and

[73] Brantôme, Oeuvres, v, pp. 59–60.
[74] A. d'Aubigné, Histoire universelle, IV, p. 178; cited by N. Yvanoff, 'Les fêtes de cour
des derniers Valois d'après les tapisseries du Musée des Offices', Revue du XVIe Siècle,
19 (1932–3), pp. 115–16.
[75] 'Ut musica poesis', p. 33.

increased visibility. Their collective role sought to put into practice the universal, cosmic aims which have often been thought of as belonging only to the domain of theorists. Finally, although a significant social position for musicians employed by the court could often be taken for granted, along with other artists they had also acquired a political function: poets and dramatists had drawn musicians and choreographers even more securely into the sphere of princely propaganda.

University of Sussex

Early Music History (1994) Volume 13

JOHN O'BRIEN

RONSARD, BELLEAU AND RENVOISY

Howard Mayer Brown's stimulating paper pays greatest attention to the centrality of Ronsard as the *fons et origo* for musical settings. One often has the impression, reading the paper, that there was no substantial problem of imitation in these settings: the composers simply took the words supplied by Ronsard and set them to music. In the comments which follow, I want to suggest a different approach to this question of imitation within Renaissance poetry and to ask what effect the issue of imitation itself had in the dialogue between poetry and music in mid sixteenth-century France. The focus I shall be using is the *Anacreon* of 1554.

In March 1554, according to Laumonier, the young scholar Henri Estienne published his edition of the Greek lyric poet Anacreon.[1] It was one of the more famous pieces of pseudepigrapha to appear in the Renaissance. This poetry, written in loose imitation of the seventh-century B.C. poet Anacreon during the Hellenistic and Byzantine periods,[2] met with almost universal acclaim on its publication. Only two scholars (both Italian) recognised the spuriousness of the collection,[3] and the validity of

---

[1] Cf. P. Laumonier, *Ronsard poète lyrique*, 2nd edn (Paris, 1923), p. 121, repeated in his critical edition, L VI, p. 176, n. 1. Laumonier bases his evidence on the fact that Ronsard dedicates his 'Odelette à Corydon' (*loc. cit.*) to Panjas, who in April 1554 left for Rome in the retinue of the Cardinal d'Armagnac.

[2] For the dating of the Anacreontea, see most recently M. West, *Carmina anacreontea*, 2nd edn (Leipzig and Stuttgart, 1993), pp. xvi–xviii, and 'The Anacreontea', *Sympotica*, ed. O. Murray (Oxford, 1990), pp. 272–3. For a study of the Anacreontea, see P. Rosenmeyer, *The Poetics of Imitation: Anacreon and the Anacreontic Tradition* (Cambridge, 1992), and for the fortunes of the Anacreontea in Renaissance France, J. O'Brien, *Anacreon redivivus* (Ann Arbor, forthcoming).

[3] See F. Robortello, *De arte sive ratione corrigendi antiquorum libros disputatio* (1557) in G. Schoppe, *De arte criticâ* (Amsterdam, 1662), p. 119, and F. Orsini, *Carmina novem illustrium feminarum . . . et lyricorum* (Antwerp, 1568), pp. 130 ff.

their objections, although supported by Estienne's contemporary, Joseph Scaliger, went unrecognised until the nineteenth century. There were good reasons for the success of pseudo-Anacreon; not the least of these was that the work was enthusiastically received by Ronsard. It is instructive to explain why.

Ronsard's earlier adventures in Greek lyric had been unsuccessful. His imitations of Pindar which appeared in the *Odes* of 1550 and opened his poetic career had no doubt demonstrated his intellectual mastery, but were poorly received at court and did not succeed in gaining him the wide audience which he sought. Italian lyric, in the shape of the Petrarchist-inspired *Amours de Cassandre* of 1552, was to prove a better choice, based as it was on a well-established Italian model. However around the same time an anti-Petrarchist reaction set in (Du Bellay, for example, wrote against Petrarchism),[4] and Ronsard himself sought new sources of inspiration. He did so by moving from the *style élevé* represented by Pindar and Petrarch to the *style bas* represented by Anacreontic poetry, among others.[5] Indeed, Ronsard's use of the terms 'doux' and 'doux-coulant' in speaking of Anacreontic poetry underlines, by contrast with Pindaric inflation and obscurity, the lightness and musicality of *style bas* models.[6]

Thematically, these *style bas* odes by Ronsard emphasise an epicurean view of life, with particular preference for sympotic motifs: this is a poetry of wine, women and song. If accordingly these poems recall certain moods of the odes of Horace, this is no coincidence, for Estienne in his commentary accompanying his edition of pseudo-Anacreon expressly draws comparisons between Horace and the Anacreontea (unsurprising, since Horace did imitate the real Anacreon).[7] Estienne also compares pseudo-Anacreon with the Latin elegiac poets such as Ovid, with his

---

[4] See H. Chamard, *Histoire de la Pléiade* (Paris, 1939), I, pp. 274–9, quoting Du Bellay's 'A une dame' from the second edition of the *Recueil de poësie* of 1553 and his critical edition of Du Bellay, *Oeuvres complètes*, IV, pp. 205–15. This poem was remodelled and reappeared five years later in *Divers jeux rustiques* (1558) as 'Contre les pétrarquistes'.

[5] The turning point was the *Livret de folastries* of 1553, which cultivated a strong strain of Bacchic poetry. The distinctive sympotic themes of the Anacreontea reinforce this trend.

[6] For the implications of these terms, see Laumonier, *Ronsard poète lyrique*, pp. 170–1.

[7] See H. Estienne, *Anacreontis Teij odae* (Paris, 1554), e.g. pp. 76–8 on Ode XXXI (9 West), where there is an extensive analysis of the relationship between Horace, Alcaeus and Anacreon.

well-known cultivation of eroticism. Everything points to the attempt to integrate the newly discovered Greek poet into well-established poetic traditions which would have an immediate appeal for a wide audience. To these attempts to assimilate pseudo-Anacreon to a particular author or authors can be added the wish to associate him with specific genres. The 'ode légère' to which this Anacreontic poetry belongs recalls the genre of the epigram. Estienne himself draws parallels between the themes of the Anacreontea and those of the Hellenistic epigram.[8] This was encouraged by the enormous Renaissance vogue for the Greek Anthology,[9] by the fact that the Greek Anthology and the Anacreontea are thematically similar (again not surprising, since they were composed at least in part during similar periods), and by the fact that the Anacreontea are predominantly short and look like epigrams.[10] Moreover, two Anacreontic poems do appear in the Greek Anthology, thus cementing the public perception of the similarity between the two genres.[11] The final feature which must be mentioned is the invention of a distinctive style common to vernacular Anacreontics and related poetry. This style is known as *mignardise*.[12] It involves in particular the extensive use of diminutives and compound epithets (such as 'doux-coulant', mentioned earlier, which is itself one of the descriptions of *mignard* style). To speak of the *invention* of a distinctive style is in fact not strictly correct since Renaissance French poets took this idea from Catullus and their closer contemporaries Marullus and Secundus.[13] Yet there was certainly the decision to extend this style to encompass pseudo-Anacreon also.

[8] See Estienne, *Anacreontis Teij odae*, e.g. p. 68 (Ode xi [7 West], Palladas and 'Anacreon'), p. 70 (Ode xx [22 West], Dionysius the Sophist, Theocritus and 'Anacreon'), p. 80 (Ode xl [35 West], Theocritus and 'Anacreon').

[9] See the valuable work of J. Hutton, *The Greek Anthology in France and the Latin Writers of the Netherlands to the Year 1800* (Ithaca, NY, 1946).

[10] Cf. Laumonier, *Ronsard poète lyrique*, p. 94: 'on peut d'autre part considérer la plupart des épigrammes comme des odelettes monostrophiques' and A. Couat, *La poésie alexandrine sous les trois premiers Ptolémées (324–222 av. J.-C.)* (Paris, 1882), p. 173: epigrams had become 'des pièces lyriques analogues aux odes d'Anacréon'.

[11] Odes xv and xvii (8 and 4 West) appear in the Greek Anthology as *a.p.* xi, 47 and 48 respectively. Moreover Ode xi (7 West) has a parallel in an epigram of Palladas, *a.p.* xi, 54.

[12] On the vocabulary of *mignardise*, see M. Glatigny, *Le vocabulaire galant dans les 'Amours' de Ronsard* (Lille, 1976), i, p. 71, and for *mignardise* in Pléiade poetry, see most recently F. Joukovsky, *Le bel objet: les paradis perdus de la Pléiade* (Paris, 1991), pp. 163–8.

[13] See I. D. McFarlane, 'Pierre de Ronsard and the Neo-Latin Poetry of his Time',

These three factors – assimilation to an author or authors, assimilation to a genre and assimilation to a style – were fully exemplified in the work of Ronsard. Ronsard made progressive use of Anacreontic material over four collections: the *Bocage* and *Meslanges* of 1554 and 1555, and the two *Continuations des Amours* cycles of 1555–6. Each of these collections exploits similar aspects of Anacreontic idiom, although the *Continuations des Amours* have a more sharply defined preference for amorous themes alone. Moreover, at least in the two earlier collections, the presence of the Anacreontic material is indicated to the reader by the use of the title 'odelette', a diminutive which already suggests *mignardise*. In part this title is for the sake of clarity; in part it is by contrast with the large-scale Pindaric odes of Ronsard's first publications. However that may be, the polemical stance which the choice of 'odelette' implies was eventually abandoned, since the 'odelettes' are, with rare exceptions, retitled 'odes' from 1560 onwards: by that time, no doubt, Ronsard was no longer so immediately associated in the public mind with *style élevé* Pindaric material.

The *Bocage* will serve as an example of the way in which Ronsard organises his material. Its poetry is formally grouped: dedicatory and epitaphic epigrams; love sonnets; 'blasons'; 'odelettes' and other shorter odes; and finally the 'Traduction de quelques épigrammes grecs' reprinted from the *Livret de folastries*. The titles of these early Ronsardian collections are themselves significant: *Bocage*, *Meslanges*. Brown notes the occurrence of the term *meslanges* in musical circles,[14] and it seems likely that one reason for Ronsard's choice of this title would have been to create a clear link between poetry and music. The fact that the Anacreontea contain a number of poems about the lyre or referring to the lyre reinforces this point: the Anacreontea actually thematise the alliance of music and poetry.[15] And the fact that this is lyric with short lines – in supposed imitation of Anacreontic metre – is no less significant, as Brown understood. Quoting

---

Res Publica Litterarum, 1 (1978), pp. 177–205, especially p. 181 on participles and diminutives.
[14] Brown, '*Ut musica poesis*', pp. 26–7 and particularly note 60.
[15] Notably in Odes ɪ and xʟvɪɪɪ (23 and 2 West).

from Ronsard's later *Abbregé de l'art poëtique françois* (1565), he comments:

He [Ronsard] describes poems with shorter lines as 'wonderfully appropriate for music, that is, the lyre and other instruments' . . . presumably because their differing short line lengths offer the musician the opportunity for greater variety in phrase lengths. [. . .] He seems to suggest, in short, that music's real importance was for setting short lyric poems, whereas in fact his admonition to vary line lengths for the sake of music makes the most sense.[16]

If we take the thirteen poems which make up the Anacreontic 'odelette' section of the *Bocage*, we find that the first, third and thirteenth poems are heptasyllabic, the second, fourth and sixth are octosyllabic and the other six are alexandrines. Short lines but of variable length is a principle which Ronsard implicitly follows here.

What evidence do we have to suggest that Ronsard's experimentation with a new type of lyric had any effect on chanson composers? Brown's Appendix 2 provides ample evidence of the composers' interest in this freshly available material. Four composers have recourse to the Anacreontic odes. Blancher sets 'Tai toi, babillarde arondelle' (*Meslanges*, L VI, pp. 230–1) and Durand sets 'Corydon, verse sans fin' (*Bocage*, L VI, pp. 102–3), while Du Tertre and Lassus both choose 'La terre les eaux' (*Meslanges*, L VI, p. 256).[17] It would be instructive to know why these poems were selected for attention, for they are not the most notable or the most memorable in these collections by Ronsard, as perusal of them (printed below) will show:

Odelette

A l'arondelle

Tai toi, babillarde arondelle,
Par Dieu je plumerai ton aile
Si je t'empongne, ou d'un couteau
Je te couperai ta languette,
5   Qui matin sans repos caquette
Et m'estourdit tout le cerveau.

---

[16] Brown, '*Ut musica poesis*', p. 8.
[17] All references to Ronsard's poetry in the text are to the *Oeuvres complètes*, ed. P. Laumonier, revised and completed by R. Lebègue and I. Silver, 20 vols. (Paris, 1914–75); abbreviation: L, followed by volume number.

John O'Brien

Je te preste ma cheminée
Pour chanter toute la journée,
De soir, de nuit, quand tu voudras:
Mais au matin ne me reveille,
Et ne m'oste quand je sommeille
Ma Cassandre d'entre mes bras.

10 (on the fourth line)

(Be silent, chattering swallow, by heaven I shall pluck your wing if I get hold of you, or cut out your little tongue with a knife, since you chatter ceaselessly in the morning and make my head ache. I'll lend you my chimney to sing all day long, at evening or by night, as you wish. But don't wake me up in the morning and, when I'm sleeping, don't take Cassandre from my arms.)

Odelette
A Corydon

Corydon, verse sans fin
Dedans mon verre du vin,
A fin qu'endormir je face
Un procés qui me tirace
Le coeur & l'ame plus fort,
Qu'un limier un sanglier mort.
    Apres ce procés icy,
Jamais peine ne souci
Ne feront que je me dueille,
Aussi bien vueille ou non veuille,
Sans faire icy long sejour,
Il fault que je meure un jour.
    Le long vivre me desplaist:
Malheureus l'homme qui est
Acablé de la vieillesse,
Quand je perdrai la jeunesse,
Je veus mourir tout soudain
Sans languir au lendemain.
Ce pendant verse sans fin
Dedans mon verre du vin,
A fin qu'endormir je face
Un procés qui me tirace
Le coeur & l'ame plus fort,
Qu'un limier un sanglier mort.

(Corydon, pour endless wine into my glass, so that I can put to sleep a lawsuit which plagues me, body and soul, more relentlessly than a bloodhound does a dead boar. After this lawsuit, no troubles or cares will distress me; whether I will or no, after only a brief stay, I must die one day. I do not like a long life. Unhappy the man who is burdened with old age. When I lose my youth, I want to die straightaway, without

204

languishing for the morrow. Meanwhile, pour endless wine into my glass, so that I may put to sleep a lawsuit which plagues me, body and soul, more relentlessly than a bloodhound does a dead boar.)

Odelette

La terre les eaux va boivant,
L'arbre la boit par sa racine,
La mer eparse boit le vent,
Et le soleil boit la marine.
5   Le soleil est beu de la lune:
Tout boit, soit en haut ou en bas:
Suivant cette reigle commune
Pourquoi donc ne boiron nous pas?

(The earth drinks up the waters, a tree drinks water through its roots, the disparate sea drinks the wind, and the sun drinks the sea. The sun is drunk by the moon: everything drinks, whether down on earth or up above in the sky. Following this common law, why don't we drink, too?)

From the literary standpoint, the interest of these poems is relatively limited, especially the weak 'La terre les eaux': poems of equivalent length in the Anacreontea can frequently have much more to offer. The first poem recalls medieval French poems, often about the nightingale who rouses the poet from his amorous slumbers,[18] and it was perhaps because of this popular tradition that it found favour with the composers. The most interesting of the three is the second, with its Virgilian dedicatee. Ronsard makes extensive changes to the original here, introducing the theme of the lawsuit which is absent from the Greek. However, on the whole, the purely literary qualities of these poems were clearly not the overriding criteria for the composers.

Equally from the point of view of literary scholars, the composers display a limited range of interest as compared with the great variety of genres, forms and metres characteristic of Ronsard's work in the *Bocage*, *Meslanges* and the two *Continuations*. The composers have a special liking for poems specifically designated 'chanson' by Ronsard, and there is the enduring cultivation of the sonnet form. By contrast, what Brown's list does demonstrate is that Ronsard was wholly successful in strengthening or indeed even relaunching his career as a lyric poet. Although the list

[18]   See Laumonier, *Ronsard poète lyrique*, pp. 450–3 and 602–3.

covers the period 1550–65, the bulk of the musical settings are drawn from the two collections entitled *Continuations des Amours*, and particularly from the *Nouvelle continuation*. Of the settings listed, no fewer than fourteen are from the *Nouvelle continuation*, with a further three from the *Continuation*; almost every composer listed made settings of at least one poem from these two collections. Moreover, in addition to the Anacreontic material drawn from the *Meslanges*, other *Meslanges* material proved no less popular, above all to Goudimel who set three pieces from the *Meslanges* and one from the *Bocage*. Thus the total amount of *style bas* material is extensive, in striking contrast to the limited enthusiasm with which the composers greeted Ronsard's Pindaric odes. Indeed the only consistent enthusiast of those early *style élevé* poems is Clereau. Even then, in common with other composers, he often selects only parts of longer poems; for instance, his setting *Le comble de ton sçavoir* is the epode of the ode 'A la roine' (L I, p. 69). Clereau was likewise drawn to other idioms. His *La lune est coustumiere*, although taken from the 1550 *Odes*, is nevertheless not a celebratory poem in the grand public manner of Pindar, but a love poem to Cassandre; and Clereau too was to come under the influence of the *Nouvelle continuation*, as two of his settings show. The overwhelming preference of the composers, one concludes, is for pieces which fall within the domain of love poetry.

II

There is a further aspect to Ronsard's Anacreontic activities in the mid 1550s. Quite a number of his Anacreontic odes are translations rather than imitations. The point of this observation becomes clear when it is understood that the years 1549–51 (the very years when the Pléiade began to publish) were marked by a polemic over the question of the relative merits of translation and imitation.[19] The polemic was launched by Du Bellay's *Deffence et illustration*,[20] to be followed by Ronsard (although by no other

---

[19] The controversy is too well known to require special treatment here. See T. Cave, *The Cornucopian Text: Problems of Writing in the French Renaissance* (Oxford, 1980), pp. 60 ff., and G. Norton, *The Ideology and Language of Translation in Renaissance France and their Humanist Antecedents* (Geneva, 1984), pp. 290–302.

[20] See T. M. Greene, *The Light in Troy: Imitation and Discovery in Renaissance Poetry* (New

member of the Pléiade). The distinction Du Bellay and Ronsard drew was between imitation – the true domain of the poet – and translation, an inferior and improper mode for the revival of classical antiquity. This position was the reverse of the attitude widely adopted towards translation (translation was, on the standard view, a form of imitation) and provoked strong ripostes from contemporary literary figures such as Barthélemy Aneau and Guillaume des Autelz.[21] Without retracting their statements, the two leading members of the Pléiade subsequently returned to translation, at least as a propaedeutic to imitation. Du Bellay published a translation of the fourth book of the *Aeneid* as early as 1552. Ronsard, less enamoured of the format, did nevertheless publish translations in the *Bocage* and the *Meslanges* of poems from the Greek Anthology and the Anacreontea. These translations, in his work, are juxtaposed with imitations and it is frequently extremely difficult to decide, without further information from Ronsard, whether a particular piece is a translation or an imitation. Often enough Ronsard maintains the ambiguity of a poem or, in subsequent editions, shifts its status to one side or the other of the dividing line.

These facts about the Pléiade and translation are worth mentioning because the history of the Anacreontea in the French Renaissance is a history of translations. In the two years 1554–6, there were two Neo-Latin translations[22] and two vernacular translations of the work – a selection by Ronsard and a full translation, expressly designated as such, by Belleau, which appeared in 1556 (at the same period, therefore, as Ronsard's *Continuations des Amours*).[23] For comparative purposes, we may cite

Haven, 1982), pp. 189 ff., M. W. Ferguson, *Trials of Desire: Renaissance Defences of Poetry* (New Haven, 1983), pp. 18–53, and Norton, *The Ideology and Language of Translation*, pp. 292 ff.

[21] Aneau wrote a critique of Du Bellay's *Deffence* under the pen name 'le Quintil Horatien': extracts from it are included in Chamard's standard edition of the *Deffence*. For Des Autelz's criticisms of Du Bellay, see *Replique de Guillaume des Autelz, aux furieuses defenses de Louis Meigret* (Lyons, 1551), pp. 58–9.

[22] The Neo-Latin translations are a partial translation by Estienne himself, included in his *editio princeps*, and a full translation by Elie André (Helias Andreas).

[23] On Belleau as a translator of Anacreon, consult Chamard, *Histoire de la Pléiade*, II, pp. 87–95, and A. Eckhardt, *Remy Belleau: sa vie – sa 'Bergerie': étude historique et critique* (Budapest, 1917), pp. 164–8. References in the text are to the new edition of Belleau's *Odes d'Anacréon* by K. Cameron and J. O'Brien (Paris, forthcoming); abbreviation: COB, followed by Ode number.

Belleau's version of the Anacreontic poems which proved popular with composers in Ronsard's versions:

L'arondelle

Ha vraiment je vous puniray
Babillarde, et vous rougnerai
De mes cizeaux l'une et l'autre aelle,
Ou bien comme la main cruelle
5   De Terée a fait autrefois
Vous tondray la langue et la vois,
Qui tousjours las! quand je sommeille
Devant le point du jour m'esveille,
Et de son importun babil,
10   M'arrache du sein mon Bathyl.

(COB xii [10 West])

('The Swallow'. Ah, truly I shall punish you, you noisy chatterer, and I shall clip both your wings with my scissors, or, as Tereus' cruel hand once did, I shall shave your tongue and your voice which alas! always wakes me before daybreak when I am sleeping and with its untimely chatter wrests my Bathyllus from my bosom.)

Qu'il faut boire par necessité

La terre noircissante boit,
Et les arbres, boivent la terre,
La mer, boit les ventz qu'elle enserre,
La mer, le Soleil qui tout voit,
5   De luy, la Lune se dessoive,
Pourquoy donc empeschés vous tous
Veu que tout boit, que je ne boive
Mes compaignons de ce vin dous?

(COB xix [21 West])

('That drinking is a necessity'. The darkening earth drinks, and the trees drink the earth, the sea drinks the winds which it encircles, the sea drinks the sun which sees everything, the moon quenches its thirst on the sun. Seeing that everything drinks, why then do you all prevent me, my companions, from drinking some of this sweet wine?)

Du plaisir qu'il a de boire

Quand je boy la tasse pleine,
Tout travail, et toute peine,
Et tout chagrineux despis,
En moi dorment assopis,
5   Qu'ai-je affaire de me plaindre,
Puis que mort me doit esteindre!
Et en despit de mon vueil

Me coucher en un cercueil?
Faut il que je me soucie?
10 Faut il que j'erre en ma vie?
Non non je burai dautant,
Compaignons, or' sus avant,
Puis qu'en buvant tasse pleine,
Tout travail et toute peine
15 Et tous chagrineux despis,
En moy restent assopis.

(COB xxv [45 West])

('Of the pleasure he has in drinking'. When I drink the brimming goblet, all troubles, all cares and all vexatious anxieties fall asleep within me. Why should I bother to complain, since death will extinguish me and against my will lay me to rest in a tomb? Ought I to worry? Ought I to wander around in my life? No, no, I shall drink all the more – come, companions! – since in drinking the brimming goblet, all troubles, all cares and all vexatious anxieties slumber within me.)

Whereas Ronsard had a discernible effect on Belleau's translation (although not in the three poems just examined, with the possible exception of the word 'babillarde' in the first poem), it would be interesting to know whether Belleau's translation itself had any effect on composers. The question is not motivated by curiosity alone, but because one's impression is that Ronsard (and the Pléiade in general) acted as 'official' interpreters or disseminators of Anacreontic material, and one would like to know how far this 'official' influence extended.

III

A test case in this respect is Richard de Renvoisy, whose settings of a selection of Anacreontic odes were published by Breton in 1559 and again by Le Roy and Ballard in 1573.[24] Thirteen odes are translated, in no recognisable order.[25] The interests of the translator and the

---

[24] All references in the text are to the first edition, *Quelques odes d'Anacreon poete ancien, nouuellement mises en francoys apres le grec, les nombres gardez: et depuis mises en musique par maistre Richard Renuoysy, maistre des enfans, et chanoyne de la saincte chapelle du roy à Dijon* (Paris, 1559). I am grateful to Frank Dobbins for lending me his photocopy of this edition.

[25] The poems in the order followed by Renvoisy's 1559 edition are these: 'Sus le delicat arbrisseau' (Ode IV [32 West]), 'La rose que les Dieux' (Ode V [44 West]), 'En ceste premiere saison' (Ode LIII [55 West]), 'Trop amer est il de n'aymer' (Ode XLVI [29, 29A West]), 'De Giges de Sarde prince' (Ode XV [8 West]), 'Attendu que suis nay' (Ode XXIV [40 West]), 'Quand du bon vin ie boy' (Ode XXV [45 West]), 'Vulcan

composer are well defined and are epicurean in character: transience, *carpe diem*, poems on birds and flowers, on the fleeting joys of love and the pleasures of wine. More than any composer we have examined so far, Renvoisy assimilates a coherent range of Anacreontic themes and ideas (he pays attention to sympotic motifs, for example). More important, he also chooses poems which are intrinsically interesting as well as being well-known representatives of the Anacreontic idiom. The following, which also appeared in the Greek Anthology, is an excellent example.

> De Giges de Sarde prince,
> Le renom mon coeur ne pince:
> De l'or ie ne me soucye,
> Au roy ie n'ay point d'enuie.
> 5   L'un des soucys qui m'atache
> C'est apres ma mousetache,
> Pour l'adoucyr de senteurs,
> L'autre soucy qui m'arreste
> C'est à couronner ma teste
> 10   D'un chapeau de belles fleurs.
> Je n'ay nul soucy ny cure,
> Sinon passer l'aduanture
> Du iourd'huy qui peult cognoistre
> Quel le lendemain doibt estre.
> 15   Pendant que courent tes ans,
> Boy et pren tes passetemps,
> A fin que quelque mal chault
> Sans y penser ne te vienne
> Qui de plus boire te tienne
> 20   Disant jeuner il te fault.

(fols. 10^r–11^r)

(The renown of Gyges, prince of Sardis, does not trouble my heart. I do not worry about money. I do not envy the king. Of principal concern to me is my moustache, to sweeten it with perfumes. My other chief concern is to crown my head with a garland of beautiful flowers. I have no worry or care, except to take what today brings. Who knows what tomorrow will be? While you are still alive, drink and take your ease, lest some malady catches you unawares and prevents you drinking any more, saying: 'Now you must be abstemious.')

fondz dedans ton four' (Ode xvii [4 West]), 'Quand Bacchus entre en moy' (Ode xxvi [48 West]), 'Mignarde colombelle' (Ode ix [15 West]), 'Un matin qu'amour cuidoit' (Ode xl [35 West]), 'Un soir enuiron la minuict' (Ode iii [33 West]), 'Si la vie nous venoit' (Ode xxiii [36 West]).

Compare Ronsard:

> Du grand Turc je n'ay souci,
> Ny de l'empereur aussi,
> L'or n'attire point ma vie:
> Aux roys je ne porte envie:
> 5   J'ay soucy tant seulement
> D'oindre mon poil d'oignement:
> J'ay soucy qu'une couronne
> De fleurs ma teste environne.
> Le soin de ce jour me point:
> 10   Du demain, je n'en ay point:
> Et qui sçauroit bien cognoistre
> Si un l'endemain doit estre?

(L v, pp. 79–80)

(I do not care about the Sultan of Turkey, nor about the Emperor of Germany. Money does not attract me. I do not envy kings. My only concern is to anoint my hair with unguent. My concern is to wreathe my head with a garland of flowers. I concentrate on today; I do not worry about tomorrow. Who could know whether there will even be a tomorrow?)

and Belleau:

> Ni Gyge prince de Sarde
> Ni l'or, ny l'argent, retarde
> Mon plaisir d'un petit point.
> De cella ne me chaut point.
> 5   Aux rois je ne porte envie,
> Seullement je me soucie
> De parfumer de senteurs
> Ma barbe, et de mille fleurs,
> Faire un tortis à ma teste,
> 10   C'est le soing qui plus m'arreste.
> Dès le matin jusqu'au soir
> Je souci, non de l'espoir
> Du lendemain, car qui est-ce
> Qui de le voir ait promesse?
> 15   Boi donc et pren ton plaisir
> Pendant qu'en as le loisir,
> De peur qu'une malladie
> En te grippant, ne te die,
> Il vous faut mourir, or' sus
> 20   Amis, vous ne beurés plus.

(COB xv [8 West])

(Neither Gyges, Prince of Sardis, nor gold, nor silver hinder my pleasure one iota. I don't care about that. I do not envy kings. I am only

worried about perfuming my beard with scents; making a garland for
my head out of myriad flowers is my chief concern. I care from
morning to night. I do not worry about tomorrow, because who can
be guaranteed of seeing it? Drink then and take your pleasure while
you can, lest some illness grips you and says: 'Now you must die, so
come, friend, no more drinking.')

Ronsard's poem appeared in the *Livret de folastries* of 1553 where it
is juxtaposed with translations and imitations of Greek epigrams,
thereby reinforcing the links between Anacreontism and the Hell-
enism of the epigram. It is significant that Ronsard's version is
quite brief, like the Renvoisy setting. By contrast, Belleau's poem
is altogether more elaborate. The advantage of his expansiveness
is clear at the close of the poem, which is immediately comprehen-
sible, whereas Renvoisy is muddy and obscure: 'sans y penser'
is awkward and best construed as 'without your thinking about
it' (i.e. foreseeing it). It would be nice to think of 'jeuner' in the
last line as an irony in the context of drinking, though that
interpretation is not secure. 'Ma mousetache' does however add
a nice touch of humour, and all this in a verbal pattern which
is even more reliant on symmetry than the original: observe the
isocola in 'ie ne me soucye' / 'ie n'ai point d'enuie' and in 'l'un
des soucys qui m'atache' / 'l'autre soucy qui m'arreste'. Rather
than give extended analyses of Renvoisy's settings, I shall cite one
further example where Renvoisy has been especially successful in
using repetition to convey what is for him the point of the poem:

> Trop amer est il de n'aymer,
> Mais aymer est trop plus amer.
> Et le plus amer que lon voye
> Est aymant faillir à sa proye.
> 5   Ne sert en amour la noblesse,
> Moins y sert vertu ou sagesse,
> Le seul argent à tout pouvoir.
> Maudit soit qui premier ayma
> Cest argent & qui estima
> 10   Plus que vertu richess' auoir.
> Pour argent on laisse le frere,
> Pour argent on laisse le pere:
> Meurtres & noyses l'argent fait,
> Et qui pis est nous amoureux
> 15   Par argent sommes malheureux,

Argent, argent nous ruyne et deffaict,
Argent, argent nous ruine et deffaict.

(fols. 8ᵛ–9ᵛ)

(Not loving is very bitter; but loving is much bitterer. The bitterest thing one can see is to fail to catch one's quarry when one loves. Nobility is no use in love; even less use are virtue or wisdom. Money alone is all-powerful. Accursed be the man who first loved money and placed riches higher than virtue. For money one deserts one's brother; for money one deserts one's father. Money causes murder and strife. What's worse, when we're in love, it's money which makes us unhappy. Money, money ruins and defeats us, money, money ruins and defeats us.)

Once again the syntax and the lexis are much simpler and less varied than either Belleau (COB xlvi) or Ronsard (L vi, pp. 162–4). The phraseology in Renvoisy has however some affinities with Ronsard's version, especially in the use of anaphora ('Pour argent . . . / Pour argent . . .'), which Ronsard deploys even more extensively. The original poem is not itself the most intelligent in the collection, since it cannot decide whether it is about the miseries of love or the iniquity of money. Renvoisy's setting develops the second from the first ('Maudit soit qui premier ayma cest argent') and again uses isocola and the very effective repetition of 'argent' to end on a strong note what is otherwise a weak, confused poem.

One should not suppose that chanson composers were interested in literary debates about the relative merits of translation and imitation. Composers would be interested in the finished product, not in the process. In any case, such debates would have died down by the time Renvoisy came to compose. The question nevertheless arises: what type of literary creation does this text by Renvoisy represent? In my view, it is a translation rather than an imitation: it recognisably follows closely the tenor of the original and seeks close approximations for its wording; at the same time, the modifications and shifts of emphasis which it makes to the original are of just the kind that characterise Renaissance translations.

The next difficulty is to ascertain the author of the translation which Renvoisy used. It is just possible that Renvoisy made it himself, but since the eighteenth century the translation has been attributed to Jean Bégat, *président* of the Parlement of Dijon, who was born around 1520 and died in 1572.[26] Renvoisy was choirmaster at the Ste Chapelle at Dijon from 1554 onwards, and contact between the two men would not be difficult to imagine. This is nevertheless an exceptional instance of a translation carried out outside Pléiade circles and indeed in the provinces. The fact that it is published in Paris, in both its first and second editions, suggests that Renvoisy had some connection with the capital. The translation is accurate enough to have been made directly from the original; an alternative is that this French translation was made from the Neo-Latin versions of Estienne and André. In either case, the vogue for Anacreontism in the mid 1550s provided the stimulus which might otherwise have been lacking: the Bégat translation is very much of its time and no change of substance was made to it when it came to be reprinted by Le Roy and Ballard.[27]

Finally, given that Bégat's translation is not heavily indebted to Ronsard or Belleau, what are we to think of Ronsard's influence on music in the late 1550s and after? Was there, as Howard Brown suggests, a gradual parting of the ways between poets and musicians? On the contrary, as Jeanice Brooks has shown, there was sustained interest in setting Ronsard's *style bas* poetry.[28] Brooks argues that Ronsard's influence spread outside the capital after 1559, with foreign composers such as Lassus taking up his work. Moreover the 1570s saw a spate of settings of Ronsard, among which Anacreontics have their place: Briault (1569) set 'Tai toi, babillarde arondelle' (L vi, pp. 230–1), Costeley (1570) and Caietain (1571) both set the popular 'La terre les eaux' (L vi, p. 256), and Lassus (1571) set the final part of 'Lors que Bacus entre chés moy' (L vi, pp. 243–4). Castro and Monte

---

[26] See the information contained in F. Dobbins, 'Renvoisy, Richard de', *The New Grove Dictionary of Music and Musicians*, ed. S. Sadie, 20 vols. (London, 1980), xv, pp. 744–5.

[27] Dobbins notes that the order of the pieces was altered, and the rhythm and spelling occasionally modified. Most important of all was the omission of the short preface in which Renvoisy disclaimed in his own life any of the 'lubricité' of Anacreon.

[28] See J. Brooks, 'French Chanson Collections on the Texts of Pierre de Ronsard, 1570–1580' (Ph.D. dissertation, Catholic University of America, 1990), chapter 1, 'Ronsard Settings in the late Sixteenth Century', pp. 5–61. I am grateful to Jeanice Brooks for allowing me to have sight of this material. The information which follows in my paper is indebted to her.

both set further Ronsardian Anacreontics: Castro (1575 and 1576) chose 'Verson ces roses prés ce vin' (L VII, pp. 189–92) and 'Je suis homme né pour mourir' (L VII, pp. 195–6), while Monte (1575) opted for 'Corydon, verse sans fin' (L VI, pp. 102–3) and 'Pour boire dessus l'herbe tendre' (L VI, pp. 103–4). The second edition of Renvoisy ties in with the renewed attention to this material, as does the second edition of Belleau's *Odes d'Anacréon*, published in 1573. It seems clear, then, that Ronsard's position in the composers' repertory was strengthened and extended throughout his working career. But it is also clear that we may be looking in the wrong place if we seek only or principally Ronsard's verbal influence on French poetry. What seems to have had just as lasting an effect was his championing of a genre and a style – the *ode légère*, the *style bas*. From that perspective, Ronsard's influence may easily have extended well beyond the actual settings made of his poetry.

University of Liverpool

Early Music History (1994) Volume 13

JEAN-MICHEL VACCARO

GEOMETRY AND RHETORIC IN ANTHOINE DE BERTRAND'S *TROISIESME LIVRE DE CHANSONS*

Howard Mayer Brown was correct in his understanding that a complete knowledge of the French chanson from the second half of the sixteenth century must take in the provincial activity in this genre and its rapports with Paris, for it is essential to study the ties that connected the centre with its periphery. During the 1570s in Toulouse, the Auvergne-born Anthoine de Bertrand and his 'friends'[1] formed one such provincial school, which was strongly attached to the personality of Pierre de Ronsard and to the poetic ideals of the Pléiade. Complementing the praise given to the composer by Henry Expert, who believed as early as 1926 that his works merited a complete edition,[2] Howard Brown considered Bertrand 'one of the very best composers' of this music.

These flattering words from the pen of a musicologist of comparable distinction serve to strengthen my own intuition about these works, formed many years ago when I devoted my first academic work to a study of the chansons of Anthoine de Bertrand.[3] Since that time my understanding of the absolutely central position held by Bertrand within the history of the French chan-

---

[1] I have borrowed this term from Geneviève Thibault, who employed it in her study of the prefatory material to Bertrand's collections published by Adrian Le Roy and Robert Ballard, in 'Anthoine de Bertrand, musicien de Ronsard, et ses amis toulousains', *Mélanges offerts à M. Abel Lefranc* (Paris, 1936), pp. 282–300.

[2] 'Today forgotten and unknown, Anthoine de Bertrand will undoubtedly be viewed tomorrow as one of the most personal, lively, and seductive master-musicians of our [French] Renaissance'. See Expert's prefatory *Avertissement* in his edition of the *Premier livre des Amours de Pierre de Ronsard*, Monuments de la Musique Française au Temps de la Renaissance (Paris, 1927).

[3] 'Musique et poésie à l'époque de la Pléiade, Anthoine de Bertrand (*ca.* 1540–1581)' (diploma thesis, Centre d'Études Supérieures de la Renaissance, Tours, 1965).

son in the Renaissance has deepened. In particular, I have come to see how he represented a certain modernity of his time, not so much by his attempts at writing in a more experimental way[4] as by his radical stance against the application of unprescribed accidentals and ornamentation.[5] He represents, in sum, a wholly new type of composer, one who developed outside the traditional line of cleric musicians appointed to chapels and courts. A rural nobleman, living off his land,[6] he devoted his leisure time to pursuing the arts and culture in a provincial academy and, for purely personal reasons, devoted himself to musical composition. Through his combining of Ronsard's sonnets of the *Amours* with music, Bertrand joined the poet in celebrating his own *amours*, and invited those who performed his works to participate in the same game of love:

> Ainsi qu'en mes amours me suis servi des tiennes
> Quelcun de mesme aussi pourra faire des miennes.[7]

Indeed, he even dedicated the music of his *Second livre* 'A une sienne maistresse' ('To one of his own mistresses'):

> Marie a celle fin que le siecle advenir
> De noz jeunes amours se puisse souvenir
> . . .
> Je vous consacre ici le plus galliard de moy
> L'esprit de mon esprit qui vous fera revivre
> Ou long temps ou jamais par l'aage de ce livre

But it was Anne (Anne Carriere) whom he married, and who, moreover, remained a widow after his assassination in 1581.[8]

---

[4]   Such as his attempts at composing works based on the chromatic and enharmonic genera along the lines of Vicentino, implying vocal performance in quarter-tones.

[5]   On this subject, see J.-M. Vaccaro, 'Les préfaces d'Anthoine de Bertrand', *Revue de Musicologie*, 74 (1988), pp. 221–36. This issue contains studies on the theme of the 'Musiciens de Ronsard' by members of the musicology department at the Centre d'Études Supérieures de la Renaissance at Tours.

[6]   According to Père Michel Coyssard, Bertrand owned several farms in the Toulouse area. Indeed, this famous Jesuit and author of the *Traicté du profit qu'on tire de chanter les hymnes et chansons spirituelles en vulgaire* (1608), in writing about the violent death of the composer, caused by 'the cruelty of those who disliked those ecclesiastical hymns', specifies: 'Thus they massacred Anthoine Bertrand as he was leaving Toulouse to go to one of his farms.'

[7]   *Second livre des Amours de P. de Ronsard* (Paris: Le Roy and Ballard, 1578): 'l'auteur à Monsieur de Ronsard', a *dizain* by the composer among the introductory pieces in this collection.

[8]   This information comes down to us from a sentence pronounced by the parliament of Toulouse, dated 5 July 1583, and condemning 'Anne Carrière, veufve a feu

218

Thus we may recognise embodied in Anthoine de Bertrand a relatively new type of Renaissance musician (though a type that becomes increasingly common throughout Europe during the last quarter of the sixteenth century) among the prevalent social classes of singers, choirmasters, organists and other regular instrumentalists. This new class of musician, represented in the figure of the gentleman composer, is naturally compatible with the new musical aesthetic based on the rhetorical union between word and music. It is mainly along these lines that Bertrand's music has been studied, with scholarship viewing him as one of the important masters of the 'French madrigal'.[9]

The present study, devoted to the less well-known compositions by Bertrand that appear in the *Troisiesme livre de chansons*,[10] will focus instead on observing the mathematical aspects of his contrapuntal style and technique. To this end, I shall seek to validate a 'geometry' underlying the writing, which appears to be determined primarily by the need to represent the semantic meaning of the texts. Further, I propose to show the existence in these works of a strong, permanent mathematical structure and, consequently, the presence of a rational sense of organisation that goes far beyond a theoretical formulation, as noted wisely by Brown in the opening pages of his study.

Music has never ceased to be considered, at least in theory, a 'vray pourtrait de la Temperance', in Pontus de Tyard's delightful phrase. It is a perfect and stable balance resting on the Pythagorean virtues of number, an audible expression of the quadrivium, but it has also been used increasingly towards serving the desire for rhetorical expression. It is this latter aspect that submits most willingly to analysis today. With some exceptions, this kind of analysis examines the relationships of pitch, favouring the study of modes, genera, contrapuntal and harmonic schemes, or the 'representative' and 'figurative' elements that were suggested to the composer by the text.

Anthoine Bertrand, mere et legitime administraresse de ses enfants, filz et héritiers dudit feu Bertrand' (Archives Départementales de Haute Garonne B.88, fols. 204 ff.).

[9] This term is used by Frank Dobbins in his article 'Les madrigalistes français et la Pléiade', *La chanson à la Renaissance*, ed. J.-M. Vaccaro (Tours, 1981), pp. 157–71.

[10] The publication history of Bertrand's books by Le Roy and Ballard is as follows: *Premier livre des Amours de Pierre de Ronsard* (1576, 1578, 1587); *Second livre des Amours* ... (1578, 1587); *Troisiesme livre de chansons* (1578, 1587).

Here, I would like to draw attention instead to issues of metric organisation, which serve to govern the counterpoint and even the form of the pieces in Bertrand's *Troisiesme livre*. I hope to show the relationship that might exist between poetic forms and the metric organisation of the music. Would it not be reasonable to imagine that composers of the second half of the sixteenth century, being preoccupied with the linearity of the sense of the poem, composed their music along the threadline of the text? Were they not also attentive to the circularity of poetic metres applied to the verse, the strophe and the entire poem? Did they indeed draw up a compositional plan that reveals at the highest level their awareness of the variety of formal constraints proposed by the text? Theoretical sources of the time are, to my knowledge, completely silent about these types of compositional procedure, their importance notwithstanding. It is important, therefore, that we confront the music itself and attempt to understand mechanisms that produce this type of formal elaboration.

A CASE ANALYSIS

Chanson xix of the *Troisiesme livre*, *Pucelle en qui la triple grace*, is particularly instructive and will serve here as a case study. Taking as a starting point the transcription made by Henry Expert in 1927, it is relatively easy to provide an analytical reduction of this chanson, one that accounts for the overall structure of the piece through verticalising the elements that can be considered homologous and in respecting, under the different mensurations, the basic length of the tactus as always shown in the same space (see Example 1). The alternation of dotted and undotted barlines corresponds to the alternation of breves (tempus) and longs (modus) in the mensuration ₵3 and the alternation of semibreves (prolatio) and breves (tempus) in the mensuration C. The transcription for four voices is compressed here onto two staves so that the larger texture of the work can be seen at a glance. Regrettably, this results occasionally in difficulties in following the part-writing. The example should be read system by system across all five pages.

The key to this analytical chart is found in Table 1, for which some detailed explanation is necessary. To the left may be seen

Example 1. Anthoine de Bertrand, *Pucelle en qui la triple grace*

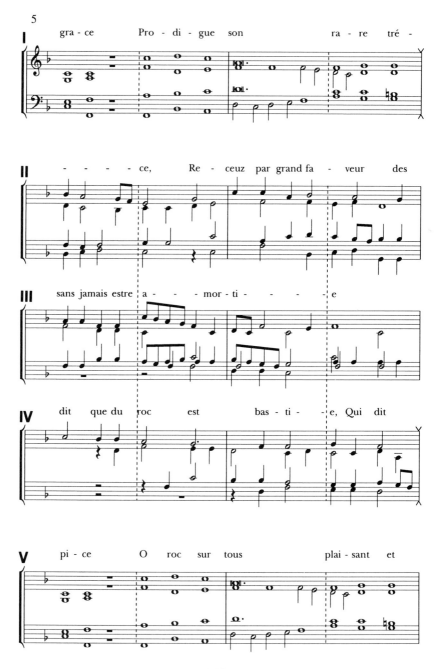

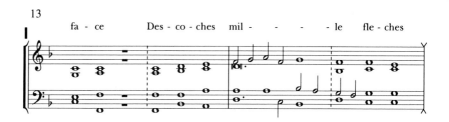

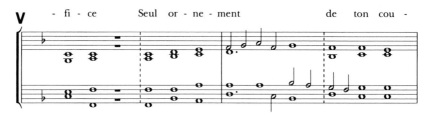

Table 1   Analysis of 'Pucelle en qui la triple grace'

Section	Group	Mensuration	Cadence	Minims ♦	Prolatio ◇	Tempus ◻	Modus ◻	Maximodus ◻
X	A	₵3	(f) MM	24				
	B		do MM	24 48	24	8◻·	4◻	2
	A		(f) MM	24				
	C		F MM	24 48	24	8◻·	4◻	2
	C		F MM	24 24 120	12 60	4◻· 20◻·	2◻ 10◻	1 5
Y	D	C	C pr.	10 ⎱	8	4◻		
	E		D T	6 ⎰	6	3◻		
	F		C T	12	8	4◻		
	G		f T	16 44	8 22	4◻ 11◻		
	H		C pr.	30	15	7,5◻		
	I		f pr.	12	6	3◻		
	D'		C T	18	9	4,5◻		
	G		f MM	16 76 120	8 38 60	4◻ 19◻ 30◻	10◻·	5
X	A	₵3	(f) MM	24				
	B		C MM	24 48	24	8◻·	4◻	2
	A'		(f) MM	24				
	C		F MM	24 48	24	8◻·	4◻	2
	C		F MM	24 24 120	12 60	4◻· 20◻·	2◻ 10◻	1 5
				360	180			15

Text lines:
1 Pucelle en qui la triple grace
2 Prodigue son rare trésor
3 Pucelle qui d'entour ta face
4 Descoches mille flèches d'or
5 Pucelle qui des ta naissance
6 Receuz par grand faveur des dieux
7 L'honneur, la beauté, la puissance
8 Qui t'accompagnent en tous lieux
9 Vy sans jamais estre amortie
10 Et ton nom soit illustre et cler
11 Qui dit que du roc est bâtie
12 Que force ne peut esbranler
13 Et toy, roc, sois tousjours propice
14 O roc sur tout plaisant et beau
15 Soutenant ce noble édifice
16 Seul ornement de ton coupeau

*12+

(·12 / +12) → (·◻)final
→ ◻

*transition final

the poem's construction in four eight-syllable quatrains of regularly alternating strong and weak rhymes. In column 1 (numbering from after the line of text) the capital letters designate musical sections corresponding to verses of the poem; these sections are each characterised by an individual motive and are punctuated by a cadence. Three overall groups, X, Y, X, result from the configuration of the sections, the hierarchy of their cadential endings, and above all, from the contrast of mensurations ₵3, C, ₵3, which are indicated in column 2. A summary analysis of the cadences appears in column 3. 'F' designates a cadence on a chord without a third, which acts as the most conclusive since it is employed at the end of the piece; 'f' designates a chord that includes a third, and '(f)' is used for a weak ending, as in the word *grace*. As concerns cadential notes, abbreviations are used to indicate the point of cadential rests within the mensural scheme in which the counterpoint is inscribed: pr. = cadence of prolation; T = cadence of tempus; M = cadence of modus; and MM = cadence of maximodus. Column 4 gives the number of minims in each group and also regroupings as long as these are justified by symmetries or repetitions.

Two numbers given in the table require some explanation: the *12 preceding group A at the return of the triple-time mensuration (verse 13) corresponds to an added transitional element; and the 12 crowned with a fermata gives the final note value of the chanson. It will be noticed that the sections of music are always counted up to the pre-cadential value, the cadential value being counted with the following element. This procedure, consistently and rigorously followed, allows for a clearer understanding of the relative proportions of the different musical sections and explains how the ultimate final value finds itself somewhat pushed outside the structure as a whole. Finally, columns 5, 6, 7 and 8 show the equivalents of those minim values according to the hierarchy of mensural values – expressed in numbers of semibreves, breves, longs and maxims, taking into account this time the issue of metric groupings, or quality[11] (the dotted values designate perfection; those without a dot, imperfection). Thus,

---

[11] In this article 'quantitative' is used in referring to the quantity and type of metrical units (e.g. 24 minims), while 'quality' or 'qualitative' refers to the particular way in which these larger units are grouped (8 × 3).

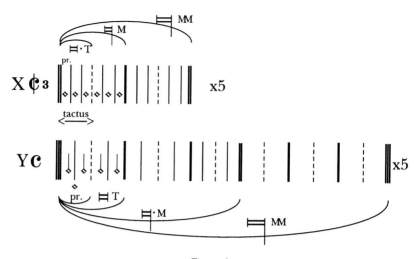

Figure 1

the couplet formed by A + B, which is duplicated by A + C, makes a total of 48 minims, forming a set of 24 imperfect semibreves, themselves derived from a collection of 8 perfect breves resulting from a subdivision of 10 imperfect longs or 5 imperfect maxims. This last metrical unit of music corresponds to the metrical poetic unit of the octosyllabic verse. In sum, the large-scale purpose of this analysis is to show that the entire chanson is composed of a whole number of perfect or imperfect longs that correspond here to a whole number of maxims. What is more remarkable, the three groups X, Y, X have equal quantitative lengths even though they are in opposing metric groupings.

Figure 1 shows superimposed the two types of mensuration used in opposition, and, naturally, coordinated by the same tactus. The varying of measures in triple, duple etc., allows for synchronising different metrical units. During the course of the piece, each of the sequences shown here is repeated five times. It is therefore possible to give the formal matrix of the chanson according to the schema of Figure 2.

Finally, Figure 3 attempts a graphic representation of the geometry of the composition. Two points should be stressed. The first is that the two imperfect longs to the right of the overall structural framework of fifteen maxims form a sixteenth maxim that is used for a transition and for the final duration. The

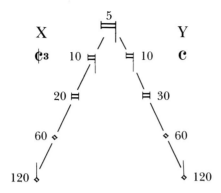

Figure 2   Formal matrix of *Pucelle en qui la triple grace*

second and more essential point underscores the hard contrast between sections X and Y. On the one hand, there is a perfect coincidence between the musical unity of the section and the structural metrical periodicity, which results in what might be called a 'phrase'. On the other hand, there is also a non-coincidence between these elements resulting in a classic case of enjambment in the disposition of musical groups by way of the disposition of metrical units, seen here up to the cadence of group G, where coincidence reappears once again. Here the full richness and subtlety of the composition can be seen at its highest and most important level.

The contrast of elements described above between patterns of coincidence and non-coincidence is mirrored by a contrast in musical textures: note-against-note counterpoint versus imitative counterpoint. In Bertrand's *Troisiesme livre de chansons* it is not uncommon to find entire passages written homorhythmically, in which the 'phrase' is inscribed within the metrical scheme that guides the overall work. Example 2 illustrates one case among others involving the third chanson of the collection, *Jamais on n'a que tristesses*: the phrase here is aligned with the imperfect long. Before proceeding further and fleshing out these observations in the chansons of the *Troisiesme livre*, it is worth emphasising that the chanson just examined displays a care for rational order within the qualitative and quantitative organisation of note durations, an order based on the mathematical handling that inscribes the counterpoint within a real geometry of the musical

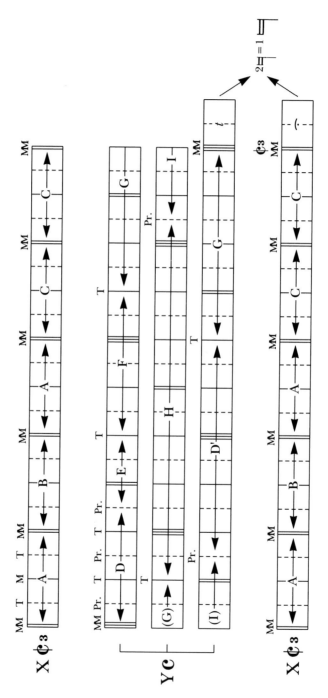

Figure 3

Example 2. Anthoine de Bertrand, *Jamais on n'a que tristesses*, verses 3–8, groups CD, CD, EE, FG, HH

space. It is quite possible that the ternary structures, which shift the metre to different values according to the sections of the chanson, are associated, this time on a semantic plan, to the 'triple grace' evoked in the first verse of the poem.

THE TWENTY-FIVE CHANSONS OF THE *TROISIESME LIVRE*

The set of twenty-five pieces in this collection have been subjected to the type of analysis just demonstrated. These analyses are reproduced in schematic form as an appendix to this article. They should be read from left to right and consist of the following: number and text incipit; mensuration signs; indication of the principal sections, designated W, X, Y, Z; names of the groups, A, B, C etc.; and cadential degrees (a horizontal arrow denotes the connection of two groups without a cadence in the voice parts, and a note in parentheses denotes a weak ending). In addition, the length of each group is shown by a number indicating the total number of semibreves, partial sums corresponding to subsections and sections; these durations are expressed whenever possible with the values immediately above, breves and longs. Quantitatively, the metrical organisation is thus executed sometimes at the lowest value (prolations), and qualitatively towards the highest value (the number of tempus and modus). With chanson XIX it is possible to see that a qualitative organisation can be extended to an overall construction at the value of the maxima, although this is an exception.

It still remains, however, to find the main metrical unit for the overall organisation of the compositions. One would expect this to be expressed by a whole number. It is necessary to discover whether there exists beyond the pure succession of simple note values (as they appear in the vocal parts without other barlines) a larger metrical entity at work that both influences the counterpoint and plays a decisive role in shaping the formal outlines of the chanson. This question is ultimately of great importance. Put another way, we are asking whether there survive in the music of Anthoine de Bertrand – and of course in that of his contemporaries too – living traces of the mensural practices so clearly discernible in polyphony of the fourteenth and fifteenth centuries, and to what extent the apparent liberty in the way the music unfolds in expressing the text is governed at its most basic level by a concern for geometrical order.

The analysis thus far reveals that the twenty-five chansons fall into four groups, two central and two lateral, with respect to the question just posed. The two lateral groups reveal two opposite points of view, and the first of these was analysed at length at the beginning of this article precisely because of its revealing character. Indeed, it was pointed out that chanson XIX was conceived on a structural basis of 3×5 maxims. It is unnecessary to return to this point here, except perhaps to stress the extent to which the mathematical rationality is present. At the opposite extreme we find three chansons, nos. XVII, XXIV, and XXV, for which the spaces in the tables representing the number of breves and longs are empty – that is, tempus and modus play no structural role whatsoever. The counterpoint appears to follow the lines of the text, and by the simple addition of prolations, among which neither symmetries nor regular mathematical connections can be distinguished, the entire work is conceived in a linear, through-composed fashion. It might be said that these chansons are composed 'on prolation'; all three are written *alla breve*, and they move progressively by the addition of semibreves and, consequently, by a half-tactus. Even if the pieces do consist of a whole number of breves in the end, qualitatively the tempus has no structural role such as would be determined by the position of cadences and by the arrangement of groups and sections.

The first of the two central groups of chansons, with respect to the question posed, consists of a set of seven songs notated in *integer valor* (nos. I, IX, XI, XII, XIV, XVI and XXIII) and a further set of seven in *proportio dupla* (nos. III, V, VI, XV, XVII, XX and XXI). For these fourteen pieces, the right column of the tables representing the long, which has been considered the basic metric unit, remains empty, and even if some of these works do contain a whole number of longs (or of modus), this level of organisation cannot be considered as playing an active role in the formal organisation of the chansons. Nevertheless, the values of the breve (and tempus) play an essential role, as may be seen by studying these tables in greater detail. One example merits particular attention on this point, the chanson *en dialogue* no. XIV,

Hola Caron, nautonnier infernal. It is clear that the overall piece and its three large sections are coordinated by a whole number of breves (and, therefore, of double tactus). But that is not all. The exchanges of dialogue between the soul, seeking to cross the river Styx, and the boatman Charon, set logically in the respective voice ranges of high and low, are in whole numbers of breves, thus superimposing a different organisation on the previous structure (Figure 4). The influence of geometry is particularly noticeable in chanson xvii, set to a text by Ronsard, where the groups and sections of the song are organised in sets of 6, 12 or 24 semibreves. This exploits the dual nature of these numbers, divisible by both 2 and 3, in order to oppose binary and ternary metres within a commonly held quantity.[12]

The second of the central groups of chansons consists of seven songs (nos. ii, iv, vii, viii, x, xii and xxii) notated in *integer valor* – that is, the tactus is at the semibreve and proceeds in breve units. It can be seen in these tables that the procedures for achieving internal structure have implications in all of the

S	3 B	
C	3 B	
S	6 B + 6 B	= 18 B

C	1 B	
S	3 B	
C	1 B	
S	5 B	
C	8 B	= 18 B

S	4 B	
C	4 B	
S	3 B + 4 B + 10 B	= 25 B

$$= 61 \text{ B}$$

Figure 4   Distribution of dialogue in *Hola Caron, nautonnier infernal*
(S = Soul, C = Charon, B = breve)

[12]   For a transcription and analysis of the first two sections of this piece, see J.-M. Vaccaro, 'Las! Pour vous trop aymer', *Models of Musical Analysis: Music before 1600*, ed. M. Everist (Oxford, 1992), pp. 175–207.

columns, particularly that on the right. In its quantitative and qualitative aspects, the contrapuntal texture appears to be fundamentally guided by a metrical unity of higher value, whose implicit presence pervades the entire structure. In no. XII, which evokes an erotic dream, the composer deploys a musical imagination that is marvellously inspired, painting the words *doux*, *soupirant, je me lasse, mourant tout las*, etc., and repeating at pleasure suggestive expressions such as *nu à nu, si doucement, la folastre m'embrasse*, and *sur son tétin*. But the entire work is also organised with geometrical rigour, revealing a compositional interest of a completely different nature. The case of no. VII, *O dieux permettez moy*, is perhaps even more significant. It is composed within a tightly controlled numerical framework which is ultimately responsible for creating a perfect equilibrium in the piece. Bertrand achieves a highly expressive (erotic) setting of the text by multiple textual repetitions which, in completely breaking up the poetic verse, intensify its power of suggestion:

> Puissons nous, elle et moy, tous nuz entre deux draps
> Flanc à flanc, bouche à bouche, enlassé de noz bras
> Pratiquer de l'amour les trousses plus gaillardes.

The aim of this analysis has been to contribute towards showing that the contrapuntal designs of Anthoine de Bertrand were grounded in a strong numerical base. The composer, who has been justifiably considered one of the finest representatives of the 'French madrigal', thus emphasising his rhetorical skill in composing music with powerful effects – the music of the word – appears equally concerned with the geometric plan of his works: music of number. These interests in number are not, therefore, confined to theory. They also have a concrete practical application in the treatment of sound durations, and are expressed through the manipulation of metrical values – prolation, tempus, modus and even maximodus – in which the hierarchy of the values has a direct impact on musical form.

These reflections urge us to consider the process of composition itself. If treatises are valuable in teaching the rules of part-writing and mensural music, they say nothing about how to work with

235

a sonnet or strophic text, or how to begin creating a musical structure from a poetic one. Treatises are equally silent on the procedures of contrapuntal elaboration, for which compositional sketches and drafts are non-existent. The theory about the use of *tabulae compositoriae* (slates), documented from the treatise of Lampadius,[13] might find indirect proof in this type of analysis. If slates for writing counterpoint were vertically aligned in a way that produced regularly sized spaces corresponding to breves and longs (this is, in fact, the example given by Lampadius and by others as well), it is not surprising that this grid, strictly measuring durations, should have left its mark on the music itself. It nevertheless disappeared in the definitive version of the notation in partbooks. I am inclined to believe that, even in the absence of barlines, such counterpoint is organised according to a distinct metrical ordering that ought to be revealed by analysis and made apparent by the use of barlines in transcriptions – lines that have been eliminated by most editors in the name of historical fidelity to the original layout of the partbooks and to the 'freedom' implied in the rhythmic and melodic flow. We have demonstrated here, however, on the basis of evidence from the end of the sixteenth century and in music by a composer strongly influenced by Italy, the persistence of true 'mental barlines', through the treatment of different levels of metric organisation. We must extend and increase these types of analysis to expand the usefulness of the results we can obtain. In the case of these three chansons, for example, which appear as being organised on only an elementary level of prolation, should we consider them as pieces still insufficiently worked through by an inexperienced composer (as Bertrand alludes to himself in the short preface to this book)? Or should we, on the contrary, see in them the fruits of progress as it detached itself from the older constraints of mensural practice inherited from previous epochs of music history, with the consequent benefit of more freedom in composing, resolutely turned towards the interest in rhetoric?

Centre d'Études Supérieures de la Renaissance, Tours

---

[13] *Compendium musices* (1537). See S. Clercx, 'D'une ardoise aux partitions du XVIème siècle', *Mélanges d'histoire et d'esthétique musicales offerts à Paul-Marie Masson* (Paris, 1955), pp. 157–70, and E. Lowinsky, 'On the Use of Scores by 16th-Century Musicians', *Journal of the American Musicological Society*, 1 (1948), pp. 17–23.

APPENDIX

Tabular analysis of chansons in Anthoine de Bertrand's *Troisiesme livre*

I *Sommeillez vous, ma belle Aurore*

·**C**·

X	A	→	6				
	B	G	4		10	5	
Y	C	d	9				
	D	♭	4	13			
	E	f	10				
	F	d	3	13	26	13	
Z	G	a	10				
	H	a	8				
	I	G	16		34	17	35

II *Hastez vous petite folle*

C

X	A	d	11					
	B	G	5					
	A	d	12					
	B	G	5	33				
Y	C	d	4					
	D	→	4					
	E	→	4					
	F	♭	5	15	48		24	12
Z	G	g	8					
	H	→	5					
	I	d	2					
	J	d	8					
	B	G	5		28		14	7	19

◆ ‖ ‖

III *Jamais on n'a que tristesses*

¢

X	A	d	6				
	B	d	6				
	B'	d	6	18	9		
Y	C	g	4				
	D	g	4				
	C	g	4				
	D	g	4	16	8		
Z	E	→	4				
	E	→	4				
	F	→	4				
	F	♭	4	16			
	G	g	6				
	G	G	6	12	28	14	31

IV *Vivons, mignarde, en noz amours*

C X

X	A	→	8	8					
	B	→	3,5						
	B	→	3,5	7					
	C	G	7	7	22		11	5,5	

¢3 Y

Y	D	d	7					
	E	g	15	22	11			
	F	(g)	3					
	G	♭	3					
	F	d	4					
	G	g	4	14	7	18	9	

C X'

X'	A	→	8	8				
	B	g	3,5					
	B	g	6,5	10				
	B'	g	4	4	22	11	5,5	20

◇   ⊟   ⊣

V   *Beauté qui, sans pareille*

·C·

X	A	d	4				
	B	G	14	18	9		
	A	d	4				
	B	G	12	16	8	17	
X'	C	d	9				
	D	G	7	16	8		
	E	d	4				
	B	G	12	16	8	16	33

VI   *Cest humeur vient de mon oeil*

¢ 3

X	A	d	12					
	B	d	15					
	B	d	15					
	C	(g)	15		57	19		
X	A	d	12					
	B	d	15					
	B	d	15					
	C	G	15		57	19	38	[19]

¢

Y	D	d	10					
	E	♭	8					
	F	d	12		30	15		
	G	d	12					
	H	a	8	20				
	I	g	12					
	I'	G	8	20	40	20	35	

VII *O dieux permettez moy*

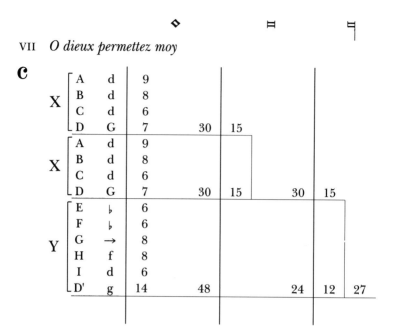

VIII *Tutto lo giorno piango*

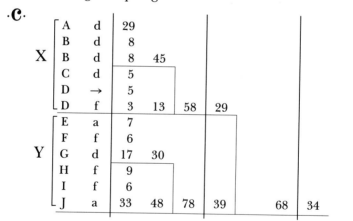

240

IX   *Je meurs, hélas!*

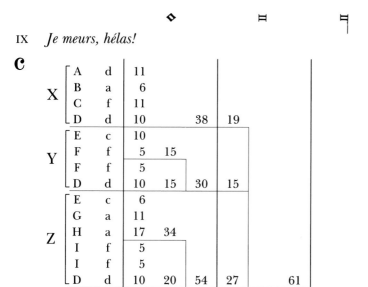

X	A	d	11						
	B	a	6						
	C	f	11						
	D	d	10		38	19			
Y	E	c	10						
	F	f	5	15					
	F	f	5						
	D	d	10	15	30	15			
Z	E	c	6						
	G	a	11						
	H	a	17	34					
	I	f	5						
	I	f	5						
	D	d	10	20	54	27		61	

X   *Tu dis que c'est, mignarde*

W	A	d	13						
	B	a	6						
	C	d	7	26	13				
X	D	f	8						
	E	a	7						
	F	c	9	24	12				
Y	G	f	8						
	H	a	9						
	I	d	5	22	11		36	18	
Z	J	f	9,5						
	K	a	8,5						
	L	d	8	26	13				
Z	J	f	9,5						
	K	a	8,5						
	L	d	8	26	13		26	13	31

◊ 𝄵 𝄴

XI   *Adieu, adieu, ma nimphette amiable*

·**C**·

X₁	A	d	6				
	B	a	4				
	C	f	6				
	D	d	11	27			
X₂	A	d	6				
	C'	a	8				
	E	f	6				
	F	a	9	29	56	28	
X₃	G	a	4				
	G	a	4				
	H	d	4				
	C'	f	8		20	10	
X₄	I	c	8				
	D	d	11				
	I	c	8				
	D	d	15		42	21	59

XII   *De nuict, le bien que de jour je pourchasse*

C

X	A	f	9						
	B	f	7						
	C	f	7						
	D	f	9	32	16				
	E	a	16						
	F	f	4						
	F	f	3						
	G	f	9	32	16	32	16		
Y	H	(f)	4						
	H	f	6						
	I	f	6	16	8				
	J	c	10						
	K	c	7						
	L	f	15						
	L	F	12	44	22	30	15	31	

◆   ⊐⊏   ⊐

XIII   *S'il est ainsi que tu m'aymes*

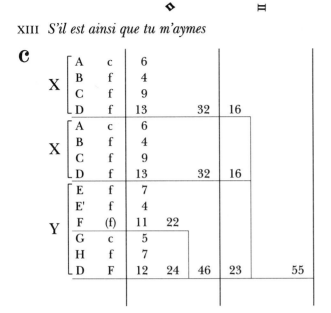

𝕮

	A	c	6					
X	B	f	4					
	C	f	9					
	D	f	13		32	16		
	A	c	6					
X	B	f	4					
	C	f	9					
	D	f	13		32	16		
	E	f	7					
	E'	f	4					
Y	F	(f)	11	22				
	G	c	5					
	H	f	7					
	D	F	12	24	46	23		55

XIV   *Hola Caron, nautonnier infernal (dialogue)*

·𝕮·

	A	→	7					
X	B	f	4,5					
	C	c	12,5					
	D	f	12		36	18		
	E	a	7					
Y	F	c	7					
	G	→	10					
	D	a	12		36	18	36	18
	H	c	8					
	I	c	4					
	J	f	3,5					
Z	K	f	6,5					
	L	c	8					
	M	c	11					
	M'	F	9		50		25	61

◆   ⊐⊏   ⊐⊏

XV *Sur moy, Seigneur, ta main pesante et dure*

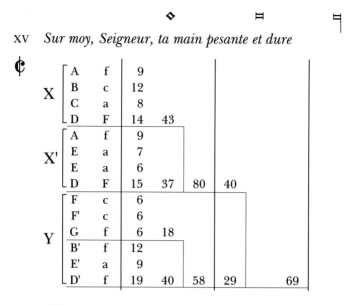

¢

X A	f	9					
B	c	12					
C	a	8					
D	F	14	43				
X' A	f	9					
E	a	7					
E	a	6					
D	F	15	37	80	40		
Y F	c	6					
F'	c	6					
G	f	6	18				
B'	f	12					
E'	a	9					
D'	f	19	40	58	29		69

XVI *Celuy qui veut sçavoir*

C

X A	f	2					
B	f	4	6				
C	f	2					
D	c	4	6	12	6		3
Y E	a	3					
F	f	3	6				
G	a	3					
H	f	3	6	12	6		3
Z I	f	12		12	6		3
J	f	6					
J	f	6		12	6		3
J'	f	2			1	25	

XVII *Demandes-tu, douce ennemie*

·¢·

Grp				◆			=		⅂	
X	A	c	6							
	B	f	6	12						
	C	c	8							
	D	f	4	12	24	12			6	
Y	E	f	6							
	E	f	6	12						
	F	c	6							
	G	F	6[+2]	12	24[+2]	12[+1]	24+1		6[+0.5]	
X	A	c	6							
	B	f	6	12						
	C	c	8							
	D	f	4	12	24	12			6	
Y	E	f	6							
	E	f	6	12						
	F	c	6							
	G	F	6	12	24	12	24		6	
Y'	E'	f	6							
	E'	f	6	12						
	F	c	6							
	G	F	6	12	24	12			6	
	G'	F	4		4	2	14	63	1	31[+0.5]

◇   ∐   ∐

XVIII *Las! O pauvre Didon*

¢

X	A	g	11		
	B	f	12		
	C	f	8		
	D	c	12	43	
Y	E	c	6		
	F	d	13		
	G	a	13		
	H	c	10	42	
Z	I	a	7		
	J	d	10		
	K	c	12		
	L	d	11		
	M	→	11		
	N	f	10		
	N	F	12	73	158

XIX *Pucelle en qui la triple grace*

¢3

X	A	(f)	12			
	B	c	12	24	8	4
	A	(f)	12			
	C	F	12	24	8	4
	C	F	12		4	2	10 → 5

C

Y	D	c	5			
	E	D	3			
	F	c	6			
	G	f	8	22	11	
	H	c	15			
	I	f	6			
	J	c	9			
	G	f	8	38	19	30	15 = 10 · → 5

¢3

X	A	(f)	[6]+18			
	B	c	12[6]+24	[2]+8	[1]+4	
	A'	(f)	12			
	C	F	12	24	8	4
	C	F	12	12	4	2	[1]+10 → 5

◆ ⎕ ⎕

XX *Devant les yeux, nuit et jour, me revient*

¢3

	A	f	12				
X	B	c	15				
	B	c	15				
	C	f	15	57	19		
	A	f	12				
	B	c	15				
X	B	c	15				
	C	f	12	54	18	37	
	D	c	7				

C

	D	c	7			
	E	f	8			
Y	F	f	3,5			
	G	c	8,5	34	17	

¢3

	H	c	21		
	H'	F	21	42	14

XXI *Le coeur loyal*

¢

	A	g	17					
X	B	C	13	30		15		
	A	g	17					
	B	C	13	30		15	30	
	C	e	14					
X'	D	g	12	26		13		
	A	g	17					
	B	C	19	36		18	31	61

XXII *S'il advient au combat*

·C·

	A	c	13				
	B	c	7	20	10	5	
X	C	g	12		6	3	
	D	c	20		10	5	
	D	c	24		12	6	19

◇   𝇇   𝄚

XXIII *Responce: Amy quand tu mourras*

C

X					
A	c	12	6		3
B	g	8	4		2
C	c	24	12		6
D	c	30	15	37	

XXIV *O doux plaisir*

¢

X							
A	d	9					
B	e	8					
B'	e	5					
C	c	7	29				
Y							
D	g	21					
E	g	13					
E'	g	9					
F	g	9					
G	g	15	67	96	48		24

XXV *Du feu chaut l'ardente fureur*

¢

X						
A	c	5				
B	g	5				
A'	c	6				
B	e	5	21			
Y						
C	c	12				
D	c	9				
E	c	8				
F	g	9	38			
Z						
G	c	11				
H	d	5				
I	c	10				
J	G	17	43	102	51	

Early Music History (1994) Volume 13

PHILIPPE VENDRIX

ON THE THEORETICAL EXPRESSION OF MUSIC IN FRANCE DURING THE RENAISSANCE

I: PROEM

It may not always seem obvious to begin a study of French music in the Renaissance with a reference from the theoretical field. By entitling his study '*Ut musica poesis*' Howard Mayer Brown attempted to remedy this shortcoming.[1] However, without in any way disparaging his work, this results in a series of paradoxes and uncertainties about the links which in France during the Renaissance period unite musical practice and musical thought, whether this be philosophical or theoretical. It is true that expressions like 'musical renaissance' or 'musical humanism', easy and pernicious terms, have a hard time in the French field. And it is precisely because these terms are easy and pernicious that they can be used in this way. For while there has never been any question of doubting the role of French composers in constructing the musical landscape of the Renaissance, it has never, on the other hand, been imaginable to write a history of humanism in French musical thinking of the Renaissance.[2] It is rather as if, causing a sudden break in the course of history, French writers and theorists of the fifteenth and sixteenth centuries had abandoned the art of sound to the practitioners, composers and performers alone. But no Western culture exists which can have a musical life without thought, and without the will to discover in it a pretext, a paradigmatic function or even

---

[1] H. M. Brown, '*Ut musica poesis*: Music and Poetry in France in the Late Sixteenth Century', pp. 1–63 above.

[2] This is not the case for Italy, as we see in the study of C. Palisca, *Humanism in Italian Renaissance Musical Thought* (New Haven and London, 1985).

an experimental field. There have certainly been periods when the importance given to the paradigmatic function has brought with it reflection upon the hidden recesses of aesthetic discourse, in which nothing allowed a glimpse of any interaction whatsoever between the reflective act and the creative, but even these rare moments have revealed a real presence of sound in writing.[3]

Thus musicology, as a victim of presupposed heresies in an idealistic vision of art, has been imprisoned within a diachronic perspective, one that makes theory the successor to practice. It is just as easy to be unfair about such a conception as it was obvious to underline the incoherence of the first. And then, even especially, the importance of number has weighed heavily, as if quantity played the role of the leading parameter of autonomy. The object of a historical study of musical theory is not articulated on subjects or actors. It extends to the conditions of the discourse, by analysing the formulation as well as the content; it is separated from numbers in favour of letters, more so in this period which is marked by the constraint of the quadrivium than in any other period. This preamble is not intended as a model of excellence, it is intended rather to fix this project within a well-determined framework: the definition of a specificity, that of the discourse on music in France during the Renaissance. However, this article seeks only to raise a number of questions, to which I will return at the end.[4]

2: THE EXTENT OF THE CORPUS

To impose geographical and chronological limits on the corpus of French music theory of the Renaissance is hazardous but essential for a definition of autonomous space/time. Chronologically, the appearance of printed treatises could serve as a point of departure. In this case, the corpus begins with a remarkable work whose influence has already been stressed many times: the

---

[3] On the place of the arts in thought and its modality of existence, see the recent book of G. Steiner, *Réelles présences* (Paris, 1992).

[4] I am preparing for the Centre d'Études Supérieures de la Renaissance an analytical and bibliographical study of the fifteenth and sixteenth centuries which is due to appear in 1995.

Musica libris demonstrata quattuor by Jacques Lefèvre d'Etaples, whose first edition dates from 1496.[5] This date at all events confirms that France did not arrive on the theoretical scene much later than its neighbours. In 1496, in Milan, Gaffurius published his *Practica musicae*; and it was only two decades earlier that Tinctoris had presented his *Terminorum musicae diffinitorium* (1473).[6] To place the beginnings of the expression of musical theory in Renaissance France at the very end of the fifteenth century rather obscures nearly a century of reflection. It is necessary to rethink French musical humanism in the light of recent studies on the emergence of new ideas during the course of the fifteenth century.[7] We may therefore attempt to apply to the field of music theory the periodisation that is generally used in describing the French humanist movement and to distinguish three generations of humanism. The first covers the transitional period between the fourteenth and fifteenth centuries. Marked by the polemic with Petrarch, this humanism undoubtedly plays a fundamental role. Both in the Collège de Navarre and in the Chancelleries, scholars and thinkers were active, producing an impressive number of works which mark a break with the Middle Ages. Music theory did not undergo any real upheavals, but it did establish the premises for new conceptions, more from an ideological point of view than from a pragmatic one. The theoretical work of Jean Gerson (1363–1429) stands as the paradigm for this movement.[8] The second humanism covers the reigns of Charles VII and

[5] On the influence of Lefèvre's treatise, see Palisca, *Humanism*, and A. E. Moyer, *Musica scientia: Musical Scholarship in the Italian Renaissance* (Ithaca and London, 1992), p. 220.
[6] Cataloguing of the manuscript sources of French music theory is under way. It poses many problems of location but promises here and now to be much reduced in number.
[7] On this subject see the two studies *L'aube de la Renaissance*, ed. D. Cecchetti, L. Sozzi and L. Terreaux (Geneva, 1991), and *Préludes à la Renaissance: aspects de la vie intellectuelle en France au XVe siècle*, ed. C. Bozzolo and E. Ornato (Paris, 1992). These two volumes pick up on research presented by A. H. T. Levi, *Humanism in France at the End of the Middle Ages and in the Early Renaissance* (Manchester, 1969).
[8] See his *Tres tractatus de canticis* which contains the *De canticorum originali ratione* (written around 1426), the *De canticordo* (written before 1423) and *De canticis* (written between 1424 and 1426). For the sources of these treatises see J. Gerson, *Oeuvres complètes*, ed. P. Glorieux, I: *Introduction générale* (Tournai, 1960). For an introduction to the work of Gerson, see J. L. Irwin, 'The Mystical Music of Jean Gerson', *Early Music History*, 1 (1981), pp. 187–202.

Louis XI (1422–83) and is marked by an undeniable decline in production.[9] This decline in France is linked to socio-political conditions: the disappearance of princely patrons, the Burgundian massacre of the protagonists of the first humanism, the dispersal and discouragement of the survivors, the war between England and France and the centralisation of Paris. Above all the kingdom had no truly influential writer capable of imposing the sense of *studia humanitatis* such as was able to develop in the states of the Italian peninsula, where both the political and religious conditions encouraged reflection on Greco-Latin antiquity. The French intellectuals of the second humanism concentrated more on the *lectio* than on the *artes*,[10] an orientation that was to have a determining influence on attitudes towards classical sources concerned with musical theory and more especially on their exploitation. This situation changed progressively during the last third of the fifteenth century, principally as the result of the new direction of humanism. First the detachment from a political viewpoint, then the affirmation in Italy of the universality of culture and no longer of its restrictive monopoly by the classical authors, allowed every country in Europe to be integrated and to belong to the humanist movement: 'Tout en se réclamant du monde commun de l'Antiquité, les humanistes européens pouvaient enfin donner libre cours à leurs préférences personnelles dans le cadre de leur propre tradition culturelle.'[11] This revival is reflected notably by the regularisation of the teaching of Greek at the Sorbonne.[12]

There was, then, during the course of the fifteenth century a break in the development of humanism. The first generation's

---

[9] E. Beltran, 'L'humanisme français au temps de Charles VII et Louis XI', *Préludes à la Renaissance*, pp. 123–62.

[10] Proof is provided by the work of Tinctoris. Thus his Latin style preceding his settling in Italy has nothing in common with the style of the works he wrote in Naples where he shows evidence of research into the quality of language. On this fascinating subject, see R. Woodley, 'Renaissance Music Theory as Literature: on Reading the Proportionale Musices of Iohannes Tinctoris', *Renaissance Studies*, 1 (1987), pp. 209–20.

[11] 'While taking as their authority the common world of antiquity, European humanists were able finally to give free expression to their personal preferences within the framework of their own cultural tradition.' Beltran, 'L'humanisme français', p. 160.

[12] George Hermonyme plays a fundamental role in this respect and an even more important one for the music theory of Lefèvre d'Etaples.

infatuation with the classics gave way to a relatively lethargic mood which allowed the infiltration and imposition of the work of the Italians. The third generation immediately sought to affirm its autonomy, both in the form of expression and in the content of reflection. The work of Lefèvre d'Etaples is the obvious point of departure for this renewal in the musical field. The other chronological pole is simpler to define, for it is marked not by gradual transformation but by a revolution in the fields of both scientific and philosophical knowledge The publication of the *Compendium musicae* by René Descartes inaugurates a new era. Some years earlier, in 1615, the appearance of the *Institutions harmoniques* by Salomon de Caus had crystallised humanist musical thought, conferring upon it a European dimension.[13]

Geographical limits present equally complex problems, in that the desire for a definition of an autonomous space must be interpreted within them. To reduce the corpus of French theory of the Renaissance to those works edited and published by Frenchmen in France can in no way give a precise idea of the speculative activity concerned with music. On the one hand, some theorists were expatriates, like Salomon de Caus, and published their works outside the frontiers of the kingdom;[14] on the other hand, some foreign theorists settled in Paris and published influential works there. (This is notably the case for Nicolaus Wollick.[15]) We should add a third category: that of theorists who published their work in the frontier regions of the kingdom of France, as is the case for certain treatises printed in Strasbourg or Geneva, in Antwerp, Louvain or Maastricht.

---

[13] The *Institutions harmoniques* of Salomon de Caus shows indebtedness to Italy in its very title, with its evident reference to Zarlino. The work was written in French and published in the Holy Roman Empire by an engineer who was fascinated by a myriad subjects. On Salomon de Caus, see C. Maks, *Salomon de Caus, 1576–1626* (Paris, 1935).

[14] The case of Johannes Tinctoris (*c.* 1435–*c.* 1511) is a special one. Born in the Brabant area, he lived in France (in Cambrai, Orléans and Chartres) before entering the service of Ferdinando I of Naples around 1472. His theoretical work, which was considerable and important for theoretical expression, is excluded from this study, first because he seems not to have written his theoretical works before going to Italy, and secondly because his work seems to have remained foreign to French theorists.

[15] See K. W. Niemöller, *Nicolaus Wollick (1480–1541) und sein Musiktraktat*, Beiträge zur rheinischen Musikgeschichte 13 (Cologne, 1956).

Table 1 shows immediately the importance of two centres of publication, Paris and Lyons.[16] This dual concentration will be discussed later in connection with the provenance of the theorists and the type of work that they produced. It was only exceptionally that theoretical texts about music were published in other towns. This distribution was conditioned by various factors, and the presence of peripheral places may be explained by particular circumstances. Jean Guyot was active in the principality of Liège.[17] In Louvain was situated one of the great musical publishing houses, that of Phalèse, which made no secret of its

Table 1   *Places of publication of*
theoretical writings on music

Place	Number
Antwerp	1
Avignon	1
Basle	1
Beaujeu	1
Caen	1
Frankfurt	2
Geneva	2
Langres	1
La Rochelle	1
Louvain	1
Lyons	9
Maastricht	1
Paris	30
Poitiers	1
Strasbourg	1
Tournai	1
Tournon	1
Troyes	1
s.l.	1

---

[16]   We still have no general study on the musical publications of Paris. It is necessary therefore to refer to several different monographs, for example G. Thibault and F. Lesure, *Bibliographie des éditions d'Adrian Le Roy et Robert Ballard (1551–1598)* (Paris, 1955), and D. Heartz, *Pierre Attaingnant, Royal Printer of Music: a Historical Study and Bibliographical Catalogue* (Berkeley and Los Angeles, 1969). For Lyons we have the excellent work of L. Guillo, *Les éditions musicales de la Renaissance lyonnaise* (Paris, 1991).

[17]   B. Even, 'Jean Guyot de Châtelet, musicien liégeois du XVIe siècle: synthèse et perspective de recherches', *Revue Belge de Musicologie*, 28–30 (1974–6), p. 112.

preference for repertory intended for plucked strings.[18] Antwerp occupied a position rather similar to that of Louvain. There were certainly commercial reasons leading to Guillaume Vosterman offering a French translation of the famous work of Sebastian Virdung.[19] Loys Bourgeois, a Protestant born in Paris, settled in Geneva in 1541 and worked there as a composer and teacher. Active in the milieux of Reformation teaching, he quite naturally printed his treatise in the city which had accepted him, knowing that his project would not gain the acceptance of everyone in France.[20] To publish a treatise in the town where the musician practised his art seems to have been characteristic of musical life in the sixteenth century. This is also true of the Holy Roman Empire, in which each important master published a treatise for the use of a particular choir school or college in his own town. In France this seems to have been the case for treatises on plainchant and for small rudimentary manuals intended for choir schools.

A number of places appear in Table 1 because works about dancing have been included in the corpus. Here also religious and/or socio-professional reasons explain the choice of peripheral places like La Rochelle and Langres. The inclusion of Strasbourg is uniquely linked to the publication of the works of Jean Gerson (1488), whose role in the formation of the first generation of French humanism has been mentioned. During the sixteenth century the Alsatian city held an important position in musical publication.[21] The treatises printed there are numerous, though belonging rather to the German world.[22]

[18] H. Vanhulst, *Catalogue des éditions de musique publiées à Louvain par Pierre Phalèse et ses fils, 1545–1578*, Académie Royale de Belgique, Mémoires de la Classe des Beaux-Arts 16/ɪɪ (Brussels, 1990), pp. xxxi–xlii.

[19] The intended readers were undoubtedly the amateur lute players, francophone or francophile, of the Low Countries: the explanation of German lute tablature is replaced here by a description of the French system. This treatise was translated into Flemish in 1568 and published by Jan van Ghelen in Antwerp, no doubt for the same commercial reasons.

[20] P. A. Gaillard, 'Nachwort' to the facsimile edition, Documenta Musicologica, 1st series, 6 (Kassel and Basle, n.d.).

[21] M. Lang, 'Bibliographie de l'histoire de la musique en Alsace', *La musique en Alsace hier et aujourd'hui* (Strasbourg, 1970), pp. 373–459.

[22] We should note the unpublished works of Cunradus Dasypodius, especially the appearance in 1612 of the *Synopsis musicae* (Carl Kieffer) of Johannes Lippius.

Table 1 also reveals the small quantity of works published. This was a peculiarity of the French corpus which Wilhelm Seidel,[23] following Albert Seay,[24] underlines, stressing the 'distance' that the French maintained in their relations with the field of theory. It is nevertheless appropriate to justify this somewhat paradoxical attitude, especially in a century preoccupied by the institutionalisation of its vernacular language and by its desire to give the visual arts the status of intellectual profession.[25] Seen from this angle, theory is effectively distinguished by its quantitative poverty. However, contrary to what Howard Mayer Brown suggests, I do not propose to make a comparison with the theoretical body of works on painting or sculpture.[26] On the other hand, turning to the domain of architectural theory seems more promising and confirms the extent of the distance that we have already mentioned.[27] Thus the anomaly disappears, giving way to a statement of uneasiness or negation.

It is with this perspective, then, that I would like to begin my discussion of French music theory of the Renaissance. It will reveal the nature of this negation or uneasiness, and equally the intention to dissemble in order to try to explain the relative exclusion of music from a system for the arts, although it appears to have a central position in the inspiration of poets. I envisage this objective rather in a hypothetical manner: as long as we do not have access to studies on all the theoretical traditions of the Renaissance, it will remain difficult to define the autonomy of French theoretical expression. And even within the French corpus, it is necessary not to centre our discussion on one work

---

[23] W. Seidel, 'Französische Musiktheorie im 16. und 17. Jahrhundert', *Entstehung nationaler Traditionen* (Darmstadt, 1986), pp. 4–140.

[24] A. Seay, 'French Renaissance Theory and Jean Yssandon', *Journal of Music Theory*, 15 (1971), pp. 254–71.

[25] G. Repaci-Courtois, ' "Art mécanique" ou "état contemplatif"? Les humanistes français du XVIe siècle et le statut des arts visuels', *Bibliothèque d'Humanisme et Renaissance*, 54 (1992), pp. 43–62.

[26] Treatises on painting and sculpture are not legion in French during the Renaissance. However, to proceed to a comparison of the modes of theoretical expression of painting on the one hand and music on the other raises questions which arise only exceptionally within the corpus of French music theory. Discourse by analogy had a much more important place in Italy in the sixteenth century. See D. Summers, *The Judgement of Sense: Renaissance Naturalism and the Rise of Aesthetics* (Cambridge, 1987), p. 365.

[27] J. Guillaume, ed., *Les traités d'architecture de la Renaissance* (Paris, 1991).

at the risk of proceeding by litotes, as would be the case were we to take as our point of reference Pontus de Tyard's *Solitaire second*.

This article attempts to answer questions intended to define the autonomy of the French domain at a precise period. I will therefore refer to general concepts and the way they were put into operation. These concepts, with one exception, could be applied to all European cultural areas of the fifteenth and sixteenth centuries: the discovery of the ancient world, the new paths of pedagogy, the legitimation of an artistic practice through the formulation of a discourse with its associated ideologies and the ordering of a system of knowledge and practice. Only the question of the confrontation of Catholic and Protestant circles has a specifically French dimension, in so far as it gave rise to a particular repertory within the French musical scene of the second half of the sixteenth century.

An analysis of the titles of the treatises affects this questioning. Table 2 divides into five categories the corpus of theoretical works on music written within the French domain in the course of the fifteenth and sixteenth centuries. Some categories give rise to normative problems: Munérat's treatise, for example, belongs both to the category of pragmatic works on plainchant and to that of works of theological reflection upon music. The chronological progression of each of these categories allows us to distinguish the major trends in theoretical expression. The first thing to note is that no compilation similar to that of Gaffurius appeared in France. On the other hand there is an affirmation of specialisation

Table 2   *Typology of theoretical works*

Type	Dance	Plainchant	Apprenticeship	General	Mathematical
Numbers[28]	1,6,12 13,17 25,26 48,52	3,5,19 24,35	2,4,7,8,9,10, 14,15,16,28,29, 32,33,36,37,39, 41,42,43,44,45, 47,49,54,56,57	11,18,22, 23,27,30, 31,34,40, 46,50,51, 53,55	20,21,38
Total	9	5	26	14	3

[28]   Numbers refer to the 'Works of French Renaissance theory' printed as Appendix 1 to Brown, '*Ut musica poesis*'.

within different subject areas. This movement is identical with that found in Italy during the years 1500–50 and which was to reabsorb Zarlino and Galilei, reintroducing general reflection into musical theory. The clearest consequence of this specialisation is found in the exclusion of music from general works on philosophy or history. Not until the seventeenth century does music theory once again serve to draw together study of the major movements of civilisations. The turning point which occurred in 1615 is thus justified as being fundamental to the evolution of the theoretical expression of music. The role of Marin Mersenne no longer requires proof.[29]

This deficiency also reinforces the statement of uneasiness or negation. The status of music as a discipline within the field of knowledge suffered serious consequences that ushered in a long period of disdain; but in parallel, this relative exclusion led to the recovery by poets of an area of knowledge that medieval tradition had anchored almost irremovably in the arts of the quadrivium. It was this recovery which obliges us to take account of poetic discussion as the source of definition for an autonomy. Literary texts themselves convey precise information on historiographic conceptions, for example, despite recourse to rhetorical figures normally foreign to scientific discourse.[30] In this particular case, it is possible to relate the progress of discourse on music with that on the plastic arts and architecture, whose autonomy (by which we mean the autonomy of discourse) was to undergo considerable meandering which delayed, at a more general level and within a European dimension, the enunciation of a philosophical aesthetic which it remained to seventeenth-century thinkers to formulate.

3: RENAISSANCE AND MUSICAL HUMANISM

The Renaissance played a part in a multitude of movements which have too often been represented in a reductionist way by

---

[29] See R. Lenoble, *Mersenne et la naissance du mécanisme* (Paris, 1926).
[30] Even if the scientific discourse of the Renaissance does not hesitate to return to the poetic figures in its formulation. See in particular F. Choay, *La règle et le modèle: sur la théorie de l'architecture et de l'urbanisme* (Paris, 1980), pp. 86–206.

the term 'humanism'.[31] This humanism has been associated with a rediscovery of antiquity and with the revival of Neoplatonism at the expense of other tendencies. For this reason, and with just cause, its centre has been seen as Italy at the end of the fourteenth and beginning of the fifteenth century. However, other movements were appearing at the same time, some of them emerging from the scholastic tradition and others radically opposed to it. Just as we refer to a theology of the south and a theology of the north, we may refer to a renaissance in musical thought of the south and a renaissance of musical thought of the north. This dichotomy does not exist only in opposition – far from it. It displays a plurality of discourse based on different postulates and conditions which nonetheless form part of Renaissance culture. Re-reading Aristotle in the fifteenth century contributed as much to the foundation of humanism as did recreating an academy of Platonist allegiance.[32] In the same way, publishing small musical treatises of an introductory nature filled an equally (or even more) important role in sixteenth-century society as did drafting vast technical surveys on compositional processes.

A commonly held belief presents the Renaissance as the place of passionate rediscovery of the theoretical works of antiquity. Italy played an incomparable role in this regard.[33] France succumbed to the philological frenzy a little later than its neighbour. However, here we will use criteria of definition for this Renaissance in a slightly different way. Rather than speaking of rediscovery it would be more correct to speak of adjustment of a tradition.[34] The French contribution must be considered more from the angle of dissemination of ancient knowledge based on

---

[31] See R. M. Ellefsen, 'Music and Humanism in the Early Renaissance: their Relationship and its Roots in the Rhetorical and Philosophical Traditions' (Ph.D. dissertation, Florida State University, 1981).

[32] See the work of Carl Schmidt recently translated into French, *Aristote à la Renaissance* (Paris, 1992).

[33] A. Gallo, 'Die Kenntnis der griechischen Theoretikerquellen in der italienischen Renaissance', *Italienische Musiktheorie im 16. und 17. Jahrhundert: Antikrezeption und Satzlehre*, Geschichte der Musiktheorie 7 (Darmstadt, 1989), pp. 7–38.

[34] For the list of works studied in university curricula see N. C. Carpenter, *Music in the Medieval and Renaissance Universities* (Norman, OK, 1958), pp. 46–75 and 140–52; M. Huglo, 'The Study of Ancient Sources of Music Theory in the Medieval University', *Music Theory and its Sources: Antiquity and the Middle Ages*, ed. A. Barbera, Notre Dame Conferences in Medieval Studies 1 (Notre Dame, IN, 1990), pp. 150–72.

Philippe Vendrix

sound philological principles than from a desire to present the work of hitherto unknown authors.[35] Table 3 illustrates the small number of classical works translated or published in France during the Renaissance. Except for Plutarch's *Moralia*, which include a treatise *De musica* whose attribution was the subject of dispute until the first half of the eighteenth century,[36] French publishers and translators concentrated their efforts on texts which served as a basis for teaching in the university faculties[37] (the *Problamera* of Aristotle[38] and the *De nuptiis* of Capella), or on the fundamental texts of mathematical reflection like Euclid's *Rudimenta musices*, on which Lefèvre d'Etaples provided abundant commentary. This situation may be associated with the reservations of the theologians of the University of Paris concerning classical culture: the programmes there were fixed and did not open doors to research into unpublished sources. The frenzy of

Table 3   *Editions and translations of ancient authors current in Renaissance France*

Author	Treatise	Edition
Aristotle	*Problamera physica*	trans. Evrart de Conty[39]
Augustine	*De musica*	Paris, 1541; Lyons, 1561
Chalcidius	*Chalcidii Timaei Platoni*	Paris, 1520
Euclid	*Rudimenta musices*	Paris, 1557
Euclid	*Le livre de musique*	trans. Forcadel, Paris, 1556
Capella	*De nuptiis*	Lyons, 1539, 1592
Plutarch	*Moralia*	Paris, 1570
Plutarch	*Oeuvres morales*	trans. Amyot, Paris, 1572
Vitruvius		

[35] On the editions of ancient authors and translations, see Gallo, 'Die Kenntnis', pp. 29–34.
[36] See P. Vendrix, 'Pierre-Jean Burette: un archéologue de la musique grecque', *Recherches sur la Musique Française Classique*, 27 (1991–2), pp. 99–111.
[37] On the philological tradition in the Middle Ages, see the texts presented in Huglo, 'The Study of Ancient Sources'.
[38] A. Gallo, 'Greek Text and Latin Translations of the Aristotelian *Musical Problems*: a Preliminary Account of the Sources', *Music Theory and its Sources*, ed. Barbera, pp. 190–6. Unfortunately Gallo fails to consider the interesting situation in France.
[39] This manuscript translation, which has never been published, is preserved in Paris, Bibliotheque Nationale, MS fr. 211. It dates from the beginning of the fifteenth century. A copy was made around 1480 and is at present in Chantilly, Musée Condé. On Evrart de Conty, see P. Chavy, *Traducteurs d'autrefois, Moyen âge et Renaissance: dictionnaire des traducteurs et de la littérature traduite en ancien et moyen français (842–1600)*, 2 vols. (Paris and Geneva, 1988).

260

the first humanists of the fifteenth century had no sequel. The movement died out in the 1420s, and the new momentum of the last third of the fifteenth century was not sustained either by an institutionalised intellectual environment or by a dynamic policy of publishing, and even less by reflection upon philological tools.

Knowledge of classical sources was clearly not restricted to these editions and translations alone. Some of the works of Italian philologists were known. Theorists could also consult the manuscripts in the Bibliothèque du Roi or in the Sorbonne library. The history of the infiltration of Italian theoretical writing remains to be written, especially for the first half of the sixteenth century.[40] Foreign influences on French theoretical writing may be allocated to two periods: before and after Zarlino. In the first half of the sixteenth century the authors cited were those whose dissemination was guaranteed by the content of their writing and by the language in which they wrote, namely Latin. Between Lefèvre and Meneheu, allusions to Gaffurius (*Practica musicae*), Glarean (*Dodecachordon*), Ornithoparchus, Froschius and Heyden abound. The numerous references to German treatises may seem surprising. They nevertheless belong to the precise framework of theoretical formulation imported into France by Nicolaus Wollick. His *Opus aureum*, and more especially the revised version which appeared in Paris under the title *Enchiridion*, introduced a new model[41] for the university treatise which was widely read in the faculties, both in the Holy Roman Empire and in the kingdom of France. This influence is related to a treatment of topics which did not upset the programme of study at the University of Paris, which remained a fairly conservative bastion of knowledge.

Pontus de Tyard played an important role in the dissemination of the work of Italian humanists in France; Cathy Yandell has shown in great detail the nature of his borrowings (see Table

---

[40] In fact we know much more about the role of Italian theory in France during the second half of the sixteenth century, thanks particularly to the *Solitaire second* of Pontus de Tyard. We also have partial translations of Zarlino dating from the last third of the century. See M. Brenet, 'Deux traductions françaises inédites des *Institutions harmoniques* de Zarlino', *Année Musicale* (1911), pp. 125–44. This deals in particular with the manuscript Paris, Bibliothèque Nationale n.a.fr. 4679, which contains a *Reigle generalle et fort familière pour cognoistre la situation des principalles cadences de tous les modes ou tons tant par b mol que par b quarre*.

[41] See Niemöller, *Nicolaus Wollick*, pp. 248–66.

261

4).[42] More than his colleagues and predecessors, Pontus de Tyard assimilated the Italian heritage.[43] He turned his back on the model set by Wollick and his successors, a model which took its direction only from treatises of a pedagogic nature. Pontus did not seek to teach the rudiments of musical practice, but rather to show how music belonged to the *studia humanitatis*. From his transalpine colleagues he derived the necessary justifications for his demonstration. Although dialogue form is found in many pedagogical treatises, here the book as a whole takes on another dimension: the dialogue adopts the expressions of a treatise.

The reading of treatises published in France in the sixteenth century immediately raises the question of the importance of lineage. Authors plagiarised each other unreservedly, sometimes even without acknowledging their sources. Thus the work of Guilliaud is little more than a reduction and French translation of two treatises by Martin, and Cornelius Blockland (de Montfort) could not conceal his debt to Guilliaud and Bourgeois. All of these were undoubtedly inspired by the treatise most frequently republished in France during the sixteenth century, Guillaume Guerson's *Utilissime musicales* (*c.* 1495, 1500, 1509, 1510, 1511, 1514, 1516, 1518, 1521, 1526, 1540, 1550).

4: A HUMANIST TEACHING?

Most French treatises of the sixteenth century have a pragmatic function. Within this group a number of different categories may be distinguished, according to whether the work was intended

Table 4   *Borrowings in Pontus de Tyard's 'Solitaire second'*

Boethius	*De musica*
Gaffurius	*Theorica musicae, Practica musicae*
	De harmonia musicorum
Glarean	*Dodecachordon*
Ficino	*In Timaeum commentarium*
Anon.	*In genialium dieruù*

[42]   C. Yandell, 'Introduction', *Pontus de Tyard: Solitaire second* (Geneva, 1980), pp. 31–52.
[43]   Particular attention should also be paid to the translation of Francesco Giorgio's *De harmonia mundi totius cantica tria*, the only translation of an Italian work dealing with music in France in the sixteenth century.

as an introduction to music (nos. 2, 9, 16, 32, 33, 37, 44, 45, 47 and 49), for instrumental playing (nos. 4, 7, 8, 28, 29, 36, 41 and 42) or for composition (nos. 10, 43, 56 and 57). Some treatises mixed several intentions: Jambe de Fer's *Epitome* served as an introduction both to reading music and to learning to play the viol and the flute, and Jean Yssandon's *Traité de musique* moves from the rudiments of reading music to the principles of writing for several voices. Apart from the diversity of destination, some common characteristics unite the French pedagogical corpus: the brevity of the works, the order of presentation, clarity of exposé and recourse to examples rather than models.[44]

The theorists state from the outset that their aim is to introduce some amateur from their circle to music. This initiation must at all costs avoid the trap of complicated and long explanations which would tire and deter the reader more than they would stimulate and hold his attention. Nearly all pedagogical works include in their title some adjective like 'brief', 'easy' or 'short'.[45] In their introductions, the authors are more specific about their aims of brevity and clarity:

Ce qui m'a occasionné de m'efforcer, & employer le peu de sçavoir que Dieu m'a donné à rechercher, & trouver une méthode, & voye plus bresve, & aisée, à fin que ceux qui la voudront apprendre cy apres, y puissent parvenir en moins de temps, & sans si grande facherie. [Blockland][46]

Ce qui m'a incité de dresser ce brief Epitome musical. [Jambe de Fer][47]

Cela m'a osté toute la crainte que i'avois d'entreprindre ceste petite Instruction familiere, par laquelle ils pourront (moyennant leu labeur, & diligence) facilement parvenir à ce que dessus ... [Menehou].[48]

---

[44] H. Schneider, *Die Kompositionslehre in der ersten Hälfte des 17. Jahrhunderts* (Tutzing, 1974).

[45] Nineteen treatises have recourse to these adjectives.

[46] 'This has forced me to make use of the little knowledge that God has given me to seek and find a method and a way that is shorter and easier, so that those who wish to may learn from what follows, and may succeed in less time and with little trouble.'

[47] 'This has prompted me to draw up this brief *Epitome musicale*.' Unlike nearly all his contemporaries, he did not specify his intentions for brevity in his title.

[48] 'This has allayed all the fears I had in undertaking this little *Instruction familiere*, by which the above aim may (with a modicum of labour and diligence) be attained ...'

The theorists did not conceal their opposition to traditional methods, those which they had apparently had to suffer themselves:

Lecteur mon ami, vous pouvez maintenant congnoistre de combien ceste mienne Instruction est plus méthodique, & plus aisé, voire plus facile pour apprendre à chanter musicalement en choses faictes, comme on dit, que celle là que les Grammairiens ont mis en avant fort opiniastrement iusques aujourd'huy, pour faire perdre le temps à la ieunesse, en comptant leurs doigts, & contemplant les rognes & citrons de leurs mains. [Blockland][49]

Several factors, then, combine to justify the brevity and clarity of these theoretical works: unwillingness to tire the reader and desire to speak out against traditional teaching methods and to reach a larger public. Certain features are not exclusive to instruction books. The use of the vernacular, for example, arises from a concern for legitimation to which I shall return. The same applies to the use of examples, which belong more to the tradition of theoretical writing than to a desire to clarify the exposé. This last point deserves closer study. The instruction books in fact offer few examples of famous compositions or composers of high repute. Yssandon, the most precise of these theorists, surprisingly offers none at all, thus in a way neutralising his discourse and at the same time conferring upon it a productive value. It is figures rather than cases which interest French theorists. Here there is an important difference between French and Italian theorists, the latter drawing broadly on a repertory of illustrations for their remarks and precepts.[50] This desire to be brief conditions the treatment of topics. The pedagogical intention itself implies a kind of formal organisation of discourse which is found in nearly all instruction books.

[49] 'Reader, my friend, you can now see how much more methodical and easier my Instruction is, even simpler for learning to sing musically in polyphony (*res facta*) as they call it, than that which the Grammarians have persistently presented hitherto, making us lose time in our youth, by counting on fingers and by contemplating the knuckles and bones of their hands.'

[50] This attitude also explains the absence of polemic in the history of French theory in the Renaissance, when Italy was marked by numerous disputes which culminated in the conflict between Monteverdi and Artusi. This atmosphere of conflict was possible only in cases where theorists referred to contemporary music. On the nature of these musical disputes see G. Cowart, *Origins of Modern Musical Criticism: French and Italian Music, 1600–1750* (Ann Arbor, MI, 1981).

It has been pointed out that the dissemination in France of Zarlino's writings marks an important stage, widely affecting the field of pragmatic theoretical writing. The name of the master from Chioggia appears for the first time in Adrian Le Roy's *Traité de musique* (1583). Following the example of his predecessors, Le Roy indicates that his work is 'summarily extracted from several treatises'; but except for this oratorical precaution, his work differs fundamentally both in its form and in its basis from Yssandon's *Traité de la musique practique* (1582). The importance of Le Roy's treatise is shown not only by its numerous later editions – in this it was exceeded only by the earlier *Utilissime* of Guerson – but also by the use made of it by theorists and composers throughout the seventeenth century.[51] The borrowings from Zarlino and their treatment has already been the subject of detailed analysis.[52] At this point we should point out the new direction of theoretical discourse.

Even though Le Roy claimed to address the readers whom his predecessors had affected, he nonetheless dealt with matters that only apprentice composers were able to make use of. He was no longer concerned with guiding the first steps in reading music, but in describing the fundamental principles of contrapuntal writing in the way that Antoine Parran was to adopt later in his *Traité de la musique théorique et pratique, contenant les préceptes de la composition* (Paris: Pierre Ballard, 1639).

5: THE INSTITUTIONALISATION OF THEORY

The characteristics of theoretical expression of music in France during the Renaissance may also be explained by the men who were responsible for writing the treatises. I drew attention earlier to the notion of institutionalisation of theoretical writing, particularly in so far as it affected instruction books for beginners. This

---

[51] There are two manuscript copies dating from the seventeenth century. The first was written in 1634 by Louys Chaveneau (Paris, Bibliothèque Nationale, MS fr. 19100, fols. 187 ff.). The second, reduced for the most part but augmented at the end by new chapters on intervals, fugue and thoroughbass, must have been copied around 1670–80.

[52] Schneider, *Die Kompositionslehre*, pp. 26–32.

institutionalisation was also strongly conditioned by the activity of the writers.

The first striking observation is the absence, with few exceptions, of authors who were both theorists and first-rate composers. One might say that this was a common characteristic for the writers of treatises throughout the Renaissance. However, in Italy there was a tradition of writing music theory which justified some composers who occupied important jobs or played an undeniable role in the evolution of musical language in taking up the pen. We need only mention two of the most famous of them, Gioseffo Zarlino and Vincenzo Galilei. It would be somewhat simplistic to establish a categorisation of French theorists according to the criterion of quality of compositions. Indeed, it is undeniable that Loys Bourgeois, for example, played an important part in the constitution of the Calvinist psalter without however leaving any enduring compositions. The same may be said of Hesdin, whose works enjoyed some dissemination in France during the sixteenth century. In this regard only Adrian Le Roy can be included in the category of composers of some stature.[53] That fact might pass unnoticed if Le Roy's treatises did not mark a break in theoretical writing with a pedagogic orientation. Just as Italy had 'need' of Zarlino to set treatises on a new track, so France had a need to include among its theorists a composer who was aware of innovations, one sensitive to the requirements of students who did not come only from the colleges or universities, but even from the lesser choir schools where musical apprenticeship took a determinedly passive or rudimentary turn.

In general we have little biographical information on the authors of the French treatises. Of Yssandon, for example, we know only that he spent twenty-five years in the service of Cardinal Armagnac in Avignon;[54] of Michel de Menehou, that he was attached to the retinue of Jean Du Bellay and was choirmaster at Saint-Maur des Fossés. There is however one important feature that shows the orientation of many French treatises: most of the theorists belong to the literary world and

[53] S. F. Pogue, 'Le Roy, Adrian', *The New Grove Dictionary of Music and Musicians*, ed. S. Sadie, 20 vols. (London, 1980), x, pp. 686–7.
[54] Seay, 'French Renaissance Theory'.

published on many subjects. Lefèvre d'Etaples published as much on mathematics and on theology; Guillaume Guerson frequently turned his attention to general questions of liturgy; Nicolaus Wollick abandoned musical theory in favour of historiography; Maximilian Guilliaud was a doctor of theology. Claude Martin and Pontus de Tyard frequented poetic circles: in the case of Martin, the salon of Jean de Brinon, and in that of Tyard the Académie of Baïf.

There is nothing surprising, then, in the determinedly general orientation of these treatises and instruction books. On the other hand mathematical research fitted in naturally with the interests of Lefèvre, Blockland and Salomon de Caus. This diversity of origin and vocation explains the apparent institutionalisation of theory. The vocabulary was unsure of itself and the turn of phrase sometimes archaic, characteristics that undoubtedly originate in the plagiarism mentioned above. In translating Martin, Guilliaud did not use a very precise French vocabulary. Some of his definitions are vague and inexact. Once again France shows itself to be behind Italy, where the work of Zarlino contributed to establishing a rich and precise theoretical vocabulary.

The institutionalisation of theory derived from a legitimation of music, but especially of the discourse on music. The two legitimations did not raise identical issues. The difficulties of legitimising music will be discussed later. The fact that they belong to a single cursus seems to have turned theorists away from any academic discourse. A kind of silence hovers over the reasons for theorising on music, quite apart from any pedagogical intentions. In Italy Tinctoris worked towards the establishment of a specific vocabulary. Alberti undertook similar work in a parallel direction for architecture, the first of the visual arts to become the subject of epistemological reflection. In France, these types of discourse were not found in literary works. Paradoxically, music was present – by its silence. This situation, while leading to an emancipation of discourse for the visual arts, carried music away onto a subordinate plane.

6: 'UT MUSICA POESIS'

The definition of music as an art results from a long process of legitimation which the Renaissance set in place. This situation is reflected more in the field of practice, however, than in that of theory. Thus it was a better and more effective legitimation of the creative act than was the creative act itself.[55] The composer was the only one to legitimise and even to legislate for a style. The work could establish itself as the place for vindication of identity, whose range exceeds the purely relational level of master and apprentice. Theoretical and even poetic discourses never reached such depths. This failure may be explained by several factors arising from a wide range of causes, sociological, ideological and theological.

6.1. The problems of a legitimation. The social identification of the musician as belonging to a group cannot be achieved by theoretical and speculative discourse. The notion of service – not of contribution – often guides the pen of the theorist. This service was rendered to the students of a college or university, or to a particular amateur who wished to become acquainted with the rudiments of music, or to Catholics and Protestants so that they could formulate their praise correctly. A form of legitimation affects the expression of the discourse more than its nature. The wish of theorists to express themselves in vernacular language became more and more marked. This increasing use of vernacular language was not exclusive to France. In Italy, but also in Spain and in the Holy Roman Empire, theorists moved towards national languages. The sixteenth century played a fundamental role in this respect.

Considérant donc la cause estre en deffaut de l'intelligence de la langue latine, i'ay prins de cela occasion de faire ce petit Traité, tiré de plusieurs Auteurs, . . . Et ay le tout reduict ensemble & mis en forme d'épitome en langue françois, afin qu'à l'advenir ils puissent plus seurement composer, & mettre par écrit leurs inventions. [Yssandon][56]

55 See H. M. Brown, 'Emulation, Competition and Homage: Imitation and Theories of Imitation in the Renaissance', *Journal of the American Musicological Society*, 35 (1982), pp. 1–48.
56 'Considering therefore the cause to be a lack of knowledge of the Latin language, I have taken this occasion to make this little Treatise taken from several Authors, . . . and I have put the whole lot together in the form of an epitome in the French language, so that in the future they may more surely compose and put their inventions down in writing.'

The mode of expression can also be considered an agent of legitimation. However, it intervenes at a level which is quite different from that of the legitimation of an art: it is rather that of the legitimation of the discourse upon art. Through using discourse in the form of dialogue theorists set down their works within a tradition of writing on music which went back to antiquity. The practice of discoursing in dialogue also responds to an establishment of theoretical expression closely linked to the intention of the treatise. The written replaces the oral in order to crystallise knowledge in a form that borrows from a pedagogical universe familiar to everyone.

6.2. The protecting myth. French theorists of the Renaissance seem to have been protected by a philosophical, or more precisely a speculative, discourse on music. This protection appeared as an avoidance of the legitimation of music as an art. The myth alone carried within itself the possibility of transparency, a transparency that was necessary to bridge the impassable gulf between music as the *imago mundi* and music as the *imago humanis*. Outside this transparency, which revealed the complex network of universal order, music could not defend its autonomy as a creative act. The problem had not been presented in these terms before, for the transparency of the two levels resulted from a uniquely logico-mathematical order, the only one that could be envisaged and conceived in so far as the individual nature of creation had not been taken into account.

To assert the strength of poetic order in order to bridge the aforesaid gulf, in other words to reveal, was to turn an order of knowledge upside down: to legitimise or know, not by an immutable order but by looking at the creative activity of the human being. This was in a way to pass from unicity to multiplicity: to break the mould to open up to and towards the infinite and to demythologise art in order to entrust it to the power alone of the individual. Music theorists contributed to this rupture much less than did the poets; but even the poets did it without making too many waves. The mythical narrative served them ideally in that it belonged to the tradition of poetic and theoretical discourse and thus served as a metaphor rich in possibilities. Over and over again theorists called on their illustrious ancestor, Orpheus, in order to justify the position of music.[57] By this means they supported the poets who, with dissimulation, claimed a new alliance between the arts.

6.3. Perception versus interiorisation.

To define music as an art requires a definition of beauty in music and therefore a borrowing of techniques from criticism rather than from theory. There is no doubt that the epistemological revolution in musical aesthetics, introduced by René Descartes, was effected by this readjustment of the discourse on music. The theorists of the Renaissance only outlined its contours, for a reason rich in implications: namely suspicion of discourse on perception.

In fact, if theoretical discourse on music in France had one characteristic, it was its neutralisation. The combination of uneasiness and negation, which had already given rise to a good deal of hesitation towards the very idea of writing about music, resurfaced and obscured the interpretation of the theoretical corpus. In Italy and in the Holy Roman Empire, the infiltration of standards of judgment appropriate to poetry led theorists towards definitions of music depending on aesthetic criteria. But France was imprisoned within a system which rejected the phenomenon of perception and was based only on interiorisation. To the theology which relied on the Law of Silence corresponded an aesthetic of silence. The mathematical and normative orders were sufficient unto themselves and justified musical practice.

This principle of interiorisation was in large measure inspired by St Augustine. The re-reading in the sixteenth century of his writings, and especially of *De musica*, is reflected in the number of editions of this work.[58] It is revealing to note the constant rejection of enjoyment which, even though it arouses mistrust, occupies despite everything a central position in the disclosures of the doctor of the church. A testimony to the attitude of the literary world was the *Cymbalum mundi*, a short work surrounded by controversy and much publicity that has been attributed to an author of a treatise on music.[59]

---

[57] See *Orpheus: the Metamorphosis of a Myth*, ed. J. Warden (Toronto, 1982).
[58] On this subject, see P. Vendrix, 'L'augustinisme musical en France au XVIIe siècle', *Revue de Musicologie*, 78 (1992), pp. 237–55.
[59] *Cymbalum mundi* is sometimes attributed to Des Périers.

Music theorists set up connections based on equivalence between nature, music and man, by maintaining among them a hierarchy ranging from the high (the most general) to the low (the most particular). It is thus directly that man may understand nature: he has only to make an effort of intellect in order to apprehend immutable principles. No matter how much the perception and the multiplicity of their conditions go beyond the basic framework, there exists but one order, a single nature which itself has engendered a unique human nature.[60]

Auditory experience is excluded from the theoretical field in Renaissance France. Practice, another form of experience, is also excluded through the absence of a vocabulary for evaluation. Judgment has no place in the world of theoretical discourse, and this refusal to take into account parameters of experience and of practice impedes any definition of music as art.

6.4. Raising the status of the ear. If *Ut pictura poesis* seems frequently to have been a subject for treatment by theorists of the arts, the reason is certainly the high esteem in which the sense of sight was held – an esteem that was not enjoyed by hearing in the long medieval tradition. But at the beginning of the sixteenth century in France this hierarchy of the senses was turned upside down, with consequences that weighed heavily upon the emergence of a philosophical musical aesthetic in the course of the seventeenth century. This upheaval was the work of a philosopher mathematician, close to Lefèvre d'Etaples, whose works greatly interested historians of science but held little interest for musicologists: Charles de Bovelle.[61] His *Liber de sensibus* appeared in 1509. In its three sections the author treats of:

1. The senses in general and their integration into his anthropological and cosmological conception.

2. The hierarchic relationship between the senses.

---

[60] The influence of Aristotle is tangible here and must be taken into account in any study of musical thought in the Renaissance.

[61] See Thomas Frangenberg's excellent article whose main lines are summarised here: 'Auditus visu prestantior: Comparisons of Hearing and Vision in Charles de Bovelle's *Liber de sensibus*', *The Second Sense: Studies in Hearing and Musical Judgement from Antiquity to the Seventeenth Century*, Warburg Institute Surveys and Texts 22 (London, 1991), pp. 71–94.

3. The parts played by hearing and sight in the acquisition of knowledge.

Trying not to present himself as against either the Platonist tradition or the Aristotelian tradition concerning the role of the senses, Bovelle nevertheless presents a hierarchy of the senses based upon quantifiable reasons. These reasons were organised in three points which progressively specify his classification:

1. The value is determined by its rarity, but touch is not restricted to a particular organ.

2. The senses activated by a medium – water or air – possess a wider field of action and operate more specifically, which is not the case with touch or with taste.

3. The more distant the organs of the same sense are from each other, the more important they are.

The two first reasons allowed him to set apart touch and taste. The third allowed him to show the place of hearing, sight and smell. Starting with a pyramidal figure, it is easy for him to prove that the leading role should be accorded to hearing. His pyramidal conception is reinforced by another idea which was accorded as little respect as anatomical truthfulness, but which fitted perfectly with a 'mathematicised' description of being and of nature. Bovelle considered that the organs of the senses derive their perceptive power from a precise point and that the lines linking the organs to their vital centre form angles. These are divided into three types: obtuse, right-angle and acute.

Charles de Bovelle's theory of the senses, unlike his other works, was not subjected to much commentary. However, Bovelle seems to have exerted an influence on two of the important thinkers of the sixteenth century: Symphorien Champier and Pontus de Tyard. The extracts from *Symphoriani Champieri Philosophici* ... (1537) quoted by Frank Dobbins exactly reflects the thinking of Bovelle.[62] The senses are considered from a numerological angle, and sight and hearing occupy equal rank in the quest for knowledge. This Aristotelian vision, which is particularly developed in his *Problamera*, was to be taken up by Pontus de Tyard in a way that was much more ambiguous and less

---

[62]   F. Dobbins, *Music in Renaissance Lyons* (Oxford, 1992), pp. 32–4.

assertive than in the work of Symphorien Champier: 'Si ne pouvez-vous, toutefois, nier que la voix ne soit plus puissante energie que la vüe, vu que la voix penetre les corps plus solides, epaiz, et opaques; comme murailles, et autres semblables entre-deux, et la vüe ne peut seulement outrepasser ce chassi de papier.'[63]

The ideas put forward by Charles de Bovelle and adopted by Symphorien Champier and Pontus de Tyard belong more to the Aristotelian than to the Platonist conception. They depend on an interiorisation of feeling and hindered the developments which would lead to rethinking the phenomenon of music at the end of the sixteenth century and the beginning of the seventeenth. They are linked to the theology based on the Law of Silence mentioned earlier, to which Des Périers often refers. But however much hearing failed to benefit from this rehabilitation, it was unthinkable to hold any discourse whatever on a musical poetic whose implications would have been able to go beyond the simple interplay of mathematical relationships.

Ut musica poesis remained an impossible goal at the time when the French chanson was enjoying its hour of glory.

University of Liège

---

[63] 'So you cannot however deny that the voice has more powerful energy than sight, given that the voice penetrates more solid, thick and opaque bodies, like walls and other such obstacles, whereas sight cannot pass through even this sheet of paper.' Pontus de Tyard, *Solitaire second*, p. 197.

REVIEWS

PETER JEFFERY, *Re-envisioning Past Musical Cultures: Ethnomusic-ology in the Study of Gregorian Chant*. Chicago and London, University of Chicago Press, 1992, ix+212 pp.

Here is a scholar possessed of a vision of future chant scholarship and an ardent desire to communicate it. He is versed in the liturgies and languages of many Christian churches (for 'chant scholarship' here encompasses the chant not only of the Latin West but also of all the Eastern churches, which were typically performed in the vernacular). He is widely read in the scholarly literature on both liturgical chant and ethnomusicology, feels that recent writing about the nature, origins and development of Western chant has failed to tap the large potential of research techniques developed by ethnomusicology, and believes he can identify the ways in which this might be done and the results which might ensue.

The panorama unfolded is vast. To investigate all its aspects is the work of a lifetime, perhaps the lifetime of many scholars. The book Peter Jeffery has written is, however, not large, amount-ing to 124 pages of text, with a further 68 for an extensive bibliography. At one point he refers to it, in fact, as an 'essay' (p. 50). A good deal of the text is taken up with summaries of previous research, which the author then subjects to critical comment before proceeding to his ideas for future lines of investi-gation. It follows that, for the present, these do indeed remain ideas. The spadework which will convert the vision into reality has not yet been done. Jeffery describes a Promised Land, where the soil seems to be fertile, the expected harvest rich and varie-gated. Presented with such a prospect, we should certainly not avert our gaze.

The decision to put forward his ideas in this way must have needed considerable courage on Jeffery's part, for inevitably he has to hold out a large number of hostages to fortune. Can he be sure that the lines of investigation he proposes will actually bring us to the desired goal? His optimism is founded in part on work of his own in progress, some of it cited in the bibliography, much more in footnotes. Some of this has since appeared in print (the joint article with Kay Kaufman Shelemay and Ingrid Monson in *Early Music History*, 12, 1993, which I have seen, and volumes of Ethiopian chant from A-R Editions, which I have not). Nevertheless, we are asked to take rather a lot on trust, for there is no practical demonstration here of how ethnomusicological methods might be applied to the analysis of any specific item in the chant repertory. (There are only two musical examples in the book, both recastings of examples first published by Treitler.) Jeffery would no doubt argue that he is here concerned with principles, and that the detailed discussion of a particular example or group of chants would need at least a whole article to itself. Still, there will remain for the time being, at least in sceptical minds, a nagging doubt about the application of his ideas.

In the course of the book Jeffery makes a large number of 'suggestions about the new directions in which I think chant research should proceed'. He continues: 'Of course I exaggerate somewhat in calling these directions "new," for in many cases both their existence and the value of exploring them has been evident to all for some time. But they need to receive new attention because of their special usefulness for studying the problem of early chant transmission'. I should guess that it was chiefly his dissatisfaction with recent writing on 'the problem of early chant transmission' which propelled him into print. The 'new directions' are principally those suggested by ethnomusicology.

Ethnomusicology is concerned with musical repertories which were and are transmitted orally. That was also the case with plainchant right up to Carolingian times. (The detail of the way in which written transmission became important or dominant, and when, remains controversial.) The best-known rethinking of chant history in order to take proper account of its oral transmission is that carried through by Leo Treitler and Helmut Hucke. As one of many striking challenges to our pre-conceived notions (or, more accurately, our laziness in failing to think through the implications of what we casually assumed) Treitler put forward the analogy of the transmission of Serbo-Croatian epic poetry. This had been investigated by Milman Parry and Albert B. Lord for the similarities it offered to the way in which Homeric poetry might have been transmitted. The analogy was brilliantly successful, partly because in the context of traditional chant scholarship it seemed so outlandish, but mostly because it did indeed appear to explain so many features of strongly for-mulaic chants such as tracts. This and other ideas – about the musical make-up of chants, the role of notation in their later transmission, and the nature and origin of notation itself – have come to form a complex in our minds which has been identified by the catch-phrase 'the new historical view' (which Jeffery gives with capital letters). Controversy has not been lacking, but the gains have been substantial.

Jeffery clearly feels an urgent need to establish his own position in relation to the 'New Historical View'. Other ways of organising the book are conceivable, but he chooses to begin with a chapter summarising the main points and implications of Treitler's and Hucke's work. On the whole, this seems to me well balanced, and the conclusion that we are still at the beginning of an extended period of working out those implications is likewise unexceptionable. The oral transmission of chant, or any other repertory, requires both a musical vocabulary and ways of deploying it, ground rules for performance. Jeffery rightly points out that 'Much more close work needs to be done to build up methodologies for extrapolating specific "rules" and organizing them into a complete reconstructed "grammar" and "rhetoric" of Gregorian melody' (p. 21). He cites some recent analytical studies of particular chant genres, and there are many older ones, too; but his assertion is correct, that, by and large, these studies have not interpreted the material with an eye to its oral transmission.

The next chapter is entitled 'Some Reflections on the New Historical View'. (In fact there is constant reference to the topic throughout the rest of the book.) Here Jeffery offers some thoughts on grammar, rhetoric, and the 'language' of formulaic chant. One important question he asks is: How far is the extensive use of formulas an exclusive characteristic of oral transmission, if at all? And having cast doubt on our ability to distinguish oral from written transmission by the criterion of formulism, he goes on to pose questions about other possible criteria and about the interpretation of melodic similarities and variation in groups of chants. Some help is promised from the study of other orally transmitted musical repertories, from ethnomusicology in fact. Yet Jeffery is right to point out that ready-to-wear methods of ethnomusicological investigation cannot be simply taken off the peg. Chant scholarship should rather be 'informed by the direct observation and evaluation of actual oral musics' (p. 47); we need to draw 'whatever assistance we can from the great stock of experience that ethnomusicologists have built up trying to understand modern musical cultures not their own' (p. 50).

The promised help is so far rather vague in outline, so the next chapter, 'Some Ethnomusicological Concerns', identifies issues which are typical of ethnomusicology and could profitably be addressed in chant studies. Jeffery first stresses the value of cross-cultural comparisons, whereby the development of other musical traditions might, by analogy, suggest ways in which the Western chant repertory was formed. He lists chant repertories still transmitted orally, such as those of the Syriac and Coptic rites, but also non-Christian traditions, such as those of Judaism. He warns against jumping too readily to the conclusion that similarities signify common origins:

[To] know these chant traditions intimately is to see clearly that they are related only on a very fundamental level – the kind of level on which all dance music or all marching music or all musical theater might be said to be related. The liturgical chant traditions of the world's major religions are similar in some respects because they are used in similar contexts to achieve similar purposes, not because one is historically derived from another. [p. 58]

Yet the case for pushing chant studies in a comparative direction (Jeffery suggests following the way liturgiology has developed) is clearly made and, in my view, fully justified.

It is not so much that, when we have got to know non-Western chant traditions better, we shall suddenly discover a host of concordant items, or even concordant models for chant types. There may be some, but experience so far suggests they are rare. Rather, we shall begin to understand better the processes by which the types and then the specific items became established. For example, if we can identify the ground rules by which Syriac repertories are still performed without music books (they have been studied by Husmann after being written down from a living, oral tradition), then we shall have a clearer idea of what it may have been possible to perform on the eve of the writing down of Gregorian chant in the (eighth or) ninth century. This is one of many places in Jeffery's book where I would have welcomed a couple of musical examples, to illustrate such a case as this. (Perhaps the author could have drawn something from his recent publications of Ethiopian chant. It is true that this material is not at all easy to take in at a first reading, and it would be correspondingly difficult to extract an example which made its point immediately, without cumbersome terminological explanations.) If there was space for reproducing musical examples by Treitler, surely space might also have been found for an illustration of how analogies between chant repertories can work.

Jeffery concentrates, however, on more general issues: the necessity for understanding the circumstances under which chant is performed, and the institutional life and training of the medieval singer. Does the latter have living counterparts in other musical traditions? What was the role of books in the performance of the liturgy, both before and after musical notation was employed? What can we learn from their role in other ritual traditions? Was liturgical chant hermetically sealed off from secular music? What musical contacts were there between clergy and laity? Does this bear on the matter of the so-called regional chant 'dialects'? Jeffery argues that comparison with other traditions will help answer such questions. He has a good deal to say about chant history on the way and touches on a surprisingly large number of topics, at least briefly, and with numerous bibliographical references. The section 'Cultural Contexts', for instance, contains a section 'Art Music vs. Folk Song in the Liturgy', which is the occasion for a review of the historical ideas put forward in support of the musical reforms of the Second Vatican

Council. It is well done, and I would not want to be without this or other digressions of the sort, even though the connection with the central theme of the essay is at times tenuous.

The last of the main chapters, 'Some Possible Means of Oral Transmission in Liturgical Chant', points to a fascinatingly wide variety of phenomena in both Western chant and other repertories which illustrate 'a possible variety or type or means of oral transmission' and are thus susceptible to the types of approach developed by ethnomusicologists. First and foremost, there is the use of melodic formulas, types, models and families. This is certainly an area where ethnomusicologists have accomplished much, duly cited by Jeffery, though as far as I am aware only Dobszay and Szendrei have carried through really extensive, and mutually fructifying, projects of melodic classification in the areas of both ethnomusicology and plainchant (Hungarian folksong on the one hand, Gregorian antiphons on the other). Here Jeffery takes the opportunity to sketch the early development of the modal system, before moving on to different phenomena: inter-polated syllables in long melismas, melodic embellishment (with reflections on the role of 'professional' and congregational singing, and tendencies towards the elaboration or simplification of chant repertories), and organum and other types of polyphony based on a pre-existing melody.

One or two features of the book troubled me, though I readily concede that they may not strike others in the same way. Jeffery sometimes formulates criticism in a manner which might easily be misunderstood. For example, he says:

It is a sad testimony to the deep chasms that divide our specialties that historical musicologists, when they begin to wonder about oral tradition in music, should find it easier to turn to the study of oral literature than to the branch of their own discipline that actually studies oral music, even though the potential value of ethnomusicology to chant studies has been pointed out before. [p. 47]

In a footnote he cites Treitler as a scholar who has 'consistently' called for 'ethnomusicological investigations of early chant trans-mission'; yet one is left wondering who are the other historical musicologists who so regrettably concern themselves with oral literature. Elsewhere Jeffery speaks of 'trying to force medieval chant into Parry's construction of the Slavic epic poem' (p. 55),

and despite his protests (p. 46) that his reflections are offered
in a 'collegial spirit', one cannot help reflecting that the number
of colleagues who have used the analogy of the Slavic epic is
actually rather small. We are, after all, dealing in large measure
in analogies, not exact replicas of a given phenomenon or context.
My impression is that Treitler has been very careful not to press
his chosen analogies too far, whereas Jeffery appears to accuse
him of doing just that.

Some of the numerous passing bibliographical references might
also have been more deftly formulated. Thus Hansen's sophisticated melodic analysis of the entire corpus of Montpellier H.159
is called an 'ambitious attempt to discern pentatonicism in
Gregorian chant', whereas 'large-scale investigation of pentatonic
and other tonal frameworks' would have sounded less derogatory
and been more accurate. Sometimes a piece of research is criticised for failing to solve a problem it was never intended to
address. There is an example of this when Jeffery mentions the
work of the monks of Solesmes in grouping sources of the gradual
according to selected points of melodic variance (*Le graduel romain*,
IV, 1962). The context is a discussion of the ranges of variability
which can attach to formulas, the relationship between underlying
structure and surface detail, the differences that arise when the
same melody is used for different texts, and 'the variants that
emerge between different sources of the same repertory'. The
Solesmes project is characterised thus: 'The most ambitious
attempt to deal with regional variants in Latin chant, however,
was published before questions about oral-formulaic procedures
had been widely raised, and envisioned the problem as one of
comparing written variants after the manner of the textual critic,
without considering the potential oral-formulaic character of the
melodies.' The 'problem' here (there is one in the previous
sentence as well) is not actually specified; perhaps Jeffery is
thinking of the way in which the variants could have arisen. But
the point is that the Solesmes project had a very specific aim,
the identification of relationships between sources, in particular
between sources with neumatic notation and those with staff
notation, so that the earliest manuscripts could be matched up
with later ones, to produce performable editions of those chants
approved for the modern Roman liturgy. No doubt the question

of how the variants came about must one day be answered; indeed, I am sure it is constantly in the minds of those of us who work with them – for I must here declare an interest, being guilty of dabbling in such matters myself, as Jeffery acknowledges in a footnote. In the mean time, however, one does not need to wait upon the answer to employ variant readings in identifying groups of related manuscripts.

I may as well round off this complaint about the treatment of the Solesmes project. For one thing, Van Dijk's criticism of the enterprise was never really fair, and it certainly need not have been repeated here (p. 44). Then again, Froger made it quite clear that the planned edition of the Roman gradual would not be based on all extant sources: 'il ne pouvait être question de réunir *tous* les manuscrits qui existent' (*Études grégoriennes*, 1, 1954, p. 153; emphasis Froger's). Yet Jeffery, taking a phrase out of context, implies that the very opposite was the case. Froger went on to speak of the 'classement' of the sources which would precede the establishment of a critical edition. And of course Froger was aware of the questions posed by the different possible types of transmission, which we, with only a fraction of his experience of working with the manuscript sources, still debate. 'Les mélodies se sont répandues d'abord par tradition purement orale et ont subi diverses modifications dans les diverses régions où elles ont pénétré. Quand les neumes furent inventés, on fixa par écrit la musique auparavant retenue de mémoire. Comment s'opéra cette transcription? Tout le problème est là.' ('The melodies were disseminated first through purely oral tradition and underwent various modifications in the different regions they penetrated. When neumes were invented, music formerly committed to memory was fixed in written form. How did this transcription take place? That is the whole problem.' *Ibid.*, p. 156.) He then speculates about the nature of the repertory which he expects to be able to reconstruct, and puts forward two possible hypotheses. It might be an archetype from which all other manuscripts are ultimately descended, 'l'exemplaire même qui est à l'origine de la diffusion du Graduel sous Pépin le Bref'. But it might equally represent a later stage in the diffusion of the repertory, 'seulement l'une de ses branches locales dans l'état où elle était à la fin du IXe siècle'. Forty years on, we don't seem to have got very much further in deciding the matter.

But enough of such quibbles. They were perhaps inevitable when the author was trying to compress so much into a small space. So, too, the rather craggy style of writing. I now look forward to work which will build on the ideas outlined here. I finished the book in an optimistic mood, for I feel instinctively that Jeffery's basic thesis is sound, and the impressively wide range of his references inspires confidence that the materials and research techniques are not beyond our grasp. Despite his remark that the directions he points out are not all new, it is certainly the case that they have never before been presented together in this concentrated form, logically ordered and forcefully articulated. And to one like myself, who works almost exclusively in the established mode of chant studies, that is, with the Western, Latin tradition, a great deal of the book is genuinely new and revealing. If that statement should seem to remove my credentials as a reviewer, I can only plead that most students of chant are, as far as I am aware, in a similar position. Peter Jeffery's book is a vigorous encouragement to us to open our minds to new possibilities for research, to march forward into the new land. It goes without saying that I hope the author will be leading from the front. He owes it now to himself, as well as to the rest of us.

David Hiley
University of Regensburg

LOUISE K. STEIN, *Songs of Mortals, Dialogues of the Gods: Music and Theatre in Seventeenth-Century Spain*. Oxford, Clarendon Press, 1993, xx+566 pp.

The *siglo de oro* of the Spanish theatre, which could be said to span the working lives of Lope de Vega (1562–1635) and Pedro Calderón de la Barca (1600–81), has long held a prominent position in Anglo-American literary studies. Hispanists of distinction, among them Crawford, Shergold, Varey, Sloman, Sullivan and Wilson, have produced extensive studies on almost every conceivable aspect of the works of these enormously prolific playwrights, and the theatre of their time, as well as some excellent critical editions. Although music has been consistently acknowledged as an integral part of seventeenth-century Spanish drama, it has received relatively little scholarly attention up till now, with the exception of the important contributions by José Subirà, Miguel Querol and Jack Sage, most of which have appeared in print in Spanish. Over the last decade, two critical editions of plays by Calderón, in the series Teatro del Siglo de Oro (published by Reichenberger, Kassel), have included detailed study and analysis of the extant music associated with them. This has been undertaken by Don Cruickshank and Martin Cunningham in the case of *La púrpura de la rosa* (1990) and by Louise Stein for *La estatua de Prometeo* (1986). Already in this introductory essay Stein displayed a formidable grasp of the subject and a willingness to confront issues that other scholars have seemed loth to tackle, partly because the difficulties imposed on them by the fact that much of the music does not survive made it all the easier for them to be intellectually evasive. This book, long and eagerly awaited, fulfils all the expectations raised by that earlier study.

Stein's *Songs of Mortals, Dialogues of the Gods* (the meaning of which is made clear in the course of the book) breaks new ground in a number of ways. First, it is the single most comprehensive study of seventeenth-century theatre music in Spain, and the only one systematically to consider the surviving repertory (Appendix II is a catalogue of extant theatre songs with over 550 entries), as well as the implications raised by the substantial amount of music that has been lost. It also brings together for the first time a large body of source material not easily available elsewhere. Second, it adopts a broadly socio-cultural approach so that, even though Stein clearly states that her main objective is to consider the textual-musical relationships within the *comedias*, the zarzuelas, the semi-operas and operas from the period, this is not undertaken without reference to the circumstances of patronage and performance; indeed, the interaction between the vicissitudes of an absolute monarchy and the cultural traditions created by popular demand proves to be potentially one of the most fascinating insights of the book. Third, Stein makes a cool, analytical, almost forensic assessment of the evidence, which contrasts strongly with the defensive tone or special pleading that has marred previous studies, notably those, it must reluctantly be said, by Spanish musicologists. Finally (and this is the nettle that writers on the subject have been most unwilling to grasp) there is Stein's determination to study the history of music theatre in Spain on its own terms, stripping away the layers of assumptions built up from and sustained by the essentially Italocentric view of the period that has dominated the history books to date.

That is no easy task. A cursory glance at the wide-ranging selection of music examples reproduced at the end of the book reveals that even the leading theatre composer of the day, Juan Hidalgo (d. 1685), could not readily be considered as inventive a composer as, say, Cavalli or Lully or Purcell. The article on Hidalgo in *The New Grove Dictionary* by John H. Baron and Jack Sage summarises received opinion in this respect: 'Hidalgo did much to popularize Italian operatic styles at the Spanish court, but his music is not as innovatory, intense or elaborate as that of his foremost Italian contemporaries.' Stein, however, would challenge the assumptions on which such a statement was based on at least two counts. First, that it would not have been Hidalgo's intention to popularise or implant Italian operatic styles. He seems to have had very little direct contact with Italian opera, and those elements he had come across became absorbed into an essentially Spanish tradition: monody and recitative, for example, were used, but generally for a specific dramatic-symbolic purpose that served the needs of Spanish theatre (more of which later). Second, that Hidalgo's musical style was developed in certain circumstances in which prevailing traditions of music theatre and conditions of performance would have influenced the composer, and that these must be considered in their own right, as a kind of *explication du style*, not in the light of whatever developments occurred in Italy where the concerns of music and drama were quite different. As Stein eloquently puts it, 'because our attitude towards seventeenth-century music has been conditioned only by the experience of non-Spanish music (largely by Italian opera), we are, at first, deafened by the strangeness of Hidalgo's music, unable to imagine or to realize its power in performance' (p. 323). She does not ask (overtly, at least) for the history books to be rewritten, just for a fresh aproach to a subject that has undoubtedly suffered neglect because, with the rather dubious benefit of historical hindsight, it did not seem interesting or important in terms of underlying (and too rarely confronted) Darwinian assumptions about progress or development in music. Hidalgo's music is 'progressive' within its own terms of reference, and was clearly successful and meaningful to the audiences for which it was intended.

As regards the transmission of Italian operatic trends to Spain, and their reception there, Stein offers little new information, but reassesses the evidence to show that it was not simply a matter of periphery versus centre. Italian-style opera was successfully mounted in Spain, but it failed to make a lasting impact in the seventeenth century. It should be borne in mind that the production aspects of Spanish opera – the mechanical techniques and visual effects – were wholly Italianate from at least the time of the court appointment of the Florentine stage designer Cosimo Lotti in 1626. Musically and dramatically, however, Italian opera would have seemed quite alien to Spanish theatre music traditions, and the circumstances in which it was introduced to the royal court in Madrid the following year were unpropitious in several ways. The Florentine embassy's desire to impress the Spanish monarchy at this time resulted in an Italian-style *favola in musica* with a libretto in Castilian by the court playwright Lope de Vega and music by the Bolognese lutenist Filippo Piccinini, a highly esteemed chamber musician in the service of Philip IV. Piccinini, however, had no experience of composing monody, and found the whole exercise so difficult that he had to enlist the help of Bernardo Monanni, a secretary at the embassy, in composing the two longest scenes. The music does not survive, but Piccinini's score may not have been the most persuasive advocate for recitative-based opera. We have no information as to who performed the opera, entitled *La selva de amor*, but generally theatre music in Madrid, in both court and corral, was performed by actress-singers with little or no formal musical training, and there was, perhaps surprisingly, almost no overlap between the musicians of the royal chapel and those hired to compose for or perform in theatrical entertainments. This is a point that could well be explored in another book, as yet unwritten, on music at the court in the seventeenth century.

Thus the circumstances of performance may well have been far from ideal. Yet, as Stein convincingly shows, there were deeper reasons why Italian-style opera failed to make a lasting impression at the Spanish court, although Philip IV himself apparently took pleasure in playing through the recitative. The pastoral setting, so central to the Florentine operatic tradition, of *La selva de amor* was itself at odds with the conventions of Spanish drama at this time as realised in the *comedias* (plays with music) of Lope de Vega. There the emphasis was on naturalness and verisimilitude: the shepherds, far from being idealised or quasi-mythological beings who conversed in a special kind of song, were labourers who spoke to one another and who sang and danced only as they might have done in real life. Lope de Vega rose to the challenge of the Florentine-inspired event by adopting the content and metres of an Italian opera libretto, but in so doing went against some of the precepts he had outlined in his *Arte nuevo de hacer comedias en este tiempo* (1609). The *comedia* was regarded as a mirror ('espejo') of life and society, or, according to one contemporary definition, 'a portrait of all that happens in the world'. Music's function within the *comedia* was thus much as it was in real life: songs and dances might, without going beyond the bounds of verisimilitude, be introduced by way of entertainment, and so formed an integral part of the play. The sylvan world of *La selva de amor* would have been seen as artificial in terms of Spanish theatrical convention and the introduction of recitative equally so.

Further, the intellectual stimulus so central to the Florentine Camerata in the forging of all-sung drama, the emulation of ancient tragedy in the recreation of the marvellous effects of music on the emotions, was quite simply a matter that did not concern seventeenth-century Spanish playwrights or musicians: 'The classicizing humanistic impulse that contributed to the development of sophisticated monody, recitative, and opera in Florence had not infected Spanish writers and musicians of this generation.' (p. 89) Instead, they adapted elements of the new musical language to serve their own purposes, and Stein reveals examples of the *concitato* style, of solo laments with an affective

287

intent, of the introduction of the structural principle of the ritornello and of music as a source of enchantment. But there was a sense of disparagement among Spanish writers and thinkers of the Italian penchant for ancient dramas, stemming from the precepts of their own theatrical tradition. Ordinary mortals did not communicate by singing to one another, but they did quite often sing *romances* (narrative poems in octosyllabic lines) or strophic songs, and these could be introduced, therefore, at appropriate points in the action. Thus, reworkings of popular songs were integral to a theatrical performance in the realistic portrayal of entertainment and the actual entertainment of the audience. The gods, on the other hand, had an elevated status, represented in visual terms by their heavenly appearances on cloud machines, setting foot on stage only when the plot dictated that they should, quite literally, come down to earth, and symbolically reinforced by music in their sung dialogue. Recitative thus served a completely different purpose in Spanish drama as a *Sprechgesang* fit for the deities. This could not be understood by mortals, so that when the gods needed to communicate with them they adopted a more lyrical, arioso style that fell somewhere between the popular songs of the earthbound and their heavenly monodic dialogue. Hence the centrality of the book's title to one of the main distinguishing features of the development of theatre music in seventeenth-century Spain.

This radically different approach to theatre music in Spain had a number of important ramifications for the musical styles predominant there: the relative simplicity, both harmonic and melodic, of the choruses and much of the solo writing (the instrumental music has been all but completely lost) owed much to the persistence of a quasi-popular idiom. This simplicity accorded with the emphasis on verisimilitude: the characters would not have been seen to sing in an inappropriately professional manner, nor did the audience have to suspend disbelief by accepting that ordinary people would have communicated through song – what happened on stage mirrored life. Consequently, there was a continued reliance on borrowed material, and especially on those popular songs that formed part of that everyday existence, and therefore the inherited musical tradition became integral to all the theatrical genres cultivated in Spain, forming the basic musical element to a greater or lesser degree according to the specific performance context. The *romance* makes a good example, as this was traditionally a narrative musical form and could serve very well in a dramatic context, obviating the need for a new piece to be specifically composed or a new style forged. A tradition for rhetorical, though not necessarily affective, word-setting is evident in the *romance* from the late fifteenth century onwards.

With the greater emphasis on grand court entertainment in the mid seventeenth century came what Stein describes as the Calderonian 'subtle expansion' of styles. Especially in the Calderón–Hidalgo mythological semi-operas (a genre singled out by Stein for the first time in discussion of Spanish theatre music), the dialogue of the gods requires the much more extensive use of monodic dialogue. But the use of music in this way is primarily symbolic, as a language pertaining to the deities who represent concord rather than in order to convey the range of human emotion. This distinctive function of monody in Spanish music drama is reflected in a striking lack of dissonance and chromaticism. Many of the examples reproduced by Stein reveal a strong reliance on repeated notes within an essentially diatonic framework and triadic patterns which, as she convincingly shows, would have been held to symbolise perfection. Affective elements such as chromatic intervals or dissonant harmonies were sometimes used in laments, but it was not the affective power of music that was most important: rather its role was seen as part symbolic, part realistic. Music did not have to be emotionally related to a scene, though it could be used to identify it through instrumentation or types of setting. This in turn owed much to broader European traditions of court spectacle and the sixteenth-century fête, not least in its most practical purpose: to cover scene changes. Music, as Stein succinctly puts it, had an important role as an 'audible prop'.

Stein elaborates the theme of the range of styles in Spanish theatre music, and the different function of music within a theatrical context in Spain, with admirable clarity. Certain areas, tangential to her main argument but nevertheless crucial to a fuller understanding of musical developments in seventeenth-century Spain, fall outside the scope of this book but cry out for further study. For example, a parallel study on court entertainment in the sixteenth century is urgently needed, as is a detailed consideration of the adherence among Spanish court composers to the *prima prattica*. It is not at all clear whether they had even heard of the *seconda prattica*, nor is the extent to which the works of Monteverdi and his contemporaries would have been circulated, or even heard of, in Spain. There appears to have been very little interest in either, even though the princely aims that helped to generate opera in Italy were also present at the royal Spanish court: 'The search for grandeur, elegance, and variety in these early Spanish court entertainments did not move towards totally sung theatre, nor did it bring Spanish theatrical musicians and court composers into contact with foreign musical styles and aesthetics' (p. 102).

Perhaps one drawback of Stein's focus on the relationship between text and music within the different theatrical genres, which are treated in turn on a broadly chronological basis, is that it is harder to gain an overall picture of the changing status of theatrical entertainment within society. The political message of the plays themselves, and the function of music in conveying that message, is brilliantly tackled by Stein, as is the role of such spectacles at court: 'Where once the king's love of theatre was used as an argument for the legitimation of theatre, after 1648 the theatre was exploited for its legitimation of the monarchy' (p. 129). It must be emphasised that it was not her intention to order the presentation of her material in this way, but there results a slight tendency to repetition from one chapter to the next. Similarly, the fascinating information that is presented *en passant* regarding other social aspects of Spanish theatre – the audience's expectations and the performers' abilities and performing resources – could have been expanded into separate, complementary chapters, but these would have made an already substantial volume unwieldy.

So, certain tasks remain to be undertaken, whether by Stein or by others following her lead, at a later date, as does a careful consideration of the tantalising parallels raised by her study with the situation in seventeenth-century England. The reassessment of Spanish theatre music in a broader European context initiated by this excellent book will take time; there is simply so much information here to absorb and to stimulate further exploration. Stein must be congratulated for taking a bold step in this direction, and for clearing the brambles (one meaning of the word 'zarzuela') that have grown up around the subject through a combination of distorted (if well-intentioned) nationalist views and judgments made on the basis of a scanty knowledge of the evidence, musical or otherwise, and on an 'unstated prejudice which assumes an operatic tradition to be the most important sign of a developed musical culture' (p. 3).

Tess Knighton
University of Cambridge

GARY TOMLINSON, *Music in Renaissance Magic: toward a Historiography of Others*. Chicago and London, University of Chicago Press, 1993, xvi+291 pp.

In *Music in Renaissance Magic* Tomlinson proposes an alternative approach to that of 'traditional' musicology to his readers, many of whom will be practitioners of that discipline. His stated aim is to construct an early modern discourse concerning music and magic and at the same time to help revise 'our own musicological and broader human-scientific discourse'. The opening and closing chapters, respectively entitled 'Approaching Others (Thoughts Before Writing)' and 'Believing Others (Thoughts Upon Writing)', are intended to provide the theoretical and methodological framework for rest of the book. According to Tomlinson, this moves on two levels of historical interpretation, the archaeological and the hermeneutic. Following Foucault, Tomlinson defines archaeological history as that which takes us 'beneath questions of authorial intent and intertextuality to the grid of meaningfulness that constrains and conditions a discourse or social practice'. Hermeneutics, on the other hand, signals 'an engagement, most generally, with the interpretation of texts so as to form hypotheses of their authors' conscious or unconscious meanings and the making of hypotheses about relationships among (and hence traditions of) texts'. This is not just any interpretation, but rather an 'intersubjective, dialogical interpretation that has emerged from the discussions of Heidegger, Gadamer,

Ricoeur, Bakhtin, and others' (p. x). What I understand him to mean is that, first, it is necessary to look at the primary sources (which are usually texts) and to try to interpret what the authors meant by them, whether intentionally or not. Secondly, one must at the same time take into account the broader context in which these texts were written and published to understand their 'proper' significance. But this is not a neutral exercise: in dealing with the past we necessarily impose our own preconceptions even as we try to reconstruct those of the period in question.

Sandwiched between two heavy and well-nigh indigestible slices of postmodernist discourse, the meat of this book is arranged into more attractively bite-sized sections within six central chapters, which each raise interesting and sometimes new ideas about the complex interrelationship of music and magic. Yet taken as a whole they hardly add up to a radical alternative to traditional approaches to this important but still little-understood aspect of early modern thought.

For Tomlinson, the crucial element of magic is that it involves the influence of the planets on earthly events, and it is no doubt for this reason that chapters 3 to 5 concentrate entirely on the connection between planets and the modes. In fact the scope of magic was much broader than this definition implies, embracing all kinds of powers and properties of things which are not regarded as magical today. Of course the author cannot be criticised for failing to address all aspects of the élite Western magical tradition. But since he evidently assumes his audience to be largely ignorant of magic, he might at least have offered some taxonomic guidelines (e.g. including definitions of terms such as 'spiritual', 'demonic' and 'occult') and a much needed introduction to the relevant bibliography on this complex subject.

It might have been helpful, for example, if he had drawn attention to the complex and changing relationships which exist between magic, which is now an inherently marginal topic, and other, supposedly more mainstream practices such as religion and science which are generally assumed to be self-evident categories requiring no explanation or justification – although our modern-day conception of science is completely different from that understood in the Renaissance. Despite some important shifts in meaning, what has remained stable in the Judeo-Christian tradition is the conception of magic as false religion and/or false science; its inherently dangerous and illegitimate nature has to be emphasised. All magic is formally condemned in canon law, but its attraction as a source of extraordinary power has always proved irresistible.

From an early modern perspective, magic was understood primarily as an art: it comprised a body of technical knowledge which a skilled practitioner could use to bring about particular effects on things or people by 'occult' or insensible means.[1] As in the case of any art, there was a whole spectrum of practice ranging from the activities of the most sophisticated practitioner to that of the lowliest and most ignorant charlatan. In other words, although the aims and methods of individual practitioners might be subjected to criticism, the efficacy of magic itself was not in question. Because magic always lay at the boundary of what was thought to be the limits of the possible and the permissible, its domain was constantly shifting. As people became accustomed to new and wondrous things, their perception of what is amazing – which must, by definition, be rare and unusual – also changed. Similarly, effective magic was always being appropriated by individuals who, once they had found effective ways of doing things, promptly claimed that it was not magic at all, a particularly useful strategy in a climate when toleration was lacking among church authorities.

Tomlinson himself observes this phenomenon (although merely in passing) in the case of Vincenzo Galilei, noting that the latter's expressive goal to exploit to varied ends 'the natural force and imitative potency of sound ... was nothing other than a restatement in a nonmagical context of a primary aim of ...

---

[1] The literal meaning of the word 'occult' is 'hidden' (Lat. *occultus*). It had always borne the sense 'hidden from public view' with its negative connotations, and this of course is the predominant meaning of the word at the present time; this has only been true, however, since the seventeenth century. It had earlier carried the principal sense of 'hidden from the human senses'; as such it was juxtaposed in scholastic philosophy with the concept of 'manifest'. See K. Hutchison, 'What Happened to Occult Qualities in the Scientific Revolution?', *Isis*, 73 (1982), 233–53; J. Henry, 'Occult Qualities in the Experimental Philosophy: Active Principles in Pre-Newtonian Matter Theory', *History of Science*, 24 (1986), pp. 335–81; *idem*, 'Magic and Science in the Sixteenth and Seventeenth Centuries', *A Companion to the History of Modern Science*, ed. G. Cantor, J. R. R. Christie, M. J. S. Hodge and R. C. Olby (London and Chicago, 1990).

Renaissance magicians' (p. 141). We are so accustomed to assuming that magic cannot work that we fail to recognise its legacy in other domains, not only that of music, but also those of the experimental sciences and technology.[2]

For a true magus or magician (a term interchangeable with 'philosopher' in the Middle Ages) was one who possessed extraordinary wisdom beyond the range of normal mortals. Like so many Renaissance figures who followed the *via activa* – the prince, the politician, the painter and the musician, among others – the magician was interested in the exercise of power and the gratification of desire. He possessed the skill to manipulate invisible and insensible forces, producing effects in things or people which went beyond what was regarded as either natural or legitimate. Such effects varied in scale and degree, encompassing the public actions of statesmen no less than the private actions of individuals in their daily lives.[3]

The hidden powers which the magician might harness for pursuing his ends fell into two basic categories, although the distinction between them was far from clear. On the one hand there was the kind of magic which relied on the intervention of supernatural, personified intelligences for bringing about particular effects; this was defined as demonic magic. On the other hand, natural, or spiritual, magic was a kind which supposedly avoided such intervention and instead concentrated on the investigation and manipulation of effects produced by insensible natural causes. Conventionally, phenomena regarded as natural were only those which occur most of the time, in nature's habit or

---

[2] S. A. Bedini, 'The Role of Automata in the History of Technology', *Technology and Culture*, 5 (1964), pp. 24–42; F. Yates, *The Rosicrucian Enlightenment* (London, 1972); W. Eamon, 'Technology as Magic in the Late Middle Ages and the Renaissance', *Janus*, 70 (1983), pp. 171–212; P. M. Gouk, 'The Harmonic Roots of Newtonian Science', *Let Newton Be! A New Perspective on his Life and Works*, ed. J. Fauvel, R. Flood, M. Shortland and R. Wilson (Oxford, 1988), pp. 101–25.

[3] 'To defend Kingdomes, to discover the secret counsels of men, to overcome enemies, to redeem captives, to increase riches, to procure the favor of men, to expell diseases, to preserve health, to prolong life, to renew youth, to foretell future events, to see and know things done many miles off, and such like as these, by vertue of superior influences, may seem things incredible; Yet read but the ensuing Treatise, and thou shalt see the possibility thereof confirmed both by reason, and example.' Extract from 'Judicious Reader!', Translator's Introduction to the *Three Books of Occult Philosophy, written by Henry Cornelius Agrippa, Translated out of the Latin into the English Tongue, by J.F.* (2nd, enlarged edn, London, 1987), p. viii.

usual course. Thus although recognised as being within the physical world, two kinds of phenomena were considered contrary to nature: the marvellous and the artificial, a category which included mechanical devices and instruments which went against the perceived natural order of things.[4] It was precisely in these realms of wonder and virtuosity, of technical power and control, that the boundaries of natural magic were contested.

Particularly in a period when Catholics and Protestants alike were questioning the very nature of true religion, the idea of a domain of natural magic which harnessed impersonal and non-demonic forces and existed independently of religion was potentially very attractive for those who were concerned with investigating and exploiting the powers of musical sound, especially for the purposes of arousing particular effects in an audience. (A notable characteristic of sixteenth-century natural magic was the deployment of instruments – including musical ones – which could be used to extend the range of the senses or to produce effects beyond those achieved without such aids.) It is surprising that Tomlinson nowhere reminds his readers that music was a highly charged subject in the sixteenth century precisely because it was understood to inflame the passions and induce all manner of responses. Certain kinds of music, especially elaborate vocal polyphony, were considered in some circles to be the ultimate manifestation of idolatrous practice, and were therefore to be banned from worship altogether. Significantly, it is most often in the context of secular courts that natural magic found most eloquent expression in this period, most notably in the writings and musico-theatrical productions of Giambattista della Porta (1535–1615). But although one or two individuals were willing to identify themselves as magicians (notoriously in the case of Agrippa), the term was more often used in a negative sense to describe the illegitimate or ineffective actions of others.[5]

---

[4]   See D. P. Walker, *Spiritual and Demonic Magic from Ficino to Campanella* (London, 1958), pp. 75–84, 'General Theory of Natural Magic'; B. Hansen, 'Science and Magic', *Science in the Middle Ages*, ed. D. C. Lindberg (Chicago and London, 1978), pp. 483–506; C. Webster, *From Paracelsus to Newton: Magic and the Making of Modern Science* (Cambridge, 1982).

[5]   The identification of both women and non-Western men with 'magical' or 'primitive' beliefs and actions in contrast to the use of 'analytic reason' well illustrates this latter tendency. See for example L. Austern, ' "Sing Againe Syren": the Female Musician

In the case of musicians, comparisons were more often drawn specifically with Orpheus or Apollo rather than with magicians as such.

The discourse of magic might be used in a number of ways, not only by people who were concerned with achieving particular new effects, but also by those who were trying to describe phenomena which by their very nature could not be put easily into words (often in the realm of what we would call psychology). As Tomlinson himself notes, the magical dimension of musical culture thrived most often in improvisatory practices that have left little or no musical trace, and which were explained by philosophers and magicians, most of whom had little theoretical training in music. Magic provided a vocabulary to describe in non-scholarly language what music does to people, especially its capacity to arouse desire and anger as well as devotion and spiritual pleasure. Performances by the lutenist Francesco da Milano, for example, were described in terms of ravishment and divine frenzy, it being generally agreed that he possessed skills which 'transported all those who were listening'.[6]

Yet Tomlinson does not take the opportunity to link up any music that his audience would be familiar with to the more lofty philosophies discussed here. He outlines 'The Scope of Renaissance Magic' with reference to the writings of a few individuals, taking as his archetypal magus Heinrich Cornelius Agrippa of Nettesheim (1486–1535).[7] Following Agrippa, he summarises the postulates every magus apparently took for granted:

that the world was hierarchically ordered, with intellectual elements occupying the highest realm; that superior elements in the hierarchy influenced inferior ones; and that the wise man might ascend through the levels of the world structure . . . to gain special benefit from these influences. At one level of analysis the whole of Renaissance occult thought proceeded from these straightforward premises. [p. 46]

---

and Sexual Enchantment in Elizabethan Life and Literature', *Renaissance Quarterly*, 42 (1989), pp. 420–48.

[6] Pontus de Tyard, *Solitaire second ou prose de la musique* (Lyons, 1555), pp. 113–15; D. P. Walker, 'Musical Humanism in the 16th and Early 17th Centuries', *Music Review*, 2 (1941), pp. 1–13, 111–21, 220–7, 288–308; 3 (1942), pp. 55–71.

[7] An interesting question which might be raised here is whether the formation of the magical canon, the works of great (male) magi, follows a course analogous to that observed in the case of music.

In fact, these premises were not limited to occult thought but applied to all aspects of Renaissance thinking. The belief in a hierarchically ordered universe was equally fundamental to theology and the domains of moral and natural philosophy. The essential difference between magic and more mundane forms of manipulative action was its source of power, a distinction which was open to many different interpretations. And although Tomlinson describes magic in this chapter as though it possessed a unique set of attributes, the reality was far more complex. Yet it is only in the fifth chapter that he makes any reference to the differences between Agrippa's taxonomy of magic, for example, and those of Campanella, Porta and Kircher who were 'conditioned by Counter-Reformation concerns to purge magic ... of its unorthodox ingredients' (p. 167).[8]

Having laid out the basic principles of magic, Tomlinson devotes the remainder of the chapter to reinterpreting Foucault's, and to a lesser extent Lévi-Strauss's, interpretations of magic.[9] Rather than engaging with these authors at length, Tomlinson might have more profitably assimilated their most important ideas, and then gone on to apply them with effect to the primary material that he knows so well. As it is, there is little sense of anything new here.

More is gleaned from the chapter on 'Modes and Planetary Song', where Tomlinson begins by reviewing the sources for the doctrines of musical ethos and celestial harmony, which from Plato through to the late Middle Ages were effectively separated within the mainstream speculative tradition. Armed with this knowledge, we are able to see more clearly what was actually new about the musical magic outlined in Bartolomeo Ramos's *Musica practica* (1482), Marsilio Ficino's *De vita coelitus comparanda* (1489), Franchinus Gaffurius's *De harmonia musicorum instrumentorum opus* (completed by 1500, published 1518) and Agrippa's *De occulta philosophia* (drafted 1510, published revised version 1533), which together represent the development of a new alliance between

---

[8] For some examples of different ways of classifying magic, see L. Thorndike, *A History of Magic and Experimental Science* (New York, 1941), especially vols. v and vi, 'The Sixteenth Century'.

[9] M. Foucault, *The Order of Things: an Archaeology of the Human Sciences* (London, 1970; first published in French 1966); C. Lévi-Strauss, *The Savage Mind* (Chicago, 1966).

the disciplines of music theory and practical magic. In these works, the age-old belief in celestial harmony was endowed with an 'ideological potency' it had not enjoyed since the end of the ancient era.

More than anyone it was Ficino who, through his translations, commentaries and treatises on the broad tradition of neo-Platonic thought, gave rise to a discourse of natural and celestial magic with music at its heart. The sources of Ficino's musical magic have already been reviewed by Walker, Copenhaver, Kaske and others; Tomlinson merely highlights some of its astrological features in his chapter on 'Ficino's Magical Songs'.[10] Apart from offering a useful summary of this material, the single most important contribution that he makes here is highly specialist in nature, but one which nevertheless has important general implications. Evidently, D. P. Walker was incorrect in claiming that Ficino's songs worked at two levels whereby music moved the human spirit through its imitative properties, but only words could reach the intellectual faculty by virtue of their rational content. According to Tomlinson (and his argument is a compelling one), Ficino in fact did not distinguish between words and music in this way. By virtue of its basis in number and proportion (*ratio*), musical sound was epistemologically and ontologically equivalent to speech. As such it could be used as a means of reaching higher intelligences, that is, in demonic magic, as well as in natural magic confined to acting on the bodily humours.

Rightly, I believe, Tomlinson emphasises the attraction of the operative power of neo-Platonic magic for Ficino and his followers. This was not merely a speculative philosophy, reflecting on the structure of the cosmos. Music, whatever the ultimate source of its potency might be, is here recognised as a powerful means of affecting the soul and mind. A renowned practitioner himself in the arts of both medicine and music, Ficino performed

---

[10] Walker, *Spiritual and Demonic Magic*, pp. 36–44; B. Copenhaver, 'Astrology and Magic', *The Cambridge History of Renaissance Philosophy*, ed. C. B. Schmitt, Q. Skinner and J. Kraye (Cambridge, 1988), pp. 264–300; *idem*, 'Natural Magic, Hermetism, and Occultism', *Reappraisals of the Scientific Revolution*, ed. D. C. Lindberg and R. S. Westman (Cambridge, 1990), pp. 261–301; *idem*, 'Scholastic Philosophy and Renaissance Magic in the *De vita* of Marsilio Ficino', *Renaissance Quarterly*, 37 (1984), pp. 523–54; *Ficino's Three Books on Life*, ed. and trans. C. V. Kaske and J. R. Clark (Binghamton, NY, 1989).

his own compositions that were designed to capture planetary emanations and thereby bring about beneficial effects on himself. While none of his own compositions survive, Ficino nevertheless bequeathed an important intellectual legacy to succeeding generations.

Tomlinson goes on to review the impact of Ficinian thought on sixteenth- and seventeenth-century musical and cultural life, claiming that his discourses 'stimulated the growth and dispersion of tacit conceptual underpinnings for questions about the nature of musical rhetoric and effect' (p. 143). The way I would say it is that the basic message of Ficinian doctrine about the power of music to affect individuals, and how it did so, was essentially as widespread then as the terms of Freudian psychology, for example, are today. I believe that he is right in suggesting that historians like Palisca and Hollander have underestimated its continuing importance across the intellectual landscape of the sixteenth and seventeenth centuries.[11] One reason why this importance has been missed, I suspect, is that since, by definition, magic has to be special and secret, the very act of popularising Ficinian doctrine itself made it less magical.

The sense of remoteness which Tomlinson cultivates is especially evident in the fifth chapter on 'Musical Possession and Musical Soul Loss'. His purpose here is 'to signal the participation of early modern Italian culture in mystical ideologies that remain widespread in non-European cultures today, ideologies concerned to foster human interactions with an unseen, supersensible world' (p. 147). He reviews some of the taxonomies used to deal with this interaction, and concludes that such phenomena are best described in terms either of spirits entering the body (possession) or of one's own spirit leaving the body (soul loss): in each case music can play a powerful role. Taking the cult of tarantism as his example of the former phenomenon, and that of the *benandanti* as that of the latter, Tomlinson argues that Ficino would have been aware of both phenomena not only through his reading of ancient sources but also through contemporary

---

[11] J. Hollander, *The Untuning of the Sky: Ideas of Music in English Poetry 1500–1700* (Princeton, 1961); C. V. Palisca, 'Scientific Empiricism in Musical Thought', *Seventeenth-Century Science and the Arts*, ed. H. H. Rhys (Princeton, 1961).

evidence.[12] That such non-élite practices may well have been a model for Ficino is an important insight, and this chapter in particular will be of interest to those concerned with anthropological and ethnomusicological approaches to western European music.

For the majority who study art music of the period, what will be notable here as elsewhere is the virtual absence of any music that it is possible to hear today. Tomlinson is not concerned so much with music as with ideas about music. The only musical 'texts' addressed in any detail are Monteverdi's famous madrigals *Sfogava con le stelle* (published in the fourth book of madrigals of 1603) and the *Lamento della ninfa* (published in the eighth book of 1638). These are used in the seventh, penultimate chapter on 'Monteverdi's Musical Magic' to show some directions that Tomlinson's proposed 'archaeological method' might take, which supposedly turn away from mainstream musical analysis and criticism. Rather than demonstrating the kind of things that the archaeological method can actually accomplish, Tomlinson is more interested in talking about it in terms of what it is not. For example, 'It is not concerned with such issues as stylistic evolution in a composer's oeuvre or across many oeuvres, the definition, emergence, and disappearance of genres, the discerning of influences, and so on'. It 'does not aim to reach judgements of aesthetic value or worth', nor does it even aim to describe 'relations between musical works and extramusical forces (poetic styles, the other arts and sciences, patronage systems, political events, etc.)' (p. 229). What then, might the reader legitimately ask, does archaeology do?

In his one example of how archaeology might be applied to music, Tomlinson seems to be using Monteverdi's madrigals emblematically: to represent the disjuncture between a magical way of construing the world (or *episteme*, as Foucault would have it) and a non-magical, rational one. Tomlinson is careful to point out that he does not believe that the contrast between these two compositions actually represents a decisive shift either in

---

[12] He draws here especially on C. Ginzberg, *The Night Battles: Witchcraft and Agrarian Cults in the Sixteenth and Seventeenth Centuries* (New York, 1985), and E. de Martino, *La terra del rimorso: contributo a una storia religiosa del sud* (Milan, 1961).

Monteverdi's own thought, or more generally among his contemporaries. 'The period around 1600 was one of wavering modes of knowledge, of multiple impulses and choices, and of complex and sometimes contradictory syncretism.' (p. 237) For all this, he still wants to show that some kind of disenchantment was taking place in Western culture, and that music constituted part of this phenomenon. (There are strong parallels to be found here in debates in the history of science, but Tomlinson does not refer to some recent work which offers new approaches to this very problem.[13])

The kind of distinction that Tomlinson is arguing for here is essentially derived from Foucault's *Order of Things*. Whether it is in fact possible to identify two such 'incommensurable epistemes' and to mark a straightforward transition from one to the other is discussed more extensively in the sixth chapter immediately preceding the one on Monteverdi: 'An Archaeology of Poetic Furor, 1500–1650'. Although he uses Foucault's analysis as his starting point, Tomlinson nevertheless suggests that 'knowledge in this period embodied an unstable interaction of alternative premises rather than resting on the single, encompassing foundation that Foucault posited for it' (p. 190). He shows, for example, the affinity between Florentine neo-Platonism and the thought of Pietro Pomponazzi (1462–1525), a leading Peripatetic philosopher. The latter's merging of erudition, observation and occultism is contrasted in the following section with the new poetic practice and poetics of Marinism, 'a revolution in literary sensibility that took shape in Italy around 1600 and eventually

---

[13] In addition to the articles already cited in note 1, see also B. T. Moran, *The Alchemical World of the German Court: Occult Philosophy and Chemical Medicine in the Circle of Moritz of Hessen (1572–1632)* (Stuttgart, 1991). For example, rather than trying to identify a once-and-for-all shift from a 'magical' to a 'non-magical' mode of thinking, historians of science are now attending more precisely to what were understood to be appropriate ways of generating scientific knowledge in the period. Many features of natural magic (including the emphasis on technical power, the ability to reproduce particular effects, the use of instruments to extend the range of the senses, and the conception of a universe where the same laws operated at both the macrocosmic and microcosmic levels) became part of the 'new natural or experimental philosophy' in the course of the seventeenth century. The emphasis that was placed on demonstration and effects bears close comparison with the development of opera in this very period. See R. Katz, 'Collective "Problem-Solving" in the History of Music: the Case of the Camerata', *Journal of the History of Ideas*, 45 (1984), pp. 361–77.

swept through most of Europe in various guises' (p. 207).[14] Its most influential vehicle was Emanuele Tesauro's *Il cannocchiale aristotelico* (1654), a text which at Tomlinson's archaeological level apparently reveals the change from magical to analytic or representational discourse. The chapter concludes with a survey of Italian writings on poetic *furor* which is intended to point up further the complexity and ambivalence of thinking on the subject around 1600. Frankly, I found the argument here impossible to follow, and remain unconvinced that Tomlinson is offering us any kind of method or new approach which might help us address such difficult issues.

Having elaborated on the distinguishing characteristics of the magical and rational epistemes, Tomlinson simply highlights the salient features of his two musical examples to make the case. Perhaps he assumes that readers already have these pieces committed to memory. But in the absence of any music here, his verbal account is insufficiently complete to be at all persuasive. In a nutshell, we are told that the madrigalisms in *Sfogava con le stelle* are 'predicated on the confidence that the world and its objects, feelings, and words were held together from top to bottom by the force of similitude' (p. 237). Each element in the song is linked to the others by the given, ontological quality of resemblance itself. From this single instance one can deduce that 'In this way, the emblematics of the sixteenth-century madrigal uncovered among music, words, and things the ternary and at the same time unitary form of signification characteristic of the magical episteme' (p. 239). In the *Lamento della ninfa*, by contrast, it is apparently the ostinato which embodied the rational episteme, and which 'heralded a new order of knowledge'. Tomlinson loads this musical device with the most weighty significance: it 'located the *Lament* at a moment of profound reorganization in the archaeology of western music, a moment when the relations between musical language and the world shifted'; it 'established for itself a new and arbitrary connection between the world and a deontologized language' (p. 239). To conclude, 'the ostinato

[14] Readers who want to know more about the relevance of this to Monteverdi are advised to consult Tomlinson's *Monteverdi and the End of the Renaissance* (Oxford and Berkeley, 1987), especially pp. 151–242.

is an emblem which does not resemble, in short; it *represents*' (p. 240).

Accepting, for the sake of argument, that these pieces are actually as different in their musical effect as Tomlinson would have us believe, I would question, first, whether two works out of the entire output of one composer (however totemic in the literature) can legitimately be used to exemplify the supposed 'chasm' which opened up between magical and non-magical thinking in Europe around 1600. Second, I would also question whether Monteverdi himself would have regarded one as magical and the other not; in each case he experimented with some very different musical devices with the purpose of bringing about particular emotional responses in the listener. Indeed, one might even suggest that the use of madrigalisms was an inferior kind of magic compared to that used in *Lamento della ninfa*, since it relied on relatively crude techniques in comparison with those he later developed to articulate emotions.

The single criterion that Tomlinson is using in this instance to distinguish between the two pieces is a highly technical, textual one, namely the supposed difference between identity and analogy.[15] In the first case – which is considered to be a magical mode of thinking – there is apparently a 'real' or 'natural' affinity between symbols and the things they represent. ('The madrigalisms are equivalent to magical metaphors in that they discover hidden connections of things that are conceived as truths about the world.') In the second, more 'rational' mode, the connection is perceived as entirely arbitrary and artificial ('The ostinato does not so much discover ontological truths as construct a new world, in which, for a moment, its arbitrary connections can thrive'; pp. 241–2).

How readers respond to this exposition is probably an accurate indicator of their response to the book as a whole. I suspect that Tomlinson's musical archaeology is most likely to appeal to scholars who already feel comfortable with intersubjective dialogues and epistemes. I think it will alienate almost everybody

---

[15] B. Vickers, 'Analogy versus Identity: the Rejection of Occult Symbolism, 1580–1680', *Occult and Scientific Mentalities in the Renaissance*, ed. B. Vickers (Cambridge, 1984), pp. 95–163.

else. For instead of showing why magic really is an important and exciting subject for those who deal with the mainstream musical tradition (something which D. P. Walker and others did so effectively a generation ago), he makes it difficult and remote. One reason for this difficulty is his extremely inaccessible style and convoluted language, replete with mixed metaphors and obscure terminology. Tomlinson is eager to demonstrate his familiarity with 'past terms like Kuhn's paradigms, Foucault's epistemes, discourses, and dispersive genealogies, Lyotard's paralogy, Bakhtin's heteroglossia, and Nietzsche's and Husserl's horizons, especially as developed by Gadamer, Jauss, and later hermeneutic theorists' (p. 4). But he is far more interested in invoking these men and the concepts distinctively associated with them than in trying to explain to other musicologists why and how they might draw on the methods of literary criticism and the social sciences in trying to understand the nature and scope of magic – or indeed why it should be relevant to them in the first place. Tomlinson here seems to be following 'the fashionable tendency to substitute for argument citation of the like-mindedness of the "community" to which one belongs' that has recently been observed in historical discourse.[16] Moreover, he adopts such a patronising and authoritarian tone that he is in danger of silencing discourse altogether, rather than widening the channels of communication between disciplines. His desire 'to evade at last the tiresome play of power by which we habitually make others submit to our ways of knowing' (p. 248) has not been fulfilled.

Throughout the book Tomlinson is so keen to demonstrate the otherness of magic that he forgets to point out its essential – and continuing – connectedness with other domains of Western knowledge and practice. Nowhere does he suggest why magic might have been so attractive to writers and musicians, and because he has concentrated almost entirely on a handful of specialised texts, it is easy to forget just how much magical

---

[16] J. Hoopes, 'Objectivity and Relativism Reaffirmed: Historical Knowledge and the Philosophy of Charles S. Peirce', *American Historical Review*, 98 (1993), pp. 1545–55. According to Hoopes, authors tend to simply cite names such as Derrida and Foucault (for example) 'as if their having stated their convictions was also a proof of them' (p. 1550).

thinking constituted part of common intellectual currency in the period.

There are many questions that remain unanswered about the relationship between music and magic in the Renaissance. Tomlinson is mostly concerned here with the role that musical ideas played in magical doctrine. But it would have been interesting if, for example, he had considered the process by which magical discourse and practice seem to have made their impact on the production and consumption of art music. This might have had the effect of narrowing the yawning gap between 'ourselves' and 'others' that Tomlinson makes so much of here, one in which magic is located firmly on the 'other' side. But since Tomlinson wants to keep magic at a suitable scholarly distance from himself, he is of course unlikely to look at such connections very closely. Since he 'knows' that western Europeans no longer consider music to be a powerful means of contacting the spiritual world or harnessing supernatural forces, it would never occur to him that such practices do take place – or if it did he would probably dismiss them out of hand or interpret them in a non-magical way.[17] The fact that it is so difficult now even to think of magic as a serious topic is itself worth further reflection, especially for those who are concerned with historical periods when it provided a common frame of reference for the majority of the population.[18]

For example, it is evident that in the process of 'self-fashioning' their identities, some Renaissance musicians (or rather those who wrote about their skills) drew on the discourse of magic to describe the powers that they had to arouse particular effects.

[17] For example, C. J. Stone, 'Witch way out of here', *The Guardian* (29 January 1994), 'Weekend' section, p. 10, contains a report on a suburban couple practising spells and using incantations. Tomlinson describes an 'early modern culture that at all levels was capable of viewing music as a window on divine or spirit realms, again much in the manner that many non-European cultures continue to do' (p. 147) as though this is emphatically not the case in modern European culture.

[18] An alternative to searching for 'real reasons' underlying historical actors' conduct is proposed by the ethnomethodologist Michael Lynch, who suggests that scholars might describe 'the situated modes of practical reasoning, including vocabularies of motive and methods of motive ascription, used by members of historical communities' (*The Achievement Project Newsletter*, 3/2, autumn 1993, p. 2). In other words, the sort of language that people use to explain things changes over time and place, and explanations that are generally deemed convincing in one culture will not be so in another.

Such discourse is usually dismissed as purely rhetorical. Yet composers – together with stage designers, librettists and others involved in the creation of new entertainments intended to arouse wonder and awe – were drawing on a whole range of conceptual and technical resources in the experimental development of new genres that were intended to imitate and even surpass the effects of ancient music. We should remember that music does not 'evolve' or 'develop' of its own accord, but that it is consciously created in the musical marketplace by people with existing expectations and as yet unfulfilled dreams.

How did the view of music as a powerful force capable of arousing very specific emotional and physical effects actually intersect with the fashioning of new genres and musical idioms in this period?[19] What kind of impact did new theatrical productions (replete with amazing scenic and acoustical effects) have on their audiences, and how did they learn to respond to them? Why were certain kinds of instrument (e.g. the lute) associated with particular modes of behaviour? Did the process of notating improvisatory practices actually change the nature of what was performed, and if so why? Clearly, we have lost the sense of what was magical about Renaissance art music (and indeed of what is magical about Western music today). While musicians of any time or place rarely write themselves about the creative process it is evident that the goals of some musicians were partly shaped by magical texts – not just the works of Ficino, Ramos and Gaffurius themselves, but by a huge range of popular texts through which musico-magical doctrine was widely disseminated, especially in the sixteenth and early seventeenth centuries. Tomlinson is well qualified to reflect on how musicians, their patrons and their audience actually changed the way music affected people, using Monteverdi as his focus.

Penelope Gouk
University of Manchester

---

[19] In the chapter on 'The Expressive Value of Intervals and the Problem of the Fourth', *Studies in Musical Science in the Late Renaissance* (London, 1978), pp. 63–80, D. P. Walker reminds us how the moods associated with particular intervals have quite clearly changed over time (see especially the table on p. 71).